Peter Gabbitass

Melodies of the Heart

For Storm And Sunshine

Peter Gabbitass

Melodies of the Heart
For Storm And Sunshine

ISBN/EAN: 9783744752770

Printed in Europe, USA, Canada, Australia, Japan

Cover: Foto ©Thomas Meinert / pixelio.de

More available books at **www.hansebooks.com**

The Clifton Poet and his Daughter Mattie (now deceased).

HEART MELODIES:
FOR STORM AND SUNSHINE.
FROM CLIFTONIA THE BEAUTIFUL.

By P. GABBITASS, the Clifton Poet,

ONCE A CARPENTER BOY.

Author of Select Poems, graciously accepted by Her Majesty the Queen, their
Royal Highnesses the Prince and Princess of Wales, Duke of Edinburgh,
late Duke of Albany, &c., &c.

CLIFTONIA THE BEAUTIFUL.
Yes, thou art beautiful !   Thy sylvan ridge,
And Avon wide, with grand Suspension Bridge,
From old St. Vincent's rocks I scan with glee,
And all have pure entrancing charms for me.

1885.
BRISTOL, CLIFTON, AND THROUGH ALL BOOKSELLERS.

Copyright entered at Stationers' Hall.

Dedication.

TO

WILLIAM BUTLER, ESQ.,

OF CLIFTON GROVE,

A LONG-TRIED, TREASURED FRIEND, IN THE STORM AND SUNSHINE,

THIS VOLUME OF POEMS, PENNED UNDER VARIED CONDITIONS OF

LIFE, IS AFFECTIONATELY INSCRIBED BY THE WRITER.

Clifton, 1885.

THE hand that finds us in the storm,
We grasp with joy amid the waves :
And feeling it are not forlorn,
Because it is the hand that saves.

All grateful hearts will own that hand—
When sunshine comes in varied form—
That brought their drifting barque to land,
Despite the pelting of the storm.

CONTENTS.

CONTENTS—*Continued.*

CONTENTS—*Continued.*

Preface.

TO write one's own history is not an easy matter, and to do it faithfully may not always be a pleasant duty : nevertheless, if it be not so written, it had better not be penned at all—and, further, if no useful purpose be served by its production, it might well remain in oblivion.   In this brief introduction to my strange life-history, I wish it to be understood that it is written at the urgent request of a dear daughter, now deceased.   "You must write your own history, father," she said ; " it has been so varied, your experiences may be of use to many when you are gathered Home."   If such should be the case, I shall be amply repaid for my toil.   In it I shall endeavour to relate what I know *is true*, and more especially those scenes and circumstances relating to my pursuing the rough track, which for the last eleven years I have been walking in—the POET'S PATH : a path I never sought, and one in which I have had to do violence to my own feelings, many times, to tread.   Nevertheless, I certainly believe it was one marked out for me by Providence : and, believing this, I have pursued it in the storm and sunshine ; and whatever may be found in this Volume of Poems to be useful in helping mankind to better life, will give me incessant joy while I live.   But let them give all the glory to Another, Whose I am, and Whom I serve : remembering that the Treasure was placed in an earthen vessel, that the excellency of the power might be of God and not of man : for it is by His Grace alone that I am what I am, and that grace He has bestowed upon me, I trust, has not been given in vain.

Clifton, 1885.   P. GABBITASS.

THE POET'S AUTOBIOGRAPHY.

E was born at Worksop, in the county of Nottingham : a pretty little market town, near the Dukeries of Welbeck and Clumber, and noted for its timber trade, and manufactories for Windsor chairs. His father for a number of years carried on a successful business in this department, which, after his decease, was conducted by his widow until their four children, then living, were brought up to man and womanhood.

The time the subject of this sketch was ushered into being, was one cold December night in the year 1822. He was born, I presume, much after the same manner as other babies, only he was,

> Of course, their first-born baby boy—
> His father's hope, and mother's joy !

and 'tis said there was a little extra rejoicing on that account. It is authoritatively stated that, on the occasion of his christening, there was quite a dispute as to what name he should bear : some of his friends wished him to be named after his mother's relatives, others declared he should be named after friends on his father's side ; and there is no knowing where the matter would have ended, had not his father, as a third party, stepped in and settled the matter in his own peculiar way. He told the varied disputants that the baby boy should not be named after any of their relatives, but after good old Peter Godfrey, a man in their employ : and he hoped that their little one would grow up like him. That is the reason the Clifton Poet bears the name of Peter, and as truth is sometimes stranger than fiction, so it is here : for good old Peter Godfrey was a poet, and of no mean order—for it

B

is said that, through the public press, for weeks he had the mastery of
a reverend gentleman, in a poetical discussion on Water Baptism.
Of the Clifton Poet's ancestors it is not needful to say much. His
mother's parents, whose name was Foster, occupied a farm near
Womersly, in Yorkshire : where was born one of the best of mothers
to her children in the wide, wide world ; and who, at the ripe age of
eighty-four, in the year 1884, at Worksop, calmly passed away to rest.
His grandsire on his father's side was a carpenter, and for many years
worked at the bench for the Poet's father (he has given some sketches
of both his grandsires in this book, in a poem entitled " Grandsires").
His great grandsire, Robert Gabbitass, was the Town Crier and
Watchman at East Retford, and where, in gold lace uniform and three-
cornered hat, he used to parade the streets and announce the passing
hours of night—beside this he filled the post of assistant sheriff's
officer, and once had the unpleasant duty of arresting at Newstead
Abbey, in bed, the world-renowned poet, Lord Byron, for debt.   'Tis
said his lordship had loaded pistols on the table at his side, but did
not use them on the Poet's great grandsire. Of the Poet's boyhood
days it is scarcely necessary to say much, only he was like some other
boys, very full of mischief and mimicry, and could perform wonderful
evolutions on his hands, by throwing himself over in windmill-like
fashion, to the great amusement of his father's workmen.   Besides this,
he was considered rather witty for a youth, as the following incident
will testify. At the Wesleyan Sunday School he attended, it was the
custom of the elder boys, after morning school hours, to hurry into
the chapel ; and as seats were not at all times easily to be found, they
would hasten up the pulpit stairs, and, as many as could, sit there
during the preaching service. But this thing had become a nuisance,
not only in obstructing the preacher on his way to the pulpit, but also
on account of the whispering going on during the discourse. This was
made known to the teachers, who announced to the scholars that from
henceforth the pulpit stairs were to be kept clear. On the following
Sunday, however, before the teachers had left the school for the chapel,
a boy, who was to be a poet, came running in, and told them there
were twenty-four boys on the pulpit stairs already ; one of the

teachers immediately hastened to expel the intruders, when, lo! to his astonishment, he found only two there. When these had been ordered down, he came back to the informant, and wished to know why he had dared to come and tell him there were twenty-four boys on the pulpit stairs. "Oh, sir," said he, "I will soon explain that. You know those two boys are the sons of Mr. Twelve, and that twice twelve are twenty-four!" This was too much for the teacher's risible faculties to hold, and he let the culprit go scot free that time. There are two other circumstances connected with his boyhood, which made at the time wonderful impressions on his mind, and are as fresh to-day as they were then—though more than fifty years have passed away; one of them is as follows. Near the town in which he lived, it was currently reported that an otter had escaped from some place, and was making a temporary abode in an adjoining plantation, and a stream of water which flowed through it ; and at various times companies of young men had tried to secure it with dogs and other means they had at hand, but as yet it was all in vain. One Sunday morning, however, as a boy, who was to be a poet, was going to his Sunday school, he saw in the distance a number of young men coming towards him from the other end of the common, and the following thoughts, in the shape of question and answer, passed rapidly through his mind : "Who are these young men coming along ? Oh, I know. When I get near them I will ask them where they have been ; one of them, Richard Sanderson, will answer, 'We have been to hunt for the otter.' I shall then say, 'And have you caught it ?' He will answer 'Yes.' I shall then ask, 'Where is it ?' and he will answer "It is at Mr. Gilling's shop.'" When they all met, the same questions and answers as referred to were put and given by the same persons. What it was that brought all this about has been through the Poet's life an unravelled mystery. The other never-to-be-forgotten circumstance was as follows. One very stormy day, when he was about ten years old, he was standing in a large timber yard watching the sails of a neighbouring mill whirling rapidly round, when this premonition passed, as it were, in a moment through his mind : "The next time those sails go round, one of them will come off and dash through that maltkiln roof." The next time they went round one of them did come off, and went through that malthouse roof. Strange ! yes, but true ; and who can solve the problem ?

The schooldays of the Poet were, on the whole, pleasant and agreeable to him, although not of long duration—for although his father had at that time a good business, yet it was an age when fathers believed in boys going to work early, and at the age of thirteen he had to earn his father, at wood-turning by piece work, ten shillings per week—what he earned over was his own for pocket money. When near the age of fifteen, however, his father thought he would apprentice him to the carpenter's business, for the following reasons. He was in the habit of purchasing large quantities of elm timber, for the seats of Windsor chairs : these were required to be of a certain size, and all timber, unless it reached that size, was practically useless, on account of its brittle nature, for any other parts of Windsor chairs ; and his father thought, by putting him to a carpenter, he would be able to find a use, in that trade, for what he himself could not turn to practical account. Consequently he was apprenticed to an industrious village carpenter, at Blidworth, on the hill near to Newstead Abbey, the seat of Lord Byron, and the spot where Dr. Livingstone wrote his last book. More than thirty years after this, he received congratulatory letters from the present owner of Newstead Abbey and his lady, for poems written on the death of Dr. Livingstone and his last words at Muilala, which appeared in several magazines, and are in this collection of poems. He immediately wrote back and thanked them for their courtesy and kindness in corresponding with him, and, however it might surprise them, it was nevertheless true, that the writer of the poems referred to was once a carpenter boy, and very near to Newstead Abbey. Since then he has had the pleasure and honour to visit Newstead Abbey, where a guide was furnished to conduct him to all its treasured spots ; and, on his leaving there, was presented with a spray from the tree on which Byron, at his last visit to Newstead, carved his immortal name ; and for which said bough that bore this inscription, the American speculating Barnum offered £500 to the then owner, Colonel Wildman ; who sent a polite message to the indomitable showman, on receiving it, that he would be obliged to Barnum if he would at once leave the Abbey grounds.

During the writer's visit to Newstead, he went to see Lord Byron's tomb, at Hucknal Torkard Church, where the kind old sexton paid him every attention, by procuring him a ladder to correctly copy the marble tablet there, by placing him on the exact spot under which Lord Byron lay ; " And," said the old man, " I assisted in placing Lady Lovelace, Byron's Ada, here." Near the tablet were suspended wreaths, sent by eminent personages, to decorate the tomb of one of the greatest Poets of the age, and one who, had his mind been under Christian influence, might have been one of the most useful. On this visit to Newstead and Byron's tomb, he had the great pleasure of meeting a number of friends at Blidworth, and spending a pleasant day, some of them being gentlemen he worked for when an apprentice boy ; and at night, at their request, he preached to them in the Wesleyan Chapel.

But to return to his apprentice days. On his entering the village for the first time, he felt an unusual strangeness, for he felt like a stranger in a strange land ; and he will never forget the feeling that came over him the first night he crept into bed. The fact was, it was not so comfortable, although clean, as the one he left behind him ; and he could not help thinking of " Home, sweet home," and his good old mother. His apprentice days passed somewhat heavily, for he had

> Plenty of chopping and plenty of sawing,
> Plenty of planing and plenty of jawing,—

Because in those days country carpenters had often to

> Cut down very many trees,
> Which was not easy for the knees ;
> Then had to saw them up, alack !
> Which was not easy for the back.

And the Poet in his younger days has often walked eight miles per day, to and from his labour, carrying with him a large pitsaw, and by way of change, exchanging it with his fellow-apprentice for a carpenter's basket of tools. Yet even then there was hope cheering him onward to Saturday night, when he would go and sit two quiet hours with one

who was then all the world to him, and whose welcome company kept
him from joining with the giddy and thoughtless of the village, and
was one means of forming his character for life.

With her he spent thirteen years of happy married life, when,
from a severe cold taken while on a visit with her husband to her
widowed mother, she was somewhat prematurely taken to the home of
no more dying, and the land of no more pain.

With four motherless children then was the Poet left, just when
everything in life seemed to be opening out for him with a fair share
of this world's prosperity. Yet during his apprenticeship he had one
severe trial, namely, the loss of his dear father. A few short months
before, he had seen him on his bed of affliction, and received from
him his last fatherly advice, especially in reference to Intoxicating
Drink,—which advice he has endeavoured to live out, by practical
abstinence from all strong drink for now more than forty years, and
for which he can never be too thankful, as through it he believes he
has been enabled to accomplish an amount of mental labour he could
never have performed otherwise.

One noontide, while coming from a near farmstead to his dinner,
he found in his master's house one of his father's apprentices, who had
walked seventeen miles that morning, bringing with him the heavy
tidings that his father was no more. Then there was a departure for
his home, where he had to meet for the first time a widowed mother.
And then

> There was weeping within the old homestead,
>   Where fond hearts had gathered of yore,
> By a widow bereft of her husband,
>   And a lad who had father no more.

For in three short days a coffin was let down in his father's open grave.
When the time of his apprenticeship had ended, he returned to his
native town, and there by plodding industry he established a good
business, for everything he seemed to put his hand to was successful;
until unfortunately by listening to one—a lawyer, who came in the
garb of a friend—he was induced to take steps which led to the
enrichment of his apparent friend, and the ruin (for a time at least) of

himself. The fruits of years of industry were swept away for the benefit of the spoiler, who to-day lies in an unenvied grave. For, after living some years in a luxuriant style on the hard earnings of others, his day of reckoning came. He was suddenly hurried from his stately mansion, and died like an exile at a wayside inn, on a neighbouring forest; and was taken from thence, 'tis said, to his burial, not in a richly plumed hearse, as 'twas once thought, but in a heavy farmer's cart. "God's mills grind slowly, yet their grinding's sure." Some time after the death of the Poet's first wife, he was sitting in the house of his eldest sister, when a friend of theirs entered, bringing with her a lady friend from Sheffield. When they had been seated for a while, he gave a casual glance at this strange lady, and in a moment there was a something seemed to say, "That will be your wife." Immediately he turned his head aside, and muttered to himself, "Impossible." Nevertheless, in a few months after this it was even so. While conversing with her some time after on this remarkable time, she said to her it seemed a mystery altogether. For on that day she entered Worksop, she had started from Sheffield with a few friends to visit a noted old ruin, not far from thence. When they reached the station, however, at which they intended to alight, she to the utter surprise of her friends said she would go forward to Worksop, and alone ; she had never been there before. They thought her conduct strange, and so did she, as she afterwards confessed. In the compartment of the carriage they occupied sat a lady, who told her that she also was going to Worksop, but going to see her friends ; and as she had seen her before near her own home, she would be glad if she would accompany her to her friend's house, where she would be welcome for the day. This offer was accepted, and with the results the reader has been made aware of. This second marriage of the Poet was happy, but of short duration, for she was in a decline, though she knew it not ; and in one year and ten months her husband had to follow her to the tomb. She sleeps in the beautiful cemetery at Sheffield, very near the honoured dust of James Montgomery, the Christian Poet ; and their little angel boy, whom they named after him, sleeps at Dronfield, a few miles away ; but his pure spirit has

joined his mother's, and "that sweet singer's in the skies."
The ways of Providence in this world are past finding out, for here
was one who had become attached to his four motherless children,
and who appeared to care for them as though they were her own ; and
yet the homestead was again in mourning through the ravages of the
king of terrors—death.   It was during this sad bereavement that the
poem, " Kilton Wood," was penned, although the writer had but
written a few stray poems before, and but very few after, until he came
to Clifton, and stood one day on grand St. Vincent's height.   Then it
was that a something stirred within him he had never felt before, and
from that day he has been what the *Bristol Mercury and Daily Post*
truly designated him, " The indefatigable Clifton Poet."   He has been
instant in season, and I dare say out of season, to some who have no
regard for what strikes at evil and encourages what is right.   His poem
on " Kilton Wood " was published with a few others, at the request of
many friends, in his native town ; and the spot is oft visited by those
who appreciate the sentiment it contains.   There is just one pleasing
incident in connection with this poem, which the writer feels he ought
not to omit to mention.   Some six or seven years ago, while at his
poet's stand on Clifton Down, a rather elderly lady, with a young lady
and gentleman, came up St. Vincent's Rocks.   One placard on the
Poet's stall bore the following inscription :—" Kilton Wood, and other
poems."   This arrested the attention of the elder lady, who came up
and said, " Will you please allow me to look at Kilton Wood book ? "
Of course this request was readily complied with, for the Poet saw in
her the demeanour of a true born lady.   When she had received it
she opened it, read a little and then smiled, and held it out for the
young lady and gentleman to look at, when they read and smiled.   She
then looked at the Poet, and exclaimed, " And did you know Kilton
Wood ? "   He answered, " Yes, it is near my childhood's home."   She
smiled benignantly, and said, " It was near there I spent my sweet
childhood's days.   You knew Lord Surrey, did you not ? "   " Certainly
I did," the Poet cried.   " He was my father," she said ; and after
making her purchases she bade him good-bye.   It was Lady Foley ;
and the title, " Kilton Wood," had touched a something within her

that reminded her of bygone years : for Kilton Wood was part of her parental inheritance, and near her childhood's home.

Some time after his last bereavement, and before he left his native town to come to Bristol, he was, with his young family, induced to take a third wife. Their meeting was somewhat peculiar, and they married in haste, yet never repented at leisure—for the longer they lived, the better they loved, until death came twelve years afterwards and separated them for a little while. It was soon after this his great sore trouble came, for which she knew her husband was innocent. He had been too confiding ; and a few words from the district manager of a bank, who knew him well, will explain it all—and they are given here for the good of posterity. " Mr. G.," said he, " you have been too honest. Lawyers are our best customers—I tell you this in confidence ; but never trust them ! " These words are placed here very reluctantly, but they are true ; and if they are the means of leading young, industrious tradesmen, to think and act with proper discretion, they will not have been written in vain. When the spider's web had been discovered too late, his wife came, with the affection of a true-hearted woman, and clasped him in her arms, saying, " Never mind, love, I will be true to you ; I will never forsake you." Nor did she, she was true in storm as in sunshine ; and nearly the last words she said to her husband on her death-bed—and which were more to him than thousands of gold and silver—were, " I have always found you faithful." As a woman she had qualifications of a superior order, for she had a smattering of five languages, had devoted much attention to the study of botany, drawing, astronomy, and to the construction of the human frame. She was also methodical and economical in everything she did ; in fact, she was far above her husband both in culture and in every way—and he told her so many times before their marriage. But it mattered not: she loved poetry, and she loved a poet —and she had him,

> With his trials and his cares :
> Spite of a few hungry bears,
> Who'd have stopp'd them if they could—
> They did try, but 'twas no good.

After the Poet's great loss, through the villany of one man whom
he trusted as a child would its father, he put his tool basket on his
shoulder, and walked more than eight miles per day ; and never lost
one day for more than three years, at Walbeck Abbey woodyard, under
His Grace the Duke of Portland.   During this time he had again got
together a nice little home, and made it more attractive than his neighbours' : inasmuch as the minister of the church to which they belonged
said one day when entering it, "Yes, Mrs. G. ; your husband has
been trying to make you comfortable here.   But this is not your rest."
Strange words, but true : for in a few short weeks the snug little home
had to be left with its nice little garden, and pleasant look-out ; and
off for Bristol went the Poet.   The reason of this sudden transition
came about in the following manner.   Early one morning, while in bed,
he said somewhat suddenly to his wife, "I wonder, love, whether we
shall ever live in Bristol ?"   What made him say it, he cannot tell, only
he knows that it is true ; and it so surprised his wife that she exclaimed,
"Whatever, love, made you think of this ?"   He told her he did not
know—nor did he ; for, under the circumstances, he was very comfortable in his present place of employment—and, for aught he knew,
there would be work for him there for an unlimited time.   A few days
after this, a letter was received by his dear wife from a friend in
Liverpool, who owned an hotel at which commercial travellers called.
He stated in that letter that a traveller, representing a Bristol firm, had
been inquiring of him, to know if he could recommend a steady,
trustworthy man, to take charge of a timber-yard belonging to a cabinet
manufactory.   His duties would be to take charge of the timber, and
furnish certain quantities to the workmen, for the articles of furniture
they had to make.   He told him he did know of one whom he was
sure would fill such a situation ; and from future correspondence, and
testimonials furnished, the situation was secured.   The reason of the
change was this—it was the wish of his wife, and the reason she gave
appeared right.   She said, "We are comfortable now, but the time
will come when you will not be so strong as you are now—your constant
walk of eight miles a day will tell on you by-and-by.   Accept this situation in Bristol : you will have better wages, not so much hard work,

and have more opportunities for bettering your position." He yielded to his wife's solicitation ; and one cold morning in the month of March, 1864, he left his native town for a city noted for its many churches, orphan houses, varied charities, and neglect of poets. It was night when he reached old Bristol, and all appeared to him gloomy enough —for the rain was pouring down in torrents. However, he managed to find the locality where his place of business was, and went into a coffee tavern nigh at hand, where he found comfortable lodgings and a home. Their minister had prayed, before he left his home, that he might find a comfortable place of abode, until his wife joined him ; and he did, with an elderly Christian widow, with one son at home, who, alternately with the Poet, conducted family worship there until his wife joined him. Early the next morning he hurried to his duties, and on entering the timber-yard for the first time, such a scene presented itself to his view as he hopes never to witness again : for the yard was in a complete upset, and the rain was pouring down ; whilst a sorry mixture of bricks and mahogany, mortar and American birch, mud and walnut, filth and rosewood, muck and maple, stones and pine-boards, met his vision ; and the eye of his mind went back to his clean, comfortable bench at Walbeck woodyard, and he almost wished himself there again. But he thought, " Well, I am here, and must try to make the best of it ; it will perhaps be better by-and-by—I will try to let them see I can make things look different soon." And he did, for his employer, who was an acute Scotchman, and did many people brown beside the Poet, congratulated him upon the change there was for the better in his timber-yard. But matters did not remain in this state long : as the Poet, before many weeks were over, discovered there was a screw loose, or a number of them, somewhere : for there came out in one of the daily papers, with whom the manufacturer largely advertised, a most glowing description of the said establishment and its workings, from tip to toe. One that made the Poet think, when he had read it, that it must have been a

> Tremendous effort of the scribe's,
> Unless he had some heavy bribes.

And he intimated as much in a letter to his wife, who had prudently

arranged to stay behind to see how matters went on before the home
was broken up, and the goods removed to Bristol.   As he thought, so
it came to pass.   But a short time before it did, the manager came to
him privately and said, "I hope, Mr. G., you will not think of
bringing your goods to Bristol on the strength of our governor's
promise, for I do assure you he is not to be trusted; and I do not
wish you, a stranger, to be led away by him.   He is continually
advertising in the public papers for men, and when the poor fellows
come, he has nothing for them; and in many instances we have had
to make collections amongst ourselves to send them back to their
homes."   The Poet thanked him kindly for the information, and
told him he should not be the worse for giving it, nor will he: for he
has done serving employers who have no more regard for their
workmen than the dirt, only as far as their selfish interests are served;
and he is resting where the wicked cease to trouble, and the weary
are at rest.   Soon after the information was given the bubble burst,
and the Poet was sent adrift; and what step to take he hardly knew,
but at once wrote home to his sensible wife for instructions.   She
was very much surprised at the news, after the very flattering
promises that had been made as to the permanence of the situation.
Nevertheless, she wrote back at once, and her husband adhered to
her advice.   It was as follows: "To seek out for some present
employment, and then be looking after a situation" she felt he
ought to have: for she argued, "To come back to your old place, you
would have the same amount of walking to do every day, and you
are not growing younger;" and then she concluded her letter with
these words: "I feel that the Lord has a work for you to do in
Bristol."   This last declaration of hers was decisive, and he went to
Mr. F., a large building contractor near Brunswick Square, stated his
case, and showed him testimonials of character he had brought from
gentlemen of influence in his native town; and the one received
from the firm he had come to Bristol for.   When the gentleman had
read these he looked at the Poet, for he was respectably dressed; and
before he had time to speak, for he thought the gentleman was
concluding he was too well-dressed to be fond of work, he said: "Oh,

never mind, sir, my clothes ; I am not afraid to labour. I have done a great deal of hard work in my time, and can do a great deal more yet." The gentleman immediately smiled, and said, " Well, you may come on to-morrow. We are building two villas near St. Matthew's Church. You can work there until something turns out better for you." The Poet wrote off at once and told his wife, and then she prepared to come to Bristol, bringing with her their youngest boy, and leaving his two daughters in situations near their mother's friends, and his eldest son in employment in that locality. These four children were by his first wife, two of whom are yet living—his eldest son and youngest daughter ; while his eldest daughter Mattie, and his youngest son Fred, two years ago passed away to rest. Soon after his wife's arrival in Bristol she began to grow feeble, and medical aid being procured, it was found that she was suffering from cancer in the breast; and after lingering with its pain and discomfort for seven years, she calmly passed away. Nearly the last words her husband heard her repeat the night before, while conversing with her on death, were : " Jesus can make a dying bed feel soft as downy pillows are." On the next morning at seven o'clock, after he had left her much as usual at a quarter to six, he was fetched from his office at Keynsham, where he was managing a business. She had fallen asleep in Jesus. A short time before her death she had come into possession of a small cottage property at Sutton Bridge, in Lincolnshire, her native place. This she had made over by will to her husband with her own hand, and which since her death—for he never touched a shilling before, for he felt it was hers—he has been using in bringing out his little books, and but for this he would have been at the end of the chapter long ago ; for the world has yet to learn that a Poet who writes for the good of humanity should be supported while he is doing his work. Providence, however, has enabled him to use this little money, so that what he has done, although not remunerative now, will be of service to his family when he is gone. It is for this, among other reasons, that he is keeping at his work, believing in an adage he has often given to many questions on this subject, that *doing right always pays.* His being left a widower the

third time was not in itself so distressing as in the other instances,
for as by some providential arrangement his daughter Mattie, who
was over twenty years of age, had come home only a few months
before her stepmother's death. She had not been strong for some
time, and she wrote home and told them so. Her stepmother said
at once she should come home, and her father wrote and told her this,
hoping the change might do her good. Then she came, and it was
while Mattie was at Keynsham growing stronger, that her stepmother
passed away. During the time her mother had Mattie with her she
was pleased, for she discovered a something in her that she loved,
and nearly her last request to her husband was : " Father, buy Mattie
a harmonium with my money when I am gone." She had
discovered that there was in Mattie an ear and love for music, and
her wish was complied with ; while oft at eventide and on the
Sabbath has the Poet's mind been cheered by the music of his Mattie,
who seemed to know when the tune of " Shall we gather at the
river ? " and " There is a better land above," would be welcome to her
sire. For some time she continued housekeeper for her father at
Keynsham, where they were very happy together ; and thought that
even there would be their dwelling-place for the residue of their days ;
but there is nothing certain underneath the sun, for the business he
was overlooking then was given up, and the Poet had to seek out
for somewhere else to go. Before he left Bristol to overlook that
business, his employer told him if he was not comfortable he was to
come back—there was the same place for him again; but he was
comfortable at Keynsham, for during the five years he was there his
employer and himself never had one unpleasant word ; and had it
not have been for an unfortunate building speculation, he would
undoubtedly have been there yet. But on being free to go, he went
and laid his case before the gentleman whom he had left previously.
He told him to come at once and resume his duties. Then there
was another removal of his goods and another home to make. This
was done very near to Clifton Down, where all went on pleasantly for
a time, when all of a sudden this employer gave up his building
business, and removed to Weston-super-Mare. The reason for this,

it is told, was the following : He had formerly purchased a large quantity of land near to Stoke Bishop, and intended filling it with new villas ; and this being discovered by a neighbouring gentleman, who found out that some of them, which were to be in close proximity to his own mansion, would not only lessen its value, but be a continual annoyance to himself, he after a deal of change ringing on both sides, bought up all the land and unfinished villas, and thus put a stop there to the building operations of the Poet's employer. He himself told the Poet that the other party had had many opportunities of purchasing the land before, and cheap. They had let the opportunity slip, and now had to purchase it very dearly. This evidently was true, for it enabled the builder to appear like the gentleman, although for aught he seemed to care his workmen might become beggars ; for there was no temporary provision made for them until they could secure employment elsewhere, as all the work was stopped at a few hours' notice, and the Poet sent adrift again. For weeks after this he was trying to procure an over-looker's situation, but nothing seemed to turn up, although he was in the meantime doing his best to turn something up himself; for he paced Bristol city day after day till he was tired, footsore, and faint. He advertised in the public papers for a place of trust and responsibility, but nothing came ; and yet while all this was going on, kind friends were saying : " I am sure there are scores of gentlemen who would put you in a good situation, if they knew." Well, many of them did know, and a few of them exercised their influence ; but it did not come to pass, until one day he determined in the following week to go and seek work as a journeyman carpenter, and try to do what good he could in a quiet way on a Sunday. On the Sunday morning following this resolve he had to go out into the country to preach twice ; and it being a very rainy morning, he put on a pair of boots with thicker soles than those he usually wore, and what with hurrying over Kingsdown, and the slippery state of the roads, on his way to meet the conveyance at the bottom of the hill, he had a fearful fall ; and although it did not entirely disable him, it made his left arm for a time powerless, though it was not dislocated. Nevertheless, it disqualified him for working at the bench for a time, had a situation been found for him. He went forward that morning, however, to his preaching duties ; took the service in the morning with his clothing all bespattered with mud, and his painful arm. Before the evening service, his friends with drying and brushing had made him more becoming to appear in public—although for the next few weeks he was for all laborious purposes comparatively useless. It was at this time that the Teignmouth Catastrophe occurred, on June 18th, 1874. An excursion from Bristol of the *employés* of Robinson and Co. went down to Teignmouth, when a party of young people went out for a short sail with a boatman who had unfortunately a boat that was unseaworthy : for when a short distance from the shore she began to fill with water, and in a short time all the occupants of the boat were in the sea—in sight of hundreds who could render them no assistance. The young men in the boat saved themselves by swimming to shore, with the exception of one Walter Lovell, aged 17. He also could have done this, but he heard the voice of one he was engaged to, Agnes Saunders, aged 17, calling from the water, " Walter ! Walter ! " and he went back to try to save her ; but 'twas all in vain, and they died together, firmly clasped in each others' arms, and near them three more young lady friends. This sad occurrence filled the City of Bristol, from whence they started, with the most pungent grief ; and it was resolved to give them a public funeral. They were brought back to Bristol, and at their interment a most affecting and numerous procession wended its way to Arno's Vale. The Poet was among the spectators, and he felt acutely on the subject ; and that night and the next morning early, there were thoughts in reference to them rising from his soul. Then he hurried from his bed, nor did he rest until he had placed the Teignmouth Catastrophe Poem on his breakfast table. After breakfast, he read it to his daughter Mattie, who gave him her opinion of it in the following words : " Oh, that is good, father. Have a thousand copies printed ; and if they will but do good and pay the printer, we will be satisfied." It was just with that feeling it went to press, and it astonished both the Poet and the public, for in four weeks from its appearing in print, twenty thousand copies had been issued from the press, and most of them sold. This thrilling circumstance seemed to convey to the mind of the Poet this truth, " Now you are to have different employment from toiling with the plane and saw. Poetry is your work. Here is a proof. What you have written is evidence that your lines are appreciated by the public. You have heard that readers of this poem, at the windows of booksellers in the city, have in the public streets been moved to tears. This is your path. You will succeed, only persevere." And from that day to this he has been endeavouring to do this, very often amid many discouragements ; and had it not been for some encouraging words from men of mark, not only for worldly position, but mental culture, *and a sense of duty*, he would have given it up long ago. Soon after his " Teignmouth Catastrophe " poem came out, he published a number of others, which although not so remunerative as this, kept him clear of the printer's books ; and as they invariably inculcated good lessons, they were not written in vain. One day, while on St. Vincent's in summer-tide, he felt a something unusual stirring within him, and he sat down before the grand panorama, and penned his poem, " Cliftonia the Beautiful." The title of the poem was attractive, and being entirely new, it procured for it a ready sale. It struck the Poet just after he had written this poem, if he could but procure an engraving of the Suspension Bridge to place on the sheet with it, it would make it somewhat attractive, and help to sell the same ; yet how to obtain one was to him a mystery, for he had no experience in these matters. One day, however, before the poem was printed, he had the manuscript in his pocket ; and shortly took a stroll near the Observatory, gazing on the matchless beauties of the scene. While there he thought he would take a seat for a short time, and just look over his manuscript again. While he was thus employed, a strange gentleman came and took a seat beside him. There they both sat silently for a time, until the stranger made some remarks on the magnificent scene that lay before them. Then the Poet told him he had been trying to depict the same in the poem that he held in his hand ; and he invited the gentleman to read it, who told him that

C

he always felt interested in descriptive poems. The Poet told him
that he had thought of having it printed, and had also thought, if he
could have an engraving of the Suspension Bridge to have gone with
it, that it would have been an advantage. He immediately replied,
" I am sure it would ; and I am an engraver from London, and shall
be pleased to do a nice one for you." Then there was an inquiry
about the price, and an appointment made to meet the Poet at his
home next day. At the hour appointed the stranger made his
appearance, and had not been long seated, when he looked across
the room to a framed steel engraving, and said, " I see you have
my father's likeness there." " Your father's!" exclaimed the
Poet. " Yes, the Rev. E. P." " Then," said he, " if that is your
father, he is my friend." The order for the bridge was given and
executed, and it is the one that appears on the eighteen forty-two
paged books already published by the Poet. Shortly after this
poem appeared a thought struck him, that if he could but be
allowed to exhibit his poems on Clifton Down, he would secure more
readers by getting them into the hands of strangers from distant
parts. He made application for permission to do so, sending
specimens of his poems, and a letter showing that what he was
writing was all pure literature ; and had in them what would be useful
to mankind. This letter secured for him the privilege to exhibit
them on Clifton Down on a Poet's stall. This was his first effort at
being his own publisher, and his first purchaser was C. Cordeux,
Esq., Jeweller, of Clifton. The reason he adopted this mode (for this
kind of work was all new to him) of being his own publisher, was
from information he met with in *Punch* years before he began his
strange avocation. The paragraph read as follows : " Did you ever
know an author who could have oyster sauce to his beefsteak ? Did
you ever know a publisher who couldn't?" "Ah !" thought the Poet,
" there is something in that paragraph worth looking at. If I am to be
an author I will be my own publisher ; it may be slower work at first,
but if there is any harvest worth gathering at the last, my family

> Shall have the good of all my life sowing,
> If their father should be pinch'd while the seed is growing."

There was one pleasing incident connected with the first appearance of the Poet's Stall on Clifton Down. A person of very gentlemanly demeanour from the Clifton Down Hotel passed by, and gave furtive glances at it; but did not venture to stay until he had gone by several times. Then he took up some of the leaflets, for as yet the Poet had not published one book. This gentleman read some of the pieces, one of which appeared very much to interest him. It was a production by the Poet's daughter Mattie, and her first, entitled "Love's reply to affection's question." He purchased all the copies of this on the stall, and a few others, and went away; but just as the Poet was closing his stall for the night, this same gentleman came to him with a beautiful book, and wished him to present it to his daughter, remarking, that a father who owned a child who could write such beautiful lines ought to be proud of her. The Poet told him he was thankful for her, and also very much obliged to him for the kind present he had brought her. The next morning, before the Poet had well arranged his stand, the same gentleman came up, making inquiries whether he had presented her with the book. The Poet told him he had, and that his daughter was very much obliged to him for it; and she also stated that if he would not deem it intrusive, she would be pleased to know who she had the honour of thanking for it. Immediately, the gentleman raised his hat and said, "Sir Godfrey L——." From that very hour there sprung up a Christian friendship between the baronet and Poet, and while he remained in Clifton—it was his favourite resort; for having, as he stated, travelled much, he admired Clifton for its scenery more than any place in the world—they had many a pleasant chat on travels, church matters, and other subjects; and when he left Clifton for his London home he came to bid farewell to the Poet, and his parting words were: "I have one thing more to say to you, Mr. G., persevere. What you write is good, and written for doing good. Persevere, your path will open some day." Then placing a gold coin in his hand he said, "That is to help you a little in your printing. Good-bye." The Poet took encouragement from this, not merely because the speaker was a baronet, but an author as well. It was at this time that the Poet had to wheel his poem stall one mile in the morning, and the same distance home at night, for it would not have been safe to have left it on Clifton Down for many reasons ; but the time soon came when there was a way made for him to do it, and leave it well secured. One morning when he was wheeling it on his way from home, he was seen by Sir Godfrey, who came to him and said, " What a pity it is you should have so much labour to get your productions for sale." On another occasion while taking home his stall, he was accosted on the way by two would-be witty gentlemen, who wanted to know if what he was wheeling was a trough to feed sheep from. " Not exactly," said the Poet, " although I daresay there is some good food in it for both sheep and lambs." Some time after another gentleman met him with it on the road, and said, " Why, whatever is that,—is it for a coffin ? " " No, sir," said the Poet, " but there is something in it which, if rightly used, will be of service to people in helping them to prepare for their coffins." The gentleman turned up his eyes at this, and off he went. One day some time after this, another gentleman, evidently of position, if diamond rings are an evidence when on the fingers, called at his publication stall, and took up several of his little books and looked them over ; and then very sneeringly said : " You appear to be, by your books, rather religiously inclined." The Poet looked straight at him and said : " Yes, sir, rather ; and if there is nothing after this life is ended, there is something in Christianity to cheer me on my journey ; and at its ending I shall be no worse off than the unbeliever. But if there should be something more, and the Bible is true, where will the unbeliever be ? " He said no more, but he did purchase a book, and went his way. On the Poet's first coming to Bristol, he had a somewhat encouraging incident in connection with his history. It was the time when Garibaldi the brave was about to visit England. Early one morning while in bed, he was thinking on the life work of the patriot, and in a few minutes he struck off some lines as a welcome to him, and dropped them into the receiving box for correspondence at the office of the *Bristol Mercury and Daily Post*. The next day they appeared in print, and a few days after the Poet was waited upon at the Cabinet Works, St. Philip's, by a gentleman from Park Street, music-seller to the Queen, asking if he would allow the words to be published with music, to which they had been set by Leigh Wilson, Esq. ; and they would like to have them published. He of course gave his consent, for there came as it were in a moment golden visions floating through his brain ; but poetlike these hopes were doomed to disappointment, as, although they were forwarded to their London publisher they were not published, for the following reasons, as stated by Mr. C. himself: " When the lines and music arrived in London, our publisher had another on the same subject in the press ; and it was thought to publish both would injure the sale of one—although we consider that yours are the best stanzas." The Poet felt himself flattered at the frank confession, and more particularly so as the one in the press was the composition of that true Poetess, Eliza Cook. It was a short time after this that he wrote his " Blind Boy " poem. It was written a few weeks after he came to Bristol, on Sunday during the intervals of public worship, in a chamber at his lodgings, with the old Christian widow lady in St. Philip's, opposite the Avonside Engine Works ; and its subject is his own life experience. He is somewhat particular in mentioning these circumstances in reference to this poem, because it has been extensively and usefully circulated ; and also graciously accepted by Her Majesty the Queen. But to return to his little book, or rather poem stall, on the Down, for he had not yet written one book ; and his first was brought out under somewhat painful circumstances, and entitled, " Musings Poetical from the Diary of Miss Chameleon Circumstances." Owing to a severe attack of lumbago, brought on by sheltering from the rain and snow in an old cold stone cave or grotto, near the Poet's tree, some of the stanzas of this book were composed at home while he lay in the easiest position he could find— namely, on the boarded floor of his room. This book was graciously accepted by Her Royal Highness the Princess of Wales, and the first edition of one thousand being sold, a second edition of two thousand more came from the press, with an engraving of Her Royal Highness on the cover. His next venture was the " Blind Boy," and

other poems. A second edition of this book of two thousand also has
come out; his third book was "The Good Wife at home: scenes
from the life of John and Martha Careful." This book has been much
praised, its object being to show that a British workman's
wife is in her right place at home, and that her husband and family
are more benefited by her being there than going out to work. This
book has been pronounced excellent by the Editor of the *British
Workman*, who had the manuscript for review. The Poet was
requested to have it printed ten years before it was published, having
given it from memory at several social gatherings, for it was one of
his earliest productions. His "Kilton Wood" book came next, and
then "Uncle Peter," dedicated to juvenile and non-juvenile smokers:
the eleven chapters are experiences in the Poet's history. The first
scene in it occurred before a large mansion with lodge that once
stood opposite the entrance to Barton Regis, Eastville; and with the
exception of a little innocent filling up, the incidents are all true. The
Poet received the personal thanks of S. Morley, Esq., for its production, copies of which he purchased to go to London, and one of the
Laureate's brothers came, and introduced himself by fetching one;
and after perusing it said: "This is a good book, although I am a
notorious smoker." From that time they became friends, and on his
leaving Clifton, where he was then residing, he brought the Poet a
parting present of "Thomson's Seasons." Many a pleasant and
profitable chat had they together before this on Clifton Down, for he
was a believer in the teaching and doctrines recorded in the good
Old Book; and on one occasion he brought one of his brothers to
introduce to him, and since then another has been, and brought with
him two interesting young ladies, his own daughters, to see the once
carpenter boy; and Lord Tennyson himself has sent him an
autograph letter, with thanks, for his book "Evangeline;" and the
Right Hon. the Earl of Shaftesbury as well. There is one
encouraging incident in the publication of this little book, it may be
right to mention here. A Clifton gentleman who had passed by the
stall for many years without having turned aside except to just give a
nod of the head to the Poet, one night as he was closing did so, and

said, " Mr. G., will you let me have one of your little books to look
at." He was told, certainly. Then he said, " Let me have your best,
if you know it." The Poet said to him, "Please to read
'Evangeline.'" He took it, and the next morning early he was up
at the Poet's stand ; and the first words he said were: " You have
surprised me." "Surprised you ?" said the Poet. " Why?" "Oh !"
said he, " I never thought you had written anything equal to this."
" Well, sir," the writer exclaimed, "you well know that you never
came near me to see." The gentleman then said, " Why, this
poem should be in every drawing-room in the land. It is better worth
one and sixpence than to be in a threepenny book. If you will bring
it out in a nice little book by itself for drawing-rooms, and
it does not pay you, I will make good your loss." At the
request of this gentleman, it has been brought out in a nice form,
and published at sixpence. He has received many flattering letters
on this book ; and one lady who visits Clifton every year, and comes
for the Poet's last new books, said she felt that she must come back
and tell him how pleased she had been to read " Evangeline."
Another lady wished to know from him, if he did not feel proud with
such a gift. He told her, " No !" What had he to feel proud of?
It was only a gift bestowed upon him by the Almighty, and one which
he felt he would have to be accountable for the right using of. It
might be made very useful, or very dangerous. It was a power for
good or evil, and he had determined that all his writings should be
like Miss Hannah More's, only for battling with wrong and
establishing right. Many people thought her mad for a time ; but
there was method in her madness, and Providence in her last days had
rewarded her for her adherence to principle. His book, " Excelsior :
a day dream on St. Vincent's Rocks," the first poem of which
portrays his own life, has received a fair share of attention, for it has
in it an impromptu written for that popular American Poet, Will
Carleton, who spent two hours with the Clifton Poet, underneath his
tree, in summertide—and whom his American brother told it was like
coming into a new world to find him there ; and they parted
reluctantly, perchance never to meet again on earth. That book also

contains the last complete poem of his dear daughter Mattie, on the
death of our Princess Alice. One day a stranger passed the Poet's
stall, and took this little book with him to London. He was the
father of a musical composer there. When his son had seen in it two
new songs, entitled " My Mother," and " Minnie Ray," he wrote at
once to Clifton, for the Poet to write him some pieces to set to music.
This he did on several occasions, and always received from him not
only congratulation, but remuneration also. The most successful
book as yet, in point of circulation, of the Poet's, is one entitled
"Cook's Folly : a Legendary Ballad of St. Vincent's Rocks," and
written there one summertide, on a piece of board behind the Poet's
stall. The first edition was sold in sixty-two booksellers' shops in
Bristol and Clifton alone. It has passed through three editions, and
the fourth will soon be out. This book has had a glowing review from the
Western Temperance Herald, and was patronised by the late owner, H.
Goodeve, Esq., J.P., who sent a good order, and an autograph letter with
it. The Poet has deemed it right to publish this story complete in this
volume, with engraving of Cook's Folly, as it is the world-renowned
legend of " Cliftonia the Beautiful." His book, " Isabel and I : an
Old Man's Christmas Story," and other poems, has not been so much
inquired for as some other of his books that are not equal to it for
touching incident. The Poet gave it as a reading one Christmastide,
to a crowded congregation in a large chapel, and had the pleasure of
hearing it said by some ladies, that they could have sat another hour
if the story had but continued ; and one Sunday, while seated at a
farmhouse in the country, where he had gone to preach, the good lady
of the house, in the afternoon, was reading the story to some friends,
when she became so affected that she sobbed aloud, and had to lay
the book down for another friend to finish it for her. Some time
before this the Poet received a beautifully bound volume of poems
from a popular poet at Lymington, — Doman, Esq., and also a very
interesting letter, in which the author gave the following pleasing
testimonial :—" We keep your little books on our table, Mr. G., and
read them with much interest ; especially ' Isabel and I.' " The Poet's
book, " Miss Nancy Dare," was brought out for the special purpose of

showing the wilful ways of some young ladies, who dare to do what they please, as this young lady did. Nevertheless, it is shown in this humorous production that in time she became wiser, and made a very excellent wife, when *she dared to do right.* His book, "Marion's Joy," has been much appreciated, and no doubt will continue to be, when the writer has passed away. A clergyman of the Church of England, and of long experience, did the Poet the honour of saying that the story would immortalise Leigh Woods for ever. It is a true love story, and the lessons taught in it are more valuable than nine-tenths of the flaming novels of the age. It was at this time, while the Poet was busy with his labour, feeling that the more he wrote the more he must, he had to undergo one of the most painful trials of his life, namely, the loss of his dear daughter Mattie. For ten years she had been his little housekeeper, and, in all that she could, she had done her best to fill the place of her foster-mother. Consumption—that deadly foe of her own mother—touched her. Alas! and just at the time when she appeared to be beginning to live, she had to die. She had just begun to write some interesting poems, and being a district visitor for some time at Redland, had opportunities for making observations, which she was turning to good account. She had begun to bring out the Clifton penny series, "Pure ballads for the nation." Her first, "Tommy Macarthy ; or, lost and found," is a true incident, and Mattie was the person who led the poor young Irish mother from Redland Park that night, to find her little one cared for by the kind policeman at Clifton Down reserve. Her next little book, "Nellie Rae," is very much admired. Her father one day received a glowing letter from a strange gentleman in one of the Oxford Colleges, stating that "Nellie Rae" had been sent him by a friend ; how much he liked it, for it was calculated to do much good, and he hoped it would have an extensive circulation. A gentleman also in Clifton, from St. John's College, Cambridge, told Mattie's father that she reminded him more of Mrs. Browning than any writer he had ever read ; and yet she was brought up in a country village, after the loss of her mother, with an aunt, with scarcely any advantages for culture or refinement, which seemed to be so very

essential for her.   When she began to write a few poems, her father, to
encourage her, had inserted in his threepenny books a few of her own
productions.   Her first piece, " Love's reply to affection's question,"
" We shall meet her once again," " Our Princess Alice," " Emily
portrayed," " The angels mind him now," these she would oft read
over to her father, as he oft did to her his own ; and this was done for
the mutual advantage of them both.   She had another little book in
hand at the time of her death, entitled " Patty Cree's angel whisper."
This was her own life history ; and, strange to say, before she had
concluded it, the angels whispered her away.   At her request her
father finished it for her, she giving him what she wished to be
inserted in reference to her, and it is now added to her penny series.
Long before she appeared to be sinking, this thought would oft come
across her father's mind, " Who would perform those duties for her at
such a time, that he felt only a loving mother could bestow upon her
child ? "   Could he have but known what afterwards came to pass, such
thoughts need never to have troubled his mind : for in her affliction she
had every attention from many kind friends, who valued her for her quiet
and unobtrusive spirit, and who had been touched by the simple
pathos of her lays.   On the 16th day of June, 1880, she sweetly fell
asleep in Jesus, without a struggle or a sigh ; and dying, as she wished,
in her father's arms.   She rests, at least what is mortal of her, at
Keynsham, Somerset, in the same burial ground as the Poet's third
wife.   After this great loss he had to keep himself more than ever
diligently employed at his writing, lest his mind should become
desponding under the trial ; and for a time he wrote almost
incessantly to give him heart relief for a father's pungent grief.   His
little book, " What News is the Postman bringing to-day ? Ten scenes
from real life," came out soon after, which is being read with interest,
and appreciated by soldiers and sailors ; some of the incidents being
true—for the Poet with his varied life experiences seems to be never
short of subjects to write upon.   The great difficulty with him at
times was, which to select, and so to use them as to make them useful,
and also to pay him for their publication.   And he will never forget
the heartfelt gladness of a poor old widow who had a boy at sea,

after she had read his No. 2 sketch in the above named little book. And some time ago he had a letter from a ship's captain for some of his books, and who told him how much they were prized by the men aboard ship.   His book, " The Poet's Tree ; or, secrets of a year," will always be interesting to those who read it.   This book was written to give an account of many influential personages who had been under the tree where the Poet had his stall, and their varied conversations with him.   The idea was taken from the Laureate's " Talking Oak," he thinking that by this means he might show the object of his mission ; and also the varied treatment he had received there, while trying to carry it out.   " Howe'er it be, it seems to me " that he has in some measure immortalised the tree, for the little book is being much read, and leaves from it are being taken to the four quarters of the globe.   In this collection of poems, the faded leaf and its lessons is a true story, and there are many more of a similar character that may be published some day in connection with the Poet's tree ; for the Poet, during the eleven years he has been under the shadow of it, has come in contact with more varieties of character than in all the former periods of his life ; and if there should be found a doubter of this statement, the Poet would advise them, if they want convincing, to open a publication stall for the same number of years with their own productions only ; and he feels assured that before half the time is expired, these would readily admit that what Thomas Carlyle said of the generality of human kind, was not an immeasurable distance from the truth ; for there the Poet has had such a variety of minds to contend with, and a great deal that was not mind at all, but a something that is always calculated, in the age where useful intelligence may be obtained, to irritate and annoy any person with ordinary common-sense.

> For 'tis indeed, though some are sage,
> A very nickel silver age ;
> And poets would have glad surprise,
> If some folk would become more wise.

Some time after this, the Poet wrote and brought out his book on "God's Orphan Homes," Ashley Down, Bristol.   He had oft longed to write a book on this Christlike institution, but seemed as if he could never get on with it until he went through the whole five houses and saw the wonderful provision made for the 2,050 orphans there; and after he had seen them at their varied employments and enjoyments, he felt he could have written anything that was good in reference to them. He had three reasons for writing this book. One was, he thought, that it might receive a fair share of attention, and repay him for its publication. Another was, he had been asked, by ladies and gentlemen visiting Clifton, for full information respecting them, and he could not give it; and therefore thought, if he could personally visit them, go into every room, and put in verse every particular, he could then tell them he had been and seen; and, if they thought well to have his little book for threepence, it was all there. The third reason was, he thought, that he could so write it, that the Almighty might in His own way influence the minds of the wealthy and others to visit the Homes, and thus coming in contact with the happy orphans, would help those who were in a measure helpless, from a sense of duty to Him who was the Bestower of their wealth. The Poet deems it right to state here, that in composing and bringing out this book, he had no solicitations from any of the conductors, or Mr. Müller himself. He wrote it from a sense of duty, and just because he felt he must; it has been the means of many going there, and will be again. A very wealthy lady in Clifton, who had purchased one of the Orphan Home Books, came to the Poet and said, " I have read your charming little book; I feel I must now go through the Homes—tell me the best way to go there." And so it is Providence uses man as an instrumant for the accomplishment of its purposes. But the age has yet to learn that we are to live by each other for the true purposes of life, and not on each other for our own selfish aggrandisement. There have been at times under the Poet's tree some very singular incidents; and it may be right here to refer to a few of them. One very hot summer's day, three gentlemen came to overlook the Poet's stand. They had on new fashionable straw hats with white streamers attached. They could not see anyone in charge of the stall, for the Poet was concealed behind it, writing in the shade. After passing varied remarks on the unusual things before them, one of the gentlemen evidently had his attention drawn to some photos of the Poet in the glass case before him : for he observed rather jocularly to his companions, if the photographer, when he took that face, thought he was photographing a fool, he made a grand mistake. The Poet smiled at this remark in his hiding-place, and remained there until they went rejoicing on their way. The Clifton Poet's political views and proclivities are well known in the locality where he resides. Although he has always avoided parading them before the public at his Publication Stall, unless he has been compelled to do so by those entertaining opposite opinions, he has had for some time two distinguished names there of gentlemen who have accepted his productions, and on this account he has been often twitted by some peculiar gentlemen. The names referred to are those of the Hon. W. E. Gladstone and the Hon. J. Bright. A singular gentleman once, in passing and observing them, said, " Mr. G., those are the wrong names for Clifton." " Never mind, sir," said the Poet ; " they seem to be right for the country." At another time a stranger to the Poet passed, although from his frequent appearance in that locality he might be a resident or constant visitor. He was very tall and somewhat consequential in appearance, and was invariably sucking a cigar. This morning he said somewhat haughtily to the Poet, " I understand that you are a supporter of Mr. Gladstone." The Poet answered, " I am a supporter, sir, of everyone who is trying to do right ; and it is for this reason alone that I am a supporter of Mr. Gladstone." He said no more, but went from the Poet's stall down old St. Vincent's Hill, looking as pleasant as an old crab-tree, or, to use one of the Poet's father's expressions, as if " he owed him a quarter's rent." It was the selfsame gentleman to whom the impromptu " Served him right," in this collection, was written ; for the incident was true. Another time, at the Industrial Exhibition held at Hotwells, Clifton, the Poet had a stall to exhibit his productions ; and in order to make it as attractive as possible without any design of exhibiting his political views, he had among a few noted philanthropists and popular ministers of Bristol for whom he had written

" In Memoriams," and of one notable woman, Miss Mary Carpenter. In the centre of these was an incentive acrostic in gilt frame, to the Right Hon. W. E. Gladstone on his 71st Birthday. It was written as a grateful recognition of his restoration to health, with the hon. gentleman's photo in the centre, and two mottos, one on the left the other on the right hand, " I will guide thee with Mine eye ; and, " As thy day, so shall thy strength be." It was the counterpart of one sent as a present to Hawarden Castle, and while in the exhibition, from right thinking people, had its meed of praise. But one day, while this was on the Poet's stall, a very influential lady in the locality came and took a survey of the books, &c., there ; and he, without thinking he was doing anything wrong, said : " This is Mr. Gladstone's Birthday Poem." " Yes !" she tartly answered, "and it ought to be burnt, and him too." Such a reply naturally surprised the Poet, and looking her full in the face, he said : " You will excuse me, madam ; but you will have to get all such feelings out of your heart, or you will never enter into the kingdom of heaven." She immediately bowed her head and said : " I beg your pardon, sir, I feel that I have done wrong." " Done wrong !" said he. " Yes ; you, Mr. G., may have made mistakes, as we all have—for we are but human." "But a close observer of his history cannot fail to discover that his whole life service has been devoted to the true interests of his country and the universal welfare of mankind." Many similar instances of annoyance has the Poet had to contend with by having placed on the inside leaves of his book copies of some lines he had placed on his poem stand to induce strangers to stay and give them their attention. Ladies and gentlemen desired to have copies of them, and to meet their wishes, these were inserted for a time inside the covers of his little books. One of the lines read thus,

" The honoured names of Gladstone, Bright ; "

and, strange to say, that single line has caused the Poet more annoyance from some people than all the poems he has written—not from right-minded people, he admits : nevertheless, it has been even so. One day a lady came to the Poet's stall, bringing with her a young lady, evidently her daughter ; having purchased some of his books, they went and sat down upon the grass underneath the Poet's tree, and the elder lady began to read aloud to the other. After having read several of the poems, the Poet approached her, and said, " You will excuse me, madam, but you know how to read poetry—it is a pleasure to hear you : for there are some persons who make such a muddle of it, that it gives me the horrors to hear them." The lady smiled, and said she was fond of good poetry. She was then going back to Ireland with her daughter, and they had come up St. Vincent's heights for a short time, to have a look round whilst waiting for the starting of the steamboat. She then exclaimed, " I suppose you think highly of Mr. Gladstone ? " The Poet replied that he did, but that had nothing to do with his books : Mr. G.'s name was there with others simply because they had accepted his productions. She then said, " I feel that I could shoot him for what he has done in reference to disestablishing the Irish Church." The Poet immediately looked straight at her, and said, " Oh, no! you could not. I see, in your face, that you would not shoot anyone, especially Mr. Gladstone." She immediately broke out into a fit of laughter, and said, " Oh, yes ; I could, though ! " And then they had lengthy conversation on the Irish Church and the Irish people ; and before they parted, she frankly confessed that she believed eventually it would be a real benefit : for the Protestant clergy, now more than ever, felt that they had important work to do, and therefore must do it. Since that time, the lady has on several occasions come from Dublin to Bristol ; but never fails to come and see the Poet, and take back with her a few of his little books. On another occasion he had a contention that afforded him some amusement, with two apparently maiden ladies, who had been at his stall a few days before, and pur-chased some of his little books. On the following day they came to see the Poet, and wished to know if he would exchange one of them for one of another kind : they liked the book, only there was Mr. Gladstone's name in it, and that they did not like. The Poet cheerfully exchanged the book, and then wished them to give him their reasons. This they commenced doing with great volubility : for the dear old souls opened out their minds freely and fully ; but Mr. G.'s chief offence, in their opinion, was that he was in league with the Pope, and someone else whom they did not scruple to name. They were horror-struck to contemplate what the country would come to by-and-by, if he continued at the head of affairs. Then the Poet tried to get a word in edgeways, which was a most difficult thing to do. He did his best to show them that even they might be mistaken, and that Mr. G. was not half so ugly as they had tried to paint him. But no, no! the dear old ladies could not see it; they had got their peculiar glasses on, and consequently the Poet had to let them have it all their own way. When they had walked on, he sat down and wrote the poem, "What a wonderful age we live in."

To mention all the amusing and remarkable incidents in connection with the life of the Poet while on Clifton Down, would swell this autobiography to a larger size than he deems would be prudent to accompany a collection of poems; and therefore he wishes to select only those that may be serviceable to posterity—showing them that the path of a Poet is not a smooth path; and to inculcate one important lesson that the present age seems slow to learn, namely, that it is while a Poet is doing his work in life, he needs helping and caring for; and especially when he his battling with the evils of the age, and trying to uplift mankind into a purer, nobler, and a better life. And yet there are such to-day who are trying to do this, who do not meet with as much pecuniary assistance as many a crossing sweeper; and why? The Clifton Poet thinks it is because folk don't agree to live a life of purity. If they did, why don't they help to circulate that which under the Divine blessing and guidance would help to promote it? One day, while he was on Clifton Down, a group of ladies and gentlemen came past the Poet's tree; and seeing the inscription near it, one of them inquired if that was Chatterton's tree. "No, sir," said the Poet; "the books on this stall are my own productions only, and I have written a book on this tree. That is the reason it is named the Poet's tree." When they heard this, they looked at the Poet in astonishment, as though they had expected seeing an angel with wings, instead of an ordinary mortal; and then one of them exclaimed: "Oh! we have not time to stay and look at them now." "No, sir," said the Poet; "and if Chatterton himself had been here, it would have been just the same, and that is what the Poets have to contend with here—

> Doing their work, sitting alone,
> Giving full many a sigh and a groan ;
> Thoughtless ones passing them giving a grin,
> Never once caring what plight they are in."

The very exposed position of the Clifton Poet's stall to the elements has been no small source of trial in addition to the before mentioned circumstances, for he has been without any kind of shelter, with the exception of an old stone grotto near his stall, and in which he has written scores of poems while the rain and snow have been rapidly falling, and beating on his feet. For eleven years he has been thus toiling, and, he has thought, sufficiently long to have exhausted the patience of any man, unless he had faith in his mission. A Catholic gentleman, who had at different times purchased the Poet's books, not only for himself, but for friends who had come to visit Clifton, one day while passing the Poet's stall remarked :. " Mr. G., the Clifton ladies ought to put you here a pretty little Poet's shelter ; and have felt it an honour to have such a man in their midst. That is what I think." " Well, sir," the Poet answered ; " many of them yet don't seem to understand a Poet's work. Had I have driven a cab or had a wheel-chair, I have no doubt it would have been done long ago ; but they have yet to learn that a man who is spending the latter part of his life in writing books to lead folk to nobler, purer, and better life, is of as much use to society as the man who drives a horse." He answered, " You are right," and then he went his way ; while the Poet hummed over a line of one of his favourite poems :

> It seemeth to me a shame it should be,
> In a beautiful world like this.

The storms that so frequently beat upon St. Vincent's Rocks have at times proved very disastrous to the Poet, in driving over his stall, and many times sending his leaflets to the four winds of heaven. One day especially was very trying. The day previous he had the misfortune to have a breakdown with the wheel upon which he used to convey his stall at night for protection behind the rocks. Then he had to go a long journey into the city—east, west, north, and south, to find another, which he thought a suitable one. At length he appeared to have succeeded, and brought it early in the morning, and fixed it to the stall, ready as he thought for service next time. When it was tried, it brought him safely up the hill. It was, however, no sooner at the top, than the wind began to blow in hurricanes, so much so that he dare not venture to open it out, nor dare he venture to take it back, until some hours after, when the wind had a little abated. While it did so he fled to his old stone cave for protection, for the storm seemed fierce enough to tear up the very trees by the roots. When three o'clock came the Poet made an effort to try to bring his stall to a place of shelter. He was on his way down the hill, wheeling it as he thought safely, although he himself could scarcely stand upright in the tempest, when all of a sudden the new wheel broke down, and of course down went the stall on its side ; and off went the Poet's hat, while he was clinging to his crippled companion with all the energy of despair. For some time he was in this immovable position, until some unknown friends in the distance, seeing how matters stood, came to the rescue, and extricated him from his perilous position. On another occasion a tremendous storm arose, lifting many of his boxes from the stall, breaking some glass squares he had for protection, and drifting his poems broadcast.

> There was such commotion, that he had a notion
> Old Satan was trying to plague him.

And yet amid all his discouragements, he has had very many things to cheer and encourage him. A young lady came to his stall one day and said, " There is one little book that you have written, entitled ' Uncle Peter,' which has been the means of reclaiming my only brother from a life of sin. He had begun to smoke and drink, and was rather gay; but since he has read that book, he has given up smoking and drinking, and is now an earnest Christian young man." This statement of course encouraged the Poet much, and he told her that such testimony was of more value than money, however necessary that might be for the purposes of life. Another young lady came and told him that this book had been the means of a young friend to whom she was engaged giving up smoking, and also the use of intoxicating drink ; and that he was coming personally to thank him for writing it, which he did some time after, and bringing for the Poet's inspection a beautiful silver watch, purchased with money saved since he had read " Uncle Peter," that would otherwise have been expended in smoke and drink. The Poet has also been personally thanked for writing this book by S. Morley, Esq., M.P., one of our nation's Christian philanthropists ; who recently sent the Poet a very kind letter, and also a cheque for three guineas ; stating that he regarded it but as a slight recognition for valuable life service. He also received by post, from some collegian, his opinion on this little book, to whom it had been sent evidently by some well-intentioned friend. This letter was not of so pleasing a character as the last, for from the Billingsgate language used in reference to the book, it was very evident that " Uncle Peter " had struck like an arrow in a sure place ; and had this unpromising young gentleman but have forwarded his address, the Poet would have replied to his disreputable communication ; and pointed out to him that, unless his future conduct became better than the language of his epistle, he might become some day a young man who would cause his father grief and his mother shame.

During the time the Poet has been pursuing his singular avocation, he has written hundreds of private pieces at the request of ladies and gentlemen—for friends' birthdays, wedding odes, and in memoriams, and many to try to heal differences among friends ; and he has done it in some cases with success. Many odes to lovers he has penned for both sexes, and never failed to give them in those odes what would be of real service, if through their life future it was faithfully carried out. Among the numerous communications received by post, there was one from a young lady in a distant county, intimating that she understood the Clifton Poet could rule the planets, and she would be much obliged if he would forward her in the stamped envelope enclosed his charge for so doing, which she would remit, as she wanted to know her fate, and have her planet ruled. Such a request brought from the Poet a smile, and he wondered that there could be yet living in the world such fools as to believe that any living man could thus reveal the purposes of the Almighty. So, instead of sending for her money, and sending back a tissue of lies and nonsense, he forwarded her by return of post the following impromptu, which he trusts may be of service to others if there are yet living such credible beings :—

> The Clifton Poet writes Miss Fonce,
>   Not to let man befool her ;
> But send her wish to Heaven at once,
>   The only planet Ruler.

He never received a letter from this strange young lady for this good advice, which he felt was the best he could give her under the circumstances. The Poet at this time had been living more than two years alone since he had lost his daughter Mattie. It was for her sake that he had remained a widower for nearly twelve years, for they were happy together ; and he could never bear the thought of taking even a wife, and she again to leave him, and battle with the world, for she was not strong ; and if during her life he had done so, one of the conditions would have been that she should remain at home. An allwise Providence, however, removed her; and two years had fled since her decease. One of two courses was open to the Poet, for he had been living by himself until he felt it was no longer right ; and he must either take another wife, or dispose of his household goods and go to lodgings. This he did not think would add to his comfort, for he had always been happy in his married life in his own home ; aud he thought that the companionship of an affectionate wife would be better than sitting at ease, with no one to please ; and Providence provided one for him, younger than himself, 'tis true, but one that thoroughly understands him, and one that he thoroughly understands. Their marriage of few years' duration has hitherto been a happy one, for it seems to have given the Poet a new life, and something else to live for. They are blest with two little jewels—

> And Clifton, with all its abundance of wealth,
> Cannot purchase his jewels to-day.

Since their birth the poems on children have been written, and the Poet feels assured, in after years, that all right-minded persons will feel and say, that if the Poet's last marriage had only been the means of bringing out the children's poems, it would not have been in vain. A strange lady in London having seen in the *White Ribbon Army Gazette*—a Gospel Temperance periodical, in which many of the Clifton Poet's productions appear—a piece entitled " Watching Baby Sleep," wrote to him in reference to it, stating that she felt she must write ; and she was not ashamed to say while reading it she was *moved to tears*, and she thanked God there was one true Poet on the earth. The Poet smiled on reading this, and also felt assured there were many. Having, however, received such a pleasing acknowledgment from a lady, evidently a mother, induced him to insert these poems on children in this collection—although a very wealthy gentleman and an author questioned whether the poem, " Little Fingers," and some others, would be appreciated by the general public. The Poet heard him to the end, but has followed out his own convictions in publishing them for the following reasons : his friend who gave him this advice was a bachelor, and consequently not well qualified to judge in matters of this kind ; and further, the Poet feels that the children's poems will be welcome to many a father's and mother's heart. Soon after the Poet's last marriage, he was waited upon by the same meddlesome gentlemen on whom he wrote the impromptu, " Served him right;" who said, " I understand that you have had as many wives as there are fingers on my hand—one, two, three, four, five." " Then, sir," the Poet answered, "you are not the first gentleman who has been mistaken in reference to me. If it will be of any real service to you to know the truth, I will give it you. I have had four, and they have all been good ones."

> He turned aside, and went his way,
> Without another word to say :
> The Poet watched him down the hill,
> And wondered why he went so still.

Some years before this, while living at Keynsham, and with his third wife, he was accosted in the public street by one of those busybodies,

who addressed him thus : " Why, sir, they tell me you have had three
wives. Oh, dear !" said he, " is it true ?" " I dare say it is," the
Poet answered, " if it will be of any real service for you to know."
" Why," he replied, " I never knew that before." " Did you not?"
said the Poet. " Well, you might have done if you had but have
come to me and inquired. But I did not think it necessary, when I
first came to Keynsham, to give the town crier a shilling to go
through the streets and announce that I had the third good wife. If
you should meet with anyone to whom the information will be useful,
you will please let them know." A few years after this, when the
Poet had been left a widower the third time, this same Mr. Officious
came into the workshops where the Poet was foreman, and bawled out
at the top of his voice, " I say, Mr. G., you should take to yourself
another wife." The Poet looked straight at him, and said, " When I
feel it right to take another wife, I shall do so, and not go paying
clandestine visits to other people's wives." On hearing this he coloured
to his temples, and bolted from the workshops as though he had been
smitten in a sore place, followed by roaring peals of laughter from the
workmen, who thought the Poet had heard a little of the doings of
this meddlesome gentleman ; and I dare say they were right. These
apparently trivial circumstances are referred to in the Poet's history
only for the purpose of showing up these very meddlesome people,
and teaching them if they are waiting and willing to be taught, that if
they will but just look within themselves, they will find plenty of ways
where they may more usefully be employed. While the Poet
was living in Keynsham he wrote an acrostic on the Prince of
Wales' recovery, entitled " Convalescence." He read it to the Rev.
W. Pratt (Baptist Minister), who advised him to have it printed ; he
thought it would be of service. This advice was carried out. It
was printed in two colours ; and two of them were put in gilt frames,
and forwarded to Windsor Castle, and graciously accepted by Her
Majesty on behalf of herself and the Prince of Wales. Very many
persons have at various times asked the Poet if he had not received
many handsome presents from the important personages who had
accepted his productions. He has not always satisfied the curiosity of

THE POET'S AUTOBIOGRAPHY.

such inquirers, when he felt they were fishing just for the purpose of wanting to know; but he may venture here to make a frank and full confession, and the truthful answer is " No ! " And further, he never expected them, so he was never disappointed. His chief object in sending his writings to them was that they might see them, and if they could find time to read them, they would discover for what purpose they had been penned, namely, for doing good; and that those who took an interest in pure literature—that which was calculated to make people true patriots, good citizens, and true Christians—might assist him in the circulation of his little books. A few have done this, but as yet comparatively very few indeed, the gentleman to whom this volume of poems is dedicated being an honourable exception. He has indeed been a true friend to the Poet, in many times sending for his publications, and giving them to Sunday Schools and bazaars gratuitously for distribution; and he has done all this quietly and unobtrusively. And now the Poet deems it right to give honour to whom it is due; and while he does this, he feels that there are many more in wealthy Clifton who might have done the same, and in doing it would have helped the Poet in doing good; but with very few exceptions they have not done so. That was the reason his poem, " Dark Days," was published a short time ago, that those who were disposed might help him in his life's decline to toil on in a work that is far more important to humanity at large than all the exciting and unreal wonderments brought out on the stage. Some time ago, during the time that C. Thomas, Esq., was mayor of Bristol, the Poet had written a centenary poem for one of Bristol's native poets, R. Southey, Esq. He wrote this poem, which he considers his masterpiece, for two special reasons: first, because when he was a boy Southey's " Battle of Blenheim " poem made him a lover of peace, and to this day a denouncer of human butchery and hater of war; and he feels to-day, that if all the clergy of the Church of England and ministers of dissenting congregations had but been faithful to their duty, in denouncing this blot on our boasted civilisation and caricature of the religion of the Lord Jesus Christ, this hateful and accursed thing would long ago have hidden its guilty head. His second reason for writing this poem, was because he loved Southey for his kindness to poor Henry Kirk White, when earthly friends were scarce, and his poor widowed mother, while he was sinking in a decline, felt the burden far too heavy for her purse to bear. The Poet sent a copy of this poem to C. Thomas, Esq., the then mayor, who sent him a very kind letter, expressing his admiration of the purity of its style, and begged the Poet's acceptance of the half-sovereign enclosed in the letter; and the present mayor, C. Wathen, Esq., on receipt of a few of the Poet's productions, forwarded him a kind complimentary letter from the mayoress and himself, and a donation of one pound. There are also a few ladies in Clifton who have been kind in having at different times a few of his little books, for the purpose of giving them to some who could not purchase them; and while some few have done this, there are others who have been telling him for years that he is worthy of something better than being exposed to the winter's storms on Clifton Down, and yet they have never tried to lift him to that something, by helping him to circulate his books. By doing this they would have assisted him in doing good, and counteracting in some small degree the pernicious influence of what may be truly described as the silly fiction of the day; and whatever tends to this must be one of the noblest pursuits of life: for a true Old Book declares that a man's life consisteth not in the abundance of the things which he possesseth in this world.

The Clifton Poet has often been requested to give answers to the following question: as to whether the life he had been pursuing during the last eleven years was not a very pleasant one? To this question he has to answer that there are two sides to it—at times it has been pleasant, at other times the reverse. Its pleasant side consists in feeling that you have done something to be appreciated by the sensible portion of mankind; and its unpleasant side is for a whole week to be exposed to the storms of St. Vincent's height, and his takings very often not exceeding five shillings per week, and sometimes not half of that. Take from this amount the cost of printing, and you will have for sum total what the Clifton Poet has often had, for writing pure literature in the midst of a wealthy people, who can give their money without stint to what neither benefits the bodies or souls of men. After this frank avowal, those who have considered the Clifton Poet to have had a lucrative occupation, will probably change their opinion. But the greatest trial the Poet ever had, while following his somewhat singular occupation, was this—and he feels he must relate it, for its recital may be of service to posterity, to teach them to act with more thought and Christian consistency than did those to whom it specially refers, should they ever be placed in similar circumstances. Some time ago a lecture was announced to be delivered in Colston Hall, by a minister in the city, entitled "Chatterton, the Poet Boy; or, a soul adrift." Of course there was, as is usual on such occasions, a large attendance to hear how the poor lad had gone adrift, and his very fearful end; and the Clifton Poet thought that night he would have a selection of his books there on a temporary stall, at the foot of the stairs, so that when the audience retired from the lecture they might have the opportunity of seeing the productions of one who was pursuing the same path, who was once a carpenter boy, and who had been connected with the Methodist family in church fellowship for nearly fifty years, and who for the twenty years he had resided in Bristol, had preached nearly as many sermons as any minister in it, and without any earthly remuneration. And he naturally concluded that from a Wesleyan audience he would at any rate get a small share of encouragement. But judge of his surprise. The whole company passed him by without any recognition, save a few solitary nods of the head. With one exception—a gentleman, Mark Whitwill, Esq., with his daughter had passed, when the Poet saw her whispering something in his ear, and he came back and said, " Let me have two of your books, please," and he left a shilling on the stall—twice the value of the books. But the Poet saw it not until after the gentleman had passed away, for his soul was too full of something else. He was thinking, " Yes; this is what sends poets' souls adrift—cold neglect. As it was in the days of Chatterton, so it is now, and apparently ever will be, world without end.

Don't let them thrive—starve them alive—
Though they are toiling away :
Then when they're dead, it can be said,
' Oh, what a shame !   Lack a day ! '"

And the reason may be given, because mankind generally prefer seeing
their names emblazoned in the public papers on what they do, than
quietly performing acts of Christian duty, in the way the Good Master
recommended : " Let not thy right hand know what thy left hand
doeth."   The Poet, feeling it to be his duty, sent an unvarnished
statement of this evening's experiences to the minister who delivered
this lecture, but it elicited from him no reply; and, although he has
passed the Poet's stall many times, he has never yet turned aside to
give him a word of cheer—yet he knew, and well, that the Poet's
productions were written for the purpose of leading people to that
Saviour whom he professed to preach.   The Poet still thinks " What
a wonderful age we live in ! " and he further wonders if there will be
that kind of Spirit manifested in heaven !—if so, he is not particularly
anxious to go until it is all banished.   He is just reminded, while
writing down this incident, of another that deserves recording, that it
may teach some would-be-thought pastors their simple duty as citizens,
and especially as professing Christians.   One day, while the Poet was
busy at his work in his little box—made with his own hands, to shelter
him from the storm—two ministers, evidently of some Nonconformist
Church, were taking note of the contents of the Poet's stall ; after
remaining a short time, the Poet opened the door of his little sanctum
and said, " Those books, gentlemen, are my own productions, if you
will please examine them."   Without deigning to give even the
respectful answer, " No, thank you," they somewhat haughtily turned
aside, and walked away.   This touched a something within the Poet,
that made him call out to the retiring reverends, " Will it be so in
heaven ? "   This made them halt near the Poet's tree, and one of them
called out, at the top of his voice, " No, it won't be so in heaven."
" Then," said the Poet, " it has no right to be so on earth."   They
then, without answering again, went on their way—with what reflections
he knew not ; but his were, that such conduct would have been

disreputable in a chimney-sweep, who had been respectfully addressed.
And yet the Poet has not always had such reverend visitors : for he has
had from many of the Church of England, and also Nonconformists, the
greatest respect.   Some years ago, a clergyman, who has two livings in
a distant county, came to see him ; and, on introducing himself, said,
" Now I want to know, as briefly as you can give it, an account of your
life-history, when and how you began verse writing, and whatever you
can give me in that direction ; "—and then the two sat down, on that
cold, January day, on a rustic seat near the Poet's stall.   The day
before this the Poet had written there his lines on the author of " Home,
sweet home," and he read them to this stranger, who said, " I should
think you have never written anything like that before, have you ? "
" Oh, yes," said the Poet, " and many ; only I felt keenly while
writing it, because it was the truth. The author of ' Home, sweet
home ' was homeless, and starving in a city, and heard a lady from
her grand mansion sing his own sweet song.   And then, when he had
been dead for thirty-two years,

> They took his poor bones
> From under the stones,

and shipped them off to America, at the request of the American
Government, from Tunis, to have one of the grandest funerals ever
witnessed in the United States."   Then the Poet gave this clergyman
the details of his life-history, which appeared to greatly interest him ;
and then he gave the Poet the substance of his own : which was that
from once being a poor lad in the employ of Pickford & Co., at three
shillings and sixpence per week, he had, by sheer plodding, and the
blessing of Providence, worked himself up to his present position.
Then with a hearty shake of the hand, some words of encouragement,
and a something more—with a " Don't feel offended,"—they parted
as true Christian friends : hoping to meet again, if not on earth, in
heaven.   The Poet felt how different was the demeanour of this
clergyman to one he had come in contact with on another occasion.
He was a tall, severe looking specimen of humanity, appeared to be
one of those strange characters, who could preach on the Sunday
about the merciful Saviour of the world, and on Monday, whilst sitting

on a magisterial bench, feel as though he would like to give some
hungry looking wretch, who had been brought before him, three
months' hard labour for looking through a hedge at a rabbit or hare
sporting in the squire's grounds—not knowing or caring whether the
poor fellow's family wanted food or not.   This strange clergyman made
a dead halt before the Poet's stall, and said rather contemptuously
" What have you got there ? " The Poet respectfully told him they
were a few little books of his own writing. Then he exclaimed, " A
strange kind of way this to get a living." " Is it, sir ? " said the Poet,
" Does a man's life consist in the abundance of the things which he
possesseth ? My little books are written for doing good." " If they
are," said he, " why don't you ask the Lord Jesus to give you something
better than this to get a living by ? " " What else better could I
have," asked the Poet, " if I had but right encouragement ? Besides
I am a great deal better off than the Lord Jesus ever was : I have
food, raiment, friends to love me, and a comfortable home, and He had
not where to lay His Head. He was despised and rejected of men,
a man of sorrow and acquainted with grief—and would be again if He
came into this world in the garb of poverty : for there are many persons
to-day who would join the rabble multitude, and cry out : ' Crucify
Him! Crucify Him ! ' " and then looking at the clerical dignity, he
exclaimed : " Ye know not what manner of spirit ye are of.   There
is many a peasant in a thatched cottage knows more to-day of the
religion of Jesus Christ of the New Testament Scriptures, than some
of those who are professing to be masters in Israel." Such are some
of the varied life experiences of the Clifton Poet, living in the sixty-
third year of his age, and from memory alone during the last few
weeks have been committed to writing to accompany his " Heart
Melodies for Storm and Sunshine." The number of incidents might
have been increased, but he thinks that from what are here recorded,
it will be quite evident to every attentive reader that his path as a
poet has not been a smooth one ; and that the Poet who
determines to battle with the evils of the age must prepare his mind
for uphill work, and a great deal of it. Very many persons have
made remarks in reference to the uncommon name of the Poet.   He

wishes to say in reference to this, that in the Counties of Nottingham and Lincoln there are many families who bear the same name ; and Mr. W. George, of the Book Stores, Park Street, Clifton, some time ago furnished him with the following, copied from an Old Bristol Directory, proving that in and near this city there were two families who had the same name : Gabbitass and Co., gunmakers, 1, King Street, 1775 ; and a Mrs. Mary Gabbitass, Shirehampton. The Clifton Poet feels he ought not to close this history of his life without referring to the great kindness and Christian friendliness manifested towards him by the Rev. W. Chapman, late Vicar of Christ Church, Clifton, who many times came to see him, and gave him words of cheer ; and also to the Rev. Arthur Hall, Congregational Minister, of Clifton Down, who, although a stranger to the Poet, came to see him, and by many kindly acts and words has shown that he understood the work of a Christian minister to one who, although not of the same church, was working for the same Master ; and with the hope cf meeting one day in the same sweet home, where there will be no high caste feeling to contend with ; but where all those who have usefully served their generation, by turning many to righteousness, will shine as the stars for ever and ever !

Appendix to the Poet's Autobiography.

IN sending forth this VOLUME of POEMS to the world, the Writer wishes it to be distinctly understood that he has consulted with no one as to what Poems should appear, or in what order; so they will appear as doth the face of Nature—rough and smooth, hill and dale. There will also be rivulets and streams, flowing rivers and rushing cataracts; or, to change the figure, some primroses and violets, a few roses, and many thorns. But, thank God, no deadly nightshade is here; there is only that which—if rightly understood, rightly embraced, and rightly carried out—will help to make those who read them wiser and better.

CLIFTON.

The Prelude to "Heart Melodies."

GO forth, my treasures, to the wide, wide world—
Go forth, though scornful lips at ye be curl'd ;
In storm and sunshine ye were born on earth,
And came from one who was of lowly birth.
Ye are true-born, I know—go, then, and bless
Some lonely hearts, when bleeding in distress ;
Take music to them while they throb with fear,
For your true mission is the faint to cheer,
And lead the erring ones from sin to part,
By bringing sweeter music to each heart.
Ye came to me in many a weary hour,
And came, I know, from a benignant Power—
Perchance to give some weary toiler rest !
And oft, when hope was sinking in my breast,
Yet on I toil'd, where many a toiler's trod
Who work'd with earnest zeal for man and God ;
And I must labour on beneath the sun,
Till my life toiling shall with joy be done.
Go forth, my treasures : go and cheer the sire
And her who loves him—by the "sweet home" fire,
When wintertide is hovering o'er the land—
And little prattlers, who take her by the hand,
And listen to their father's welcome voice
Read from these melodies their own hearts' choice :
Of " Little fingers," with a pathos deep,
Or " Father watching little baby sleep,"—
And something in the " Merry children's noise,"
That heightens every loving parent's joys.
" Who would not love the children ? " let him read,
Until his heart re-echoes, " Who, indeed ? "—
And their hearts are made better by the strains,
'Till all the household trills the pure refrains,
And their loved homestead is secure from strife
Throughout the pilgrimage of changing life.

" Heart Melodies," go forth, with my heart song,
For to the world at large ye now belong.
Go, soothe the sad, lone heart, when hope seems gone,
And take these strains to cheer them, " Hope thou on ! "
Then to true toilers in their varied sphere,
Convey the tidings, " Only persevere;"
And unto those who work with heart and will,
This message take, " There's resting o'er the hill."
Then teach the lover of the poison cup,
That all who would be wise must give it up ;
For where strong drinks are found will sorrows come,
And griefs distressing gather in the home.
No melody for hearts where these are seen,
As where true Temperance reigneth as a queen ;
Go, then, " Heart Melodies," that men may rise,
And learn from you how to be truly wise.
Learn how to live, and in your strains descry
What will yield comfort when they have to die !
Awake new thought in some on " What is Life ?"
Is it worth living for 'mid this world's strife?
Then lead them upward, as on seraphs' wings,
To what are purer, nobler, better things—
Until mankind grows better day by day
Than when the writer laboured by the way ;
Go, take sweet strains of love in years to come,
And give true gladness in each peasant's home ;
While, in the stately mansions of the great,
Let my " Heart Melodies " reverberate,
For he who penn'd them felt himself a pen
In that wise hand of His who formed us men ;
And what he's done is but his Maker's gift,
That he his fellow-man m ight upward lift
To life that is worth living in His sight,
Who gives His creatures guidance *true and right*

TO HER MAJESTY THE QUEEN.

FIFTEEN years it is, to-day,
                    Belov'd Queen,
        Since I trill'd a sonnet lay
                    On the green—
Near old Sherwood's sylvan dales—
To a youthful Prince of Wales,
When all gladsome he had come
To fair Clumber's ducal home,
                    Belov'd Queen.

Oh, what changes from that time,
                    Belov'd Queen :
Friends are gone in manhood's prime.
                    We have seen
One—a noble duke—has fled ;
Now he sleepeth with the dead
'Neath his mausoleum dome,
Near my peaceful childhood's home,
                    Belov'd Queen.

E

And another from life's day,
     Belov'd Queen,
One I loved, has pass'd away,
     So serene :
She who penn'd what I had done
For your welcom'd royal son,
Now reclineth on a breast
Where the weary are at rest,
     Belov'd Queen.

There are trials in time's lot,
     Belov'd Queen,
Palace home and peasant's cot,
     Deep and keen :
Yet the wise can understand
'Tis a loving Father's hand ;
Then, with resignation blest,
Say, " He doeth what is best,"
     Belov'd Queen.

Treasured friends are sunder'd soon,
     Belov'd Queen.
Fairest plants oft fade at noon
     On this scene :
But the true, with Eden flowers,
Bloom in amaranthine bowers,
Free from blighting and decay,
In the climes of perfect day,
     Belov'd Queen.

We have dear ones in that land,
     Belov'd Queen.
Gathered to a peaceful strand
     In their sheen,

With our Albert pure and good,
Safe beyond the Jordan flood :
And Time's surges cannot part
Their loved image from our heart,
     Belov'd Queen.

Yet there 's solace for our pain,
     Belov'd Queen :
We shall meet the good again,
     We may glean.
Read—when we all hopeful look
In the good old Holy Book—
They await us on the shore
Where all sorrowing is o'er,
     Belov'd Queen.

Yes ! there's richer joys to come,
     Belov'd Queen :
In yon Palace angel home,
     Yet unseen,
There our lov'd ones, blest for aye,
Are inviting us away ;
Hark ! they whisper from the sky,
" Your shall join us by-and-by,
     " Belov'd Queen ! "

October 21st, 1876.

THE ELMS, BLACKFORD.

REMINISCENCES.

LOVED spot !   Of thee I think, though far away—
Thy sylvan charming haunts of rare display ;
And see thee rich in pristine rustic lore,
As I beheld thee in the days of yore.
Thy steep inclining roof I yet descry,
Where slater doth the thatcher's work outvie ;
And o'er thy lattic'd porch I see entwine
The tender, clinging, lovely jasmine !
Then gaze, as though 'twere present to my sight,
Upon thy rockery in pure delight ;
While fancy, with a rapturous feeling true,
Conveys me 'neath thy ever green old yew.
And listening, as when in thy coppice found,
I hear the crystal brooklet's rippling sound ;
Behold thy graceful elm tree branches spread,
With nestling rooks loud cawing overhead :
While thus I contemplate each treasured spot,
Thou art to me a choice forget-me-not !

H.R.H. THE PRINCE OF WALES

TO CLUMBER, 1861.

"The following chaste composition, by Mr. P. Gabbitass, of Clifton, was forwarded through His Grace the Duke of Newcastle for the Prince's perusal."
—*Sherwood and Midland Gazette.*

———

HAIL! youthful Prince, Britannia's future King,
    Our nation's hopes their centre find in thee ;
      True patriot hands sweet beauteous garlands bring,
  To wreathe thy brow, loved heir of royalty !
Oh, may kind mercy shield, with tender care,
  All the allotted days for man on earth,
Thy prayed-for life ! May it be stainless here
  As hers whose name illustrious gave thee birth.
Long may her kind, maternal, loving heart—
  As passing time's swift evolutions run—
O'erflow with joy thou only canst impart,
  Thy father's pride—Victoria's royal son !
May those pure lessons they in childhood gave
  To thy young mind with love's true tendrils cling,
That in life's coming years a people brave,
  In ecstasy, may shout, "Long live the King !"
And when thy reign o'er Britain's isle shall cease,
  Life's work accomplished, may thy spirit rise
To wear a crown of righteousness and peace,
  And sway a lasting sceptre in the skies !

THE BLIND BOY.

A FATHER'S WISDOM EXEMPLIFIED.

HE golden summer's sun was slowly sinking in the west,
And with his cheering rays of light the prairie-land had blest,
While feather'd songsters sweetly caroll'd forth their evening
song,
'Mid scenes of woodland beauty, where the swift deer pass along :
'Twas near that peaceful happy spot of forest border-land
A kind and loving father clasped his Blind Boy by the hand.

They leisurely walked on, for that father felt much joy
In cheering on their homeward way his little sightless boy :
He, while they passed along in peace, beguiled the time away,
And told his boy the grandeur then of Sol's departing ray ;
Or how the pure and limpid stream, which at their feet then ran,
The ocean reached through distant vales—just as a father can.

The path which they travers'd that day was very smooth and clear,
And for some little time at least they nothing had to fear ;
The boy enraptur'd heard it all, and felt his joy complete,
While passing o'er that mossy road that eas'd his shoeless feet.
No room for fear or doubt in him—he all could understand—
He heard his own dear father's voice, and felt his father's hand.

But ere they long had trod that path, in pleasure thought to roam
Throughout the long and winding vale that reached their cottage-home,
The father gave a sudden start—he saw what would destroy—
And on the brambled forest led his blind and shoeless boy ;
Nor did he cease his rapid strides or ever look'd back,—
The safety of his child he sought on this their rugged track.

At length, with plaintive voice and tears, the boy said, " Father, dear,
What meaneth this uneven path ?   Why do we wander here ?
I cannot see the way, you know, to shun the thorns we meet,
And yet I feel their sharpen'd points have pierced my tender feet.
O father ! tell me now," he said, " you would not me destroy,
For am I not your own dear child—your blind, yet darling boy ? "

This question touched the father's heart, and bending down with pain
He saw his shoeless boy in tears, his feet a gory stain.
Then whispered softly in his ears, " My boy, we must not stay,
But haste along—our time is short—I'll wipe thy tears away ;
And soon this rugged track will end, through which thou now dost
    roam,
And thou shalt know the reason why, when we have reached our home."

On, on they went, until at length their cottage-home was gain'd,
And then the weary boy felt glad, although his feet were pain'd ;
He said he never, never thought that they could ever come
Through such a rough and thorny path to their own happy home.
And then his father kindly said, " My boy, this will repay:
For though thy pathway has been rough, 'tis much the surer way.

" I led thee from the moss-grown path—the easy, pleasant way—
For just upon thy track I saw a deadly serpent lay ;
A few more steps, and thou, my child, by reptile's poisonous breath,
Hadst writh'd beneath a viper's sting to feed the jaws of death.
I saw thy danger, and at once (as ev'ry father would)
Remov'd thee from the lurking foe,—'twas for thy future good."

The blind boy heard with wondrous joy his father's welcome voice,
And o'er his great deliv'rance found a season to rejoice ;
Then grasping with a child like faith his parent's guardian hand,
He said, " Forgive thy poor blind child—he now can understand."
Thus feeling in his home secure, he leaned upon his breast,
And whispered softly in his ear, " My father knew the best."

Thus erring mortal man through life would walk the flow'ry way—
He never dreams of danger near where deadly serpents lay ;
And oft he in his blindness blames a loving Father's skill,
Who leads him through a thorny path to save from future ill ;
The grief and cares of life he mourns, forgetful of the love
Of Him who trod the path before, that he might live above.

But when his better home is reached—the path of life is trod,
And all his tears are wiped away by his dear Father-God,
He then will see the reason why the rugged path was given—
That he might 'scape the snares of earth to share the joys of heav'n.
Thus while he grateful tribute gives shall love's sweet anthem swell,
And sing, safe in his Father's arms, " Thou hast done all things well "

ELIZABETH'S GRAVE.

'T was Spring-time, when April its blossoms displayed,
  And Nature was clad in her livery of green ;
  While the clear evening sky, in rich beauties arrayed,
From the steep mountain turret or vale might be seen.
I wandered from home, for no comfort it gave,
To a spot more endearing—Elizabeth's grave !

I gazed on the green turf, that hid from my vision
  The form of my loved one, so lately laid there,
And mused on in silence, without intermission,
  'Till the mantle of darkness enshrouded the air.
Keen sorrow was mine, for no hope came to save
Me the sad, troubled thought—'twas Elizabeth's grave !

I mused on the days that are now past recalling,
  When with youth's blooming vigour her countenance shone ;
While, link'd hand in hand, with evening shades falling,
  We indulged cheering hopes that are now fled and gone :
But now I could see the Abbey Church nave
Threw its shadowing form o'er Elizabeth's grave !

I wept there in sadness, while fleeting thoughts hurried
    And crowded, unnumber'd, my grief-stricken breast ;
For there lay my earthly endearments, deep buried,
    And there did I anxiously long for to rest
'Neath the shades of the elm, whose foliage doth wave,
With the sweet summer breeze, o'er Elizabeth's grave !

And yet, while I sorrow'd one thought came to cheer me,
    Despite the sad grief-pangs that troubled my breast ;
It was this : that her spirit in joy hover'd near me,
    And whispered, " Don't weep ; my love, I'm at rest."
This bright cheering thought, with the comfort it gave,
Threw lustrous rays o'er Elizabeth's grave !

Farewell, then, dear spot ! For a time I must leave thee,
    To join in the business and turmoil of life ;
Though absent, the thoughts of thy charge shall relieve me,
    Remembering thou holdest a once loving wife.
And while I am tossing on Time's fleeting wave,
My mind shall oft visit Elizabeth's grave !

And when my last conflict on earth shall be ended,
    And Jordan's rough swelling triumphantly cross'd ;
When my longing spirit with hers shall be blended,
    On Canaan's calm shore, no more tempest tossed—
The only request of my kindred I crave,
    Is to lay my frail form in Elizabeth's grave.

THE CHRISTIAN HERO'S REQUIEM.

LIVINGSTONE PRAYED MUCH AT MUILALA, AND SAID,
"I AM GOING HOME!"

GOING home! the brave one falter'd, ere he sweetly passed
away;
Home, where sign of night is banish'd by refulgent endless
day.
Going home! where toiling 's ended, to the mansions of the blest;
Home, where grief and sorrow vanish, and the jaded spirits rest.

Going home from time's exploring to the bright and peaceful strand;
Home, the better country reaching, in the fertile Jordan land;
Going home to find the city wide its pearly gates unfold;
Home, where jasper walls are shining, and whose streets are purest
gold.

Going home, across the desert, where there is no scorching sun;
Home, where long-sought rest abideth, life's exhaustive labour done.
Going home, to taste sweet manna, falling from the Canaan skies;
Home, to drink the living water, where the crystal fountains rise.

Going home, beyond the river, where returning scenes are o'er;
Home, where no farewells are breath'd on the great eternal shore.
Going home to landscape beauties, fann'd by Eden's zephyr breeze;
Home, where all is calm and quiet, distant from the stormy seas.

Going home, to clasp the lov'd one, she whose spirit passed before;
Home, to greet his long-lost Mary, all the pangs of parting o'er.
Going home, to have the guerdon for the path of right he trod;
Home to meet his Elder Brother, and his loving Father—God!

Going home, to join the ransom'd where the golden harpers dwell ;
Home to see the martyrs, prophets, and their choral song to swell.
Going home, to find safe gather'd some who bow'd the servile knee ;
Home, where slave bonds cannot enter, and the people all are free.

Going home, to bathe for ever where the sparkling river flows ;
Home, to pluck the fruits ambrosial which the tree immortal grows.
Going home, to gaze with rapture on unfading lovely flowers ;
Home, to have a long reposing in the amaranthine bowers.

" Going home ! " he softly murmur'd ; then his tranquil spirit rose—
Home, from stranger land high soaring to the land of sweet repose.
Going home ! oh, blest assurance, far from keen affliction's rod ;
Home, where death nor sickness enter, in the paradise of God !

WELCOME

TO CAPTAIN AND MRS N——, ON THEIR RETURN
FROM INDIA AFTER MORE THAN TEN
YEARS' ABSENCE.

E welcome you here from the Orient land,
From over the dashing blue sea,
To beautiful scenes in Cliftonia grand,
Surrounding the woodlands of Leigh.

We wish you both joy in the opening Spring,
True rapture each morning and night,
To hear the sweet linnet and nightingale sing
In their temple of sylvan delight.

You are now far away from a climate of heat,
Inhaling the pure bracing air
On Downs all inviting as Nature's retreat,
More charming than tongue can declare.

How lovely, enchanting, inspiring and good,
  Where the Avon doth placidly flow,
And the rocks of St. Vincent for ages have stood
  O'erlooking the water below.

From mountainous steep you may view with delight
  A fairyland thrilling in power,
And see in the glen, from its famed rocky height,
  The Muses' long frequented bower,—

Where Chatterton, Southey, and Coleridge retired
  In the valley of nightingale long :
And, blest in its shading, by Flora inspired,
  Re-echo'd their service of song.

We welcome you, then, to the fairest and best
  Of all that is lovely and rare—
To an increase of health in this Queen of the West,
  With a peaceful and happy new year.

And then, when the journey of life hath it close,
  When the changes of travel are o'er,
We wish you all joy in the land of repose,
  On a bright and more beautiful shore.

January, 1877.

ACROSTIC.

IN MEMORIAM.

Rev. Dr. Jabez Burns, London : 40 years Pastor of the General Baptist Chapel ; died January 31st, 1876, aged 70 years.

RESTING at length in the palace of beauty, 'neath a fair dome
    of the temple on high,
    Entered the land of the blissful and holy, in the bright
angel-abode of the sky,
Vale of the peaceful now thou hast reached, gaining sweet home
  where the pilgrims rest.

Death the pale rider hath thee escorted to thy repose in the climes
of the blest ;

Rest, weary toiler, rest with thy Maker, basking in light of His
countenance now :

Joining the good who have passèd before thee, wearing the guerdon,
love wreath on thy brow.

All the fatigue of thy journey is ended, all the rough storms of the
voyage are past,

Blending thy song with the myriad redeemed ones, safe in the haven
eternal at last :

Earth is exchanged for streets that are golden, time for eternity's
anthem of love ;

Zion below, with its hallowed enjoyment, for the full joys of the
Zion above.

Blessing on earth, with thy own hallowed labour, noble example to all
thou hast given,

Using the talents bestowed by the Owner, now thou art rich in the
blessings of heaven ;

Reigning with Him who prepared thee for duty, hearing His plaudit,
" Welcome, well done ! "

Near thy Redeemer, the dearest beloved One, seated with Him on
His dazzling throne.

Shall we, then, mourn at thy peaceful departure, sigh just because thy
sighing is o'er ?

Lay down our harps, as in sorrowful moments, now thou hast
sorrowing moments no more ?

Onward we press, with a hope that's immortal ; faith's realising
discernment is nigh ;

Nearer to where thou art dwelling it brings us, on the plumed pinions
of love soaring high.

Drink from the crystalline river o'erflowing, nerved for fresh conflicts,
forgetting the past ;

Onward to duty, in work for the Master, 'till we shall meet thee in
heaven at last,

Never to part on the radiant shore, shining for aye in the bright evermore.

THE CITY ARABS.

SWEET St. Peter's bells were ringing with melodious strain,
And the white Old Year was listening to their loved
refrain ;
While the silver moon, though waning, threw her beaming light
O'er the beautiful old city, radiantly bright.

New Year's Eve, with smile benignant, gracefully attired,
Deck'd in hope's bright blooming costume, welcome love inspired ;
While she scattered golden treasures from her virgin breast,
Precious gems, all cheering, o'er the City of the West.

Yet within the Castle precincts, near its moated ditch,
In a cellar damp and lonely, ownèd by the rich,
Lay two wanderers, young and weary, both with shoeless feet—
Sister, brother, both forsaken—Arabs from the street.

New Year's Eve to them was dreary, pleasures they had none,
For the night police had sternly bade them both *move on ;*
And on bed of straw, affrighted, they despairing lay,
Waiting, through the hours of darkness, for the light of day.

" Willie," whispered little Nellie, " Willie, can you tell
Why we thus are forced to shelter in this gloomy cell ?
Strange that we, like other children on this happy night,
Cannot with our parents sing sweet anthems of delight."

" Nellie," said the weeping brother, 'mid his bitter tears,
" Ah ! this thought oft brings me sorrow, filling me with fears ;
Yet I think I know the reason—nay, I'm sure I do,
And will try, my darling sister, now to answer you.

" Other little children gladsome through the day we see,
But their parents both are sober—ours ? alas ! ah, me.
Father, mother, oh, how wretched their besotted life,
Drinking at the gin shop, Nellie, down the path of strife.

" Oft I wish, my only sister, you had ne'er been born,
For it grieves me, Nellie, darling, when you look forlorn ;
I would freely go in tatters, want and hunger bear,
But to see you look dejected fills me with despair.

" Nellie, sister, you are hungry, starving through the day ;
Cringing, craving for a pittance, waiting by the way ;
Caring not to tell the stranger all your childhood fear,
Just because both father, mother, take the poison—beer !

" Why they make and sell it, Nellie, I have wondered long—
Some have said it makes them cheerful ; some, it makes them strong.
But I think all would be wiser, did they but abstain,
For instead of yielding pleasure, it produceth pain.

" It has brought us sorrow, Nellie ; home, ah ! we have none :
All that made us once so happy, now for ever gone !
Lonely wanderers, ragged, wretched—people wonder why ;
'Tis the drink has done it, sister. Nellie, dear, don't cry.

" Hush, my darling, you are weary ; nestle on my breast ;
Only bed of straw to lie on,—Nellie, sister, rest ;
But before you sweetly slumber, let us sing the lay
That our fallen mother taught us, ere she went astray."

Then harmoniously their voices blended in the air,
While the Evening Hymn they carolled, sweet beyond compare, —
Asking God their heavenly Father, while they thus did sing,
That in mercy He would shield them with His shady wing.

Long they trilled their simple anthem in the silent night,
While a loving Saviour, tender, heard them with delight ;
And He whispered to the angels—His beloved three—
" Go and fetch the two forsaken ; bring the lambs to me."

Then on wings of light they vanished to that cellar drear,
Bore the lone inebriates' offspring from a world of fear :
Placed them in the fold of Eden, where the weary rest,
Shelter'd by the one Good Shepherd, on His loving breast.

New Year's morn, with light refreshing, cheered the opening day,
And in Death's sweet sleep, all smiling, these two Arabs lay ;
They had gone to fairer city, where the good repose :
All the bitter now being taken from their cup of woes.

ACROSTIC.

IN MEMORIAM.

*Her Royal Highness the Grand Duchess of Hesse-Darmstadt, Princess Alice, of
Great Britain and Ireland, died December 14th, 1878, on the 17th
Anniversary of her Father's death, aged 35 years.*

AH ! there's sorrow deep and pungent, wrought, alas ! by
Death's cold hand ;
Unmistaken grief and mourning thrill our loyal Fatherland ;
Royal palaces are saddened, Royal hearts are wrung with pain—

Princes', and a Queenly mother's, with her country's, bleed again.
Rose of our beloved nation—she has gone. But why despair?
In her virgin summer's beauty she is blooming " Over there."
Now she finds again her lov'd ones, 'cross the Jordan's swelling tide—
Clasps the darlings of her bosom,—*one for whom its mother died !*
Enter'd where she greets our Albert, raptur'd with her father now ;
She whose loving hand once kindly wip'd the death-dew from his brow.
Shall we, then, because she's joyful, rend our hearts with untold woe,

And with unresigned spirit wish her with us here below ?
Let us follow in her footsteps ; she is where the seraph sings—
In the palace home of beauty, with the Sovereign King of kings ;
Crown'd by Him, and crown'd for ever, where the ransom'd hosts adore,
Endless pleasures with them sharing—yes, where parting is no more !

In Affectionate Remembrance of
MATTIE,

The devoted daughter of P. Gabbitass, Clifton, who died June 16th, 1880, aged 32 years. She was the writer of " Nellie Rae," " Our Princess Alice," and other Poems, and died as she lived, a Christian, and as she also wished, died in her father's arms.

Interred in Bethesda Chapel Burying Ground, Keynsham, Somerset.

MATTIE's crossed the Jordan river,
Angels whisper'd her away
To the land of life for ever,
To the joys of endless day.
In the home she doth inherit
Everlasting health is given :

God her Father cheers her spirit,
And her loved ones safe in heaven.
Blest beyond our frail conception,
Beautifully clad in white,
In her Saviour's loved protection,
There she hath untold delight ;
And for ever, sweet for ever,
She is trilling mercy's lay,
Safe beyond the swelling river,
Where the tears are wiped away.

F

ROYAL INCENTIVE BIRTHDAY ACROSTIC.

MAY 24th, 1881.

TO our belov'd and gracious QUEEN, in her exalted sphere,
On this glad day we tribute pay, with mind and soul
    sincere!

How doth the nation's heart exult this May-tide's welcome morn,
Enthusiastic hail the day its sovereign QUEEN was born:
Rejoicing peals from silvery bells, in empire where she reigns,

Make melody for her to-day, as pleasant dulcet strains.
On tower and turret, mart and ship, all pointing to the sky
She sees a loyal country's joy, on banners waving high;
This day of days in palace home she takes her queenly part,

Guarded by Him who keeps her throne in a lov'd people's heart.
Rever'd good QUEEN VICTORIA is, 'neath Windsor Castle's dome,
And her lov'd name is hail'd to-day in manse and cotter's home;
Collective choirs with joyful voice will sing aloud, I ween,
In one harmonious greeting throng, "God save our gracious Queen!"
Oh, may her life be long preserv'd to grace loved Britain's throne—
Unceasingly her reign proclaim that she and we are one;
So will she gather, round that throne, brave men with sterling sense,

Mark'd for their love of right to all—a nation's best defence.
And long her path the angel Peace will strew with fairest flowers,
Just like the flowers that bloom above in amaranthine bowers;
Each birthday then will bring new joy, our own loved Queen will know,
Supplied by Him, the Source of Good, from whom "all blessings flow."
Though time from all who dwell on earth is surely ebbing fast,
Yet she may have this birthday bright and better than the last.

To her we wish sweet joy returns on this all-welcome day,
Health-giving bliss, with all that's good, attend her on her way ;
Endearing friends for her heart's need, oh ! may she ever find—

Quintessence of affection pure, to soothe her anxious mind !
Until her reign on earth shall cease, may He—the Source of Love—
Endue her with that strengthening grace that cometh from above :
Enrich'd with this, she will be free from danger and despair,
Nobly preparing for a throne, with loved ones, " over there ! "

IN MEMORIAM.

EARL BEACONSFIELD.

Born December 31st, 1805 ; died April 19th, 1881. Aged 76 years.

ARTH to earth is breathed o'er thee, one of Nature's gifted
men,
And for ever is relinquished thy prolific novel pen.
Rest in peace ! The grave that holds thee, and thy polished marble
bust,
Lessons teach to coming ages,—earth to earth, and dust to dust.

Brilliant thou, in thy endeavour to uphold Great Britain's crown,
Earnest through thy life, and clever to secure a wide renown ;
Ardent, yes ; though oft phlegmatic, when thy prestige was destroyed,
Cautious when in diplomatic mission thou hast been employed ;
Oriental in thy dreaming, dwelling oft in fairy land,
Notable for dextrous scheming, which the wise could understand ;
Senatorial skill, elating, bade thee ne'er the palm to yield,
Fearless in thy shrewd debating, coroneted Beaconsfield.
Incognito, soaring upward, wheresoe'er thy lot was cast,
Exultant in time of conquest, Time has conquered thee at last ;
Loyal to thy Queen and country, we thy life-work won't prejudge,
Death's own messenger has called thee to a righteous-judging Judge !

A Model for the Rich.   A Friend for the Poor.

MEMORIAM ACROSTIC,

For Sarah, widow of Sir John Kerle Haberfield, six times Mayor of Bristol.   Died December 5th, 1874, in her 76th year.   Buried at Arno's Vale.

Bequests to varied Charities and Lifeboat Institutions, £8,040.

LIKE the golden grain in autumn, ripened for its Garner Dome,
And with waving treasure laden, waiting for the Harvest Home ;
Death, the long expectant Reaper, came to welcome thee away,
Yonder with the Angel gleaners, in the Fatherland of Day.

High above our Ancient City, in the mansions of the blest,
All the pains of Time outliving, in thy tranquil spirit's rest,
Blest in life while soothing others, giving hope and chasing fears ;
Every form of woe relieving, drying saddened Orphans' tears.
Rest in sweet reposing, loved one, Old Bristolia guards thy fame,
Friend of helpless, needy stranger, weeping widows bless thy name :
In the Hospice, and the Lifeboat, aiding on the sea and land,
Every grateful heart shall gladden, for thy potent helping hand ;
Live thy works of Love and Mercy, written far above the sky,
Deeds of Good, like Truth's Immortelles, never wither, never die.

LOVE'S REPLY TO AFFECTION'S QUESTION.

BY A POET'S DAUGHTER (NOW DECEASED).

In the soft mellow twilight of one lovely autumn eve, near the ancient city which gave birth to a gifted Chatterton, produced an immortal Southey, and whence many of the peerless hymns of that sweet singer of Israel, Charles Wesley, were ushered into being, there sat in pleasant converse a father and his child. The messenger of death had taken from them many years ago, to the angel-land, the mother, whose loved image was vividly impressed on her she left in early childhood. Inadvertently, and somewhat playfully, the father said, "Do you love your father, Mattie?" A few days after, she presented him with the following lines, her first production, as an answer to his question, and which are now published at the earnest request of many influential friends.

D O I love thee? Ask those flowers,
　　Tinged with beauty's lovely hue,
　　If they love the glowing sunshine,
　　And the gentle morning dew.

Do I love thee? Ask that songster,
　　Trilling sweet its welcome glee,
　　If it loves the tender offspring
　　Waiting it in yonder tree.

Do I love thee? Ask the mother,
　　Gazing on her babe so fair,
　　If she loves her little treasure,
　　With its locks of golden hair.

Do I love thee? Ask yon maiden,
　　Standing by her lover's side,
　　If her heart on him is centred
　　More than all the world beside.

Do I love thee? Ask the chamber
　　Where I oft retire to pray,
　　When the eventide is waning,
　　And the ushering in of day.

Ask the spot where I have kneeled,
  Oft bedewed with many a tear,
If thy name is ever mentioned
  In my fervent pleading there.

Ask them all ; and if they answer
  " Yes " to that request of thine,
Then henceforth may this thought cheer thee,
  That same answer now is mine.

INCENTIVE ACROSTIC.

Respectfully inscribed to the Right Hon. the Earl of Shaftesbury, K.G., &c., &c., on his attaining his 80th Birthday, April 28th, 1881.

TO one we love for Christian zeal, on this auspicious day
  Of birthday cheer, with heart sincere, is sent this greeting lay.
Time flies ! Yet finds him at his post, employed as heretofore,
His labours for his Master, Christ, are treasured more and more ;
Each closing day he finds a stage of pleasant duty run,

Reminded that the night will come, when man's work will be done.
In years gone by, 'tis known and well, his toiling was for good,
God gifted for a special work, that now is understood ;
His talents have been well employed, his wealth, his time, and pen,
That peace and right might dwell on earth, and good-will among men.

How blest a life thus nobly spent, what pleasure to the mind
Outflowing from his love to God, and all the human kind.
No form of woe but his large heart sought out for it relief,
Outcasts and city Arabs found in him a friend for grief ;
Unsparing of his time and care, his faith by works did show
Right evidence of Jesu's love, who cared for man below.
And when the good Old Book was found to be the world's great need,
Beyond the pale of his own church he for its spread would plead ;
Lov'd labour for this Book of books he gave with zeal untold,
Engaged in service so divine to him was more than gold.

The climbing boys of years gone by will bless his name to-day,
Have grateful heart for him who swept their drudgery away ;
Each Ragged and Industrial School that grace our Christian land

Esteem the work that he has done, the labour of his hand.
And on this grand red-letter day will ring from training ships
Right hearty cheers and wishes good from brave young seamen's lips.
Lov'd children, homed in refuges, once sad and desolate,

On his lov'd name to-day will dwell, with mind and heart elate.
Fond mothers, too, in many a cot, who laboured once in mines,

Shall name him their " Forget-me-Not," his name their heart enshrines ;
He who, when in the damp cold pit they had to toiling come,
Assisted them to their right place,—the woman's place, at home.
From Bands of Hope, from rescued waifs, and myriad tongues beside,
There shall this day, as from one heart, joy-wishes come with pride.
Esteem for him the nation feels, who sought not worldly fame,
Staunch in his efforts for its weal, to-day all hail his name.
Blest birthday this to him, who finds the good old sacred page
Upholding him with its sweet truths to cheer his ripe old age ;
Remembered he shall be to-day at morn and even prayer,
Yes, thousands whom he lived to bless shall think upon him there.

Kind heaven grant that when on earth his last birthday shall come,
Good angels from his Father-God may bear his spirit home !

The following letters were received by the Author from the Right Hon. the EARL of SHAFTESBURY and the Right Hon. the LORD MAYOR of LONDON for this Birthday Ode ; and 2,000 copies purchased by one gentleman alone, W. BUTLER, Esq., Clifton Grove, for free circulation :—

" 24, GROSVENOR SQUARE, *May 2nd*, 1881.

"DEAR Mr. GABBITASS,—Be assured that I shall keep your Incentive Acrostic among my choice papers. I am much obliged to you for it. I fear, though, you have spoken too highly of me ; but you have, I rejoice, assigned the true motives of my public life.

" Yours faithfully,

"SHAFTESBURY."

" The MANSION HOUSE, LONDON, E.C.
" The LORD MAYOR begs to thank Mr. GABBITASS for his kindness in sending him his Acrostic on the 80th Birthday of Lord Shaftesbury."

AUTUMN LEAVES.

UTUMN leaves again are falling,
  Near the abbey church they lie ;
With their voice portentous calling—
  " Man, like us, must fade and die."

Ah ! how soon their beauty ceases,
  From the elm-tree branches fled,
Where they sang, with summer breezes,
  Requiems o'er the sleeping dead,—

Feeble, fickle, ever changing,
  Rustling loud, with meaning rife ;
Disarranged and disarranging,
  Emblem fit of human life.

Happy they, who thus beholding
  Autumn leaves in their decay,
If such vivid scenes unfolding
  Guide their feet to Wisdom's way.

Leading to a land inviting,
  To the better Eden fair ;
Amaranthine bowers delighting
  All who safely enter there.

These behold without sad looming,
  When life's desert path is trod,
Trees whose leaves are always blooming
  In the paradise of God.

LOVE'S VICTORY.

EVA, THE DYING GIRL OF CLIFTON GROVE.

HE grey clad silver twilight had kissed the waning moon,
   Then vanished from the eastern sky, one lovely morn in
      June,
And o'er St. Vincent's rocks bright Sol had thrown his opening ray,
Where balmy zephyr's choral notes inspired the welcome day.
There loved Leigh Wood's green foilage, on sylvan shady trees,
Enraptured sipped the sparkling dew, inhaled the festive breeze,
While swiftly through the Avon passed, with rapid Sea King strides,
The dashing tide beneath the bridge,—the Bridge of Suicides !

Near to this giant spanning arch, majestic and complete,
Where noble Science proudly finds a trophy at her feet,
There stands within a shady grove an oft-frequented dell,
A house designed by beauty's hand—its name I may not tell ;
Yet in that home where plenty dwells, and luxury displays
Her envied stores of wealth and ease to more than vulgar gaze,
There lay on crimson silken couch, resigned, serenely mild,
A lovely girl, with flaxen hair—a sinking, dying child.

Twelve summers bright had wreathed her brow with virgin flowers
      of joy,
But now, alas ! the fever's flush produced a strange alloy ;
Those sunken cheeks and glassy eyes, with faint and bated breath,
Foretold that she was gliding through the peaceful vale of death.
An angel voice, that summer morn, had early whispered, " Come !
I wait to take thee to sweet rest—a lovelier, better home."
While there her doting mother held one thin and wasted hand,
Watching, with all a mother's love, life's last outfalling sand.

"Kiss me, my mother dear," she said, "your Eva's dying now;
The cold death-chill has come at last, I feel it on my brow.
You must not grieve when I am gone, for I shall happy be;
Your weeping will not bring me back, but you may come to me;
And if dear father, too, would walk in heavenly wisdom's ways,
You may be joyful when I'm gone, and sing Jehovah's praise.
'Tis strange he leaves you here to mourn, and from his presence shrink,
Since he has joined with Folly's sons to take the mocking drink.

"Hush! darling mother; now I hear his footsteps on the stairs,
Perchance some angel kept him safe in answer to your prayers.
How sad, throughout the silent night, your heart grief-stricken shocks,
Fearing he might have fallen down the steep and craggy rocks.
But, no! he comes again to see his Eva ere she dies,
And I, though faint, will speak to him; come, dry your weeping eyes,
It may be our kind Friend above may check his passions wild,
And save him, mother, for your sake, through me, his dying child."

The distant sound of his known tread the winding stairs ascend;
With faltering step and heavy gait he reached the wished-for end,
And, with the guilt-stain on his brow, passed by the chamber door,
Just as the College clock commenced to strike the hour of four.
Then, gazing with bewildered look, he saw his weeping wife
Holding the hand of their one child, hope of his future life;
For her twin sister, lovely babe, grim death removed before,
And left them but fair Eva's form for their parental store.

"Eva, my child," he hoarsely said, "are you no better yet?
Come, tell your father, are you worse? Whisper, my darling pet;
For since I saw you yesterday, some sudden change has come,
As though you soon were going to leave your lovely childhood home.
Now let me take that other hand, I'll sit down in this chair;
Surely I have my Eva's love, her best affections share?
I know that I deserve them not: so fickle, changing, wild;
But Eva loves her father yet, and father loves his child."

Uplifting then her thin white hand from off the snowy sheet,
She placed it in her parent's, soon his wishes to complete,
And raising high her bright blue eyes, with pure affection's rays,
She looked on him with pitying glance, yet calm and steady gaze ;
Then whispered softly, " Father, dear, I'm glad that you are come—
I feared I should have passed away ere you returned home.
There's something pains my throbbing heart I wish for you to know,
For you will have no Eva soon—no child to love below.

" Since little sister Minnie died, and I have suffered here,
Dear mother says you leave our home and fill her full of fear ;
You seek not for the healing streams, pure from the Fount of Life,
But eager sip the wine-cup's draught—a source of pain and strife.
The good Book saith to those who mourn, from sorrow's pungent smart,
The Healer hath a sovereign balm for every bleeding heart :
Oh, promise me, your dying child, you'll seek to be forgiven,
For in that Book of Truth I read, ' No drunkard enters heaven.' "

" Eva, my dying girl," he cried, " Eva, my darling child,
Hear me in this thy room of death," he sobbed in accents wild ;
" No more I'll taste the poison Drink, the cause of untold woe,
The blighter of thy mother's peace, thy father's greatest foe."
" Bless you," she gently whispered, " now your Eva dies in peace ;
Kiss me again, my father, dear, ere these pulsations cease.
Let darling mother, too, come near, and press these lips once more ;
The tide of life is ebbing fast ; I near the golden shore."

Then with a strong parental love they clasped her to their breast,
And each the fond embrace bestowed, the last life-kiss impressed ;
While she with failing voice exclaimed, " Mother, while I am here,
Kiss father ; for your Eva's sake, forgive him, mother dear.
He feels that he has caused you pain, with grief your heart has riven :
I wish you to forgive him all, as you would be forgiven."
Then o'er that sinking, dying child, the mother's form was bent,
And token of forgiveness gave the waiting penitent.

" Bless you," she fondly, feebly said, "'tis pleasant now to die ;
Lov'd angel bands are waiting here to take me to the sky.
There's Minnie, with a crown of gold,—see ! here she comes with joy,
To guide me to the land of life, where death cannot destroy.
Calm Jordan's coast of beauty's near, fairer than our loved dell ;
The pearly gates are opening now ; my loved, adieu, farewell ! "
Then from her home in Clifton Grove, that lovely summer's day,
Like the soft breath of eventide, she sweetly passed away.

INCENTIVE ACROSTIC

RESPECTFULLY INSCRIBED TO THE

Right Hon. W. E. GLADSTONE, M.P., Premier,

On his 71st Birthday, December 29th, 1880.

WHILE myriad tongues will hail thee blest, on this auspicious
    day,
    In joy from queenly Clifton Grove comes one heart
    greeting lay ;
Let it receive a welcome smile, enhance thy natal bliss,
Love for our country's weal in thee alone has prompted this.
Illustrious is thy name to-day, our nation's great delight,
As in thy senatorial way thou tread'st the path of right ;
May heaven's love thy life preserve to thy loved land and home,

Endue thee with good health to toil for many years to come.
When keen affliction laid thee low, within the year gone by,
·And loved ones watched thee on thy couch, all fearing thou would'st
    die :
Remembered at the throne of grace thou wert by thousands here,
There went as from the nation's heart strong interceding prayer.

God heard, then answered ; and to day the Guide of all thy ways
Lays out for thee more arduous work, while adding to thy days;
And for our nation's good intends thy lengthen'd life shall be
Devoted as of yore to right by laws of equity.
Such deeds immortalise thy name and honest purpose here,
Their praise this day will be rehears'd, and thrill our hemisphere.
Oh, may kind mercy give to thee new strength for coming toil,
Nerve well thy arm for striking wrong and subtle craft to foil;
Exert in thee untiring zeal, until the right is won,
    And thou shalt hear the Master say, " It is enough ; well done !"

The above lines were printed on ornamental large card, with suitable
mottoes and photo in centre, placed in neat gilt frame, and forwarded to
Hawarden Castle, on receipt of which was received the following pleasing
acknowledgment :—

" 10, DOWNING STREET, WHITEHALL, *Dec. 24th, 1880.*

"SIR,—MR. GLADSTONE desires me to thank you for your very kind gift,
and for the honour you have done him. He wishes you a Happy Christmas.

    " I am, Sir, your obedient Servant,

        " HORACE SEYMOUR.

" MR. P. GABBITASS."

THE YOUNG INEBRIATE'S WIFE.

NOVEMBER'S chill and sombre clouds, in frosty garments
      dress'd,
    Had shrouded in their sable hue the City of the West ;
And old St. Philip's clock again, within its time worn tower,
Had slow and certainly proclaim'd the solemn midnight hour.
Close by that oft-frequented spot where rest the sleeping dead,
A hovel called a dwelling rears its uninviting head :
And in its lonely attic dwelt, not long ago, in life,
A sorrowful bestricken one—a young inebriate's wife !

She sat on this eventful night with anguish sore distress'd,
And clasped her only darling babe in frenzy to her breast :
And while she held this treasure there, her true love's precious prize,
Sad bitter tears of heart-grief fell fast from her swollen eyes.
She thought of days long past, when he who claim'd the parent's part
Had gain'd her hand and, more than that, the homage of her heart :
How kind and tender then he was, for her he all despised—
But now, alas ! and then she sigh'd, and thus soliloquised :

" 'Tis strange that William does not come; how wearily I wait.
Past twelve again, 'tis always so ; to me how very late !
He told me, when he made me his, our home should be his pride,
And he would seek my happiness when I became his bride.
No other company but mine should ever be his choice,
Together we would sweetly live, and one in heart rejoice ;
But now, ah, me ! how changed the scene—he stands on ruin's brink ;
A foe has led his feet astray—the wily demon, Drink !

" Sad fatal hour to me was this.   'Twas on our bridal eve,
False friends they urged the poison cup ; he yielded, then received.
They knew not they had done him wrong ; I felt with pungent smart—
That kind, mistaken act of theirs, it pain'd my tender heart.
Since then, alas ! the serpent's fangs have enter'd deep his soul,—
He madly walks the downward path, pursues the flowing bowl ;
Seems lost to sense of guilt and shame ; he once could sober think ;
But now bewilder'd reason's drown'd in the deceiving drink.

" Hush, thee, my babe.   'Tis only me, thy mother, do not weep ;
This cry of anguish from my soul disturbs thy infant sleep ;
I would that thou hadst ne'er been born, or that thy father's life
Were sober, as it used to be when I became his wife.
Thy future?—oh, this troubles me, my daily anxious care ;
And oft imploring eyes I raise to Heaven in fervent prayer,
That my kind Father-God would bless e'en thee, my darling son,
And save thee from thy father's fate when thy poor mother's gone.

"Oh, could he read my inmost soul, the depth of my despair,
The sleepless nights for him I pass, the days of sorrow here,—
Methinks he would his steps retrace, from the destroyer shrink,
And dash the goblet from his lips, the blighting drunkard's drink.
But, no ; he madly rushes on, although it gives him pain,
Redness of eyes and sorrow's wounds, he seeks it yet again ;
And leaves me here to weep alone, and yet we soon must part,—
The waiting grave will welcome me, and hold this bleeding heart.

"Hark ! hark ! he comes at last," she cried ; "his footsteps I can tell.
'Tis right, tho' late, that he should come and hear my last farewell."
The latch-key turn'd, the creaky door of that drink-ruin'd home
Was opened wide, and then her voice, faint faltering, whisper'd, "Come,
William, my William yet," she cried, "haste, I am dying now ;
Come to my side and wipe away the death chill from my brow.
The drink, the drink has caused my death, my anguish who can tell?
Father of mercies, bless our child ! William, a long farewell."

The drunkard stagger'd, wondered, wept—in vain, the scene was o'er.
"Mary, my Mary," loud he cried ; but Mary was no more.
He clasped her hand, 'twas cold in death ; he kissed her marble cheek ;
And then he sobb'd, 'mid bitter tears, "Oh, once more, Mary, speak !
Forgive me, I have done it all—by drink, alas ! beguiled ;
And thou hast died through me alone, and left thy darling child.
Here on my bended knees, O God, this solemn vow I make,
No more to taste the poison draught, the maddening drink partake."

That vow thus made was kept through life. He sought forgiveness late ;
But found it through the Son of God, who stands at mercy's gate :
And now he trains his Mary's child in works of faith and love,
That he with it may join again the mother safe above.
And oft to Arno's Vale they go, to see her lowly grave,
Where prayers are breath'd to Heaven above this drink-curst world
    to save ;
But while he lingers near that spot he feels the anguish smart,
That she, his wife, his early love, died from a broken heart !

MARION'S JOY:

GOOD NEWS FROM OVER THE SEA.

A BALLAD IN FIVE PARTS.

PART I.

HE Avon's tide was gliding back to sea
From fair Cliftonia, by the woods of Leigh,
And on the distant matchless mountain crest
The golden sunrays sought their place of rest;
For twilight's hour was gathering in apace
The blending beauties of that queenly place,
Where hill and dale and rocks with joy are seen
In summer's glory, on a carpet green.
'Twas in the summertide's entrancing hour
A maiden sat within a shady bower;
And near her side her only brother came,
A noble youth, one Ethelred by name.
He wished to join her, as he had of yore,
When pressing duties of the day were o'er,
In holding converse on some favourite theme,
They had for both of them true heart esteem.
But, lo! on this eventful eventide
Her brother found, when seated at her side,
That there were crystal tear-drops on her cheek;
Her heart seemed full, as though she could not speak,
And yet there was true joy-light in her eyes,
That filled young Ethelred with strange surprise.
A something that he could not understand,
For there she held a letter in her hand;

And reading it had so absorbed her soul,
Its contents had her in complete control.
She saw him not, until she heard him say,
" Dear Sister Marion, what's the news to-day ?
I long to hear it ; come, your brother tell."
And then she sweetly whispered, "All is well ! "
And what was well, may well be here inquired,
What message had young Marion inspired—
What news had filled that maiden's heart with glee ?
Oh, it was news, " Good News " from o'er the sea.
Two summertides had passed since Marion sat
On grand St. Vincent's rocks, in pleasant chat
With one she loved, a youth of noble mien,
Who lived within the shade of Leigh Woods green.
And there they watched the passing of the ships,
Till burning words rushed forth from Ernest's lips ;
Yes !   Ernest was his name, and as his due,
He had a soul with earnest purpose, too :
For there he clasped anew his Marion's hand,
With fervour she alone could understand,
And breathed aloud, " My love, while we are free,
I have resolved, and soon, to cross the sea —
Though Marion I am loth to leave behind ;
I'll tell you now the purpose of my mind.
I am not anxious for securing fame,
To win on distant shores a warrior's name ;
I go to make a home of peace and rest,
Where Marion and her Ernest may be blest.
Don't blame me, love ; but on my love rely,
And I will give to you the reason why.
The other night I sat within my room,
When father entered, in apparent gloom.
Then mother followed, with no mother's joy,
Although she'd told me long she loved her boy ;
They both looked on me with peculiar look,

G

As though preparing me for stern rebuke.
And then my father, like unthinking man,
To me in his haranguing thus began :
' We heard, my son, that you are often seen
With Marion Somerton, of Leigh Woods green ;
The orphan girl that passes by our door,
Whose parents' death has left the maiden poor ;
A lady young they term her, in her teens,
But then she has not yet a lady's means.
She may be good and virtuous withal,
And be respected here by one and all.
But goodness will not do with glowing health
For this world now, unless endowed with wealth ;
We wish for you to have through coming life,
Not only goodness, but a wealthy wife.
Seek money, Ernest, if you wish esteem,
This must be first in this wise age, I deem.'
I heard him, Marion, to this, and then
I rose upon my feet to speak again,
And blushed for shame to hear my father's voice
Wish me, his boy, to foster such a choice ;
And with my hand uplifted in the air,
I to my sire and mother did declare
That I had listened till my soul was stirred,
And from my purpose would not be deterred.
I told them that I loved you as my life,
And long had vowed to claim you for a wife ;
My heart was yours, and with true love's incline,
The heart of Marion Somerton was mine.
I reasoned with them thus.   Was life bestowed
To gather gold, like pebbles on the road ;
Or was it given that hearts might blended be,
In what alone can give felicity ?
Pure heart affection, and the ways of right,
That those who love may in true love delight ;

For this alone through time can make man blest,
And trust in Providence will do the rest.
My mother looked on me with some surprise,
Yet I saw tear-drops starting from her eyes;
And I to her with filial love express,
Breathed forth aloud in earnest soul'd address;
In presence of my father, free from fear,
For my loved mother to her boy was dear.
' My mother, you have heard my father speak,
And I saw blushes on your fading cheek;
Was it for gold he sought your heart of yore?—
For I was told when young that you were poor;
And he, my mother dear, I have been told,
When he wooed you had little store of gold;
And though you both abound in plenty now,
Was it for gold that made you make the vow
To live as one throughout the vale of life,
In state all blessed, that of man and wife?
If gold was not the object, can you prove
That it is wrong in me to wed for love?
Cannot that Providence, whose gifts are free,
That's smiling on you, come and smile on me?
I feel it will, if I pursue the right,
And in the ways of rectitude delight;
And Marion, she will join me heart and hand,
If not at Leigh Woods, in a foreign land,
Where I can rear a home without molest,
A home for Marion, one with plenty blest.
I've read of brave strong hearts who've crossed the main,
Who never saw their earthly friends again;
Yet found true friends beyond the deep blue sea,
In peaceful home of love—and why not we?
I'm young and stalwart; I can practise thrift,
And Marion never shall be turned adrift.
Our hearts are blended from the source above,

We're one in purpose, as we're one in love.
And thus united we will do our best,
And trust in Providence to do the rest.' "
" And did they chide you for this bold appeal ? "
Chimed in young Marion, with her wonted zeal.
" I little thought your parents would be sore
Perplexed, and troubled that your love was poor.
Is poverty a crime? one asked of old,
Or virtue less to be esteemed than gold ?
I know my parents left me little store
Of this world's riches, but they left me more—
An honest name, and a determined mind
To do the right and leave the wrong behind.
And with their dying breath advice was given
To heed their teaching till we meet in heaven.
And I would rather be this summer eve
An orphan girl, who had to live and grieve
O'er parents that are dead, with grief untold,
Than live with parents who but worshipped gold.
Gold well employed is useful in its place,
But when it triumphs it's a brazen face ;
And they whose souls for it are full of lust
Are en'y groping beggars in the dust,
Who while their time and useless lives away
In simply hoarding up thick yellow clay,
Until corruption's worm, with strong desire,
Eats up their flesh as with consuming fire.
The good old Book thus teaches, these will rue,
And this, dear Ernest, I believe is true."
" And so do I, my Marion," he said ;
" And this I told them ere we went to bed,
That I would never give my treasure up,
We'd pledged our love in pure affection's cup ;
Together we would live, and never part
Until the hand of death had hush'd one heart."

"And what response, dear Ernest, did they make?
Oh, tell me quickly—do, for pity's sake."
"Response, my love! My father, in a rage,
Then tried to show I disrespected age;
Said children should their parents homage pay,
It was their duty always to obey.
'And so I do!' I cried; ''tis my delight,
When parents only wish for what is right;
But when they want to mar the work of love,
Why then I look to One who lives above;
And as He dictates I resolve to go,
For He will guide me right, I've learnt to know.'
At these bold words my father stood aghast,
And gloom again on him came falling fast.
When he replied, in tones I can't forget,
They thrill my heart with indignation yet—
'If you will not discard this maiden poor,
You'll find no welcome home within our door;
You have your choice, the mixing of your cup,
If you stay here, then, you must give her up
'If these are your conditions,' I replied,
'For Marion's sake I give up all beside,
Except the love of Him who claims my love,
The one unchanging Friend who dwells above.
The world's before me, with its open door,
A week from hence I'll seek a distant shore.
I've heard that in Australia's far-off land
There's work for all who try with willing hand;
That there the strong and thrifty may succeed,
Secure a homestead for the time of need.
And there I'll go; although I have not wealth,
I've something better, I am blest with health;
Full twenty pounds I've saved from gifts of friends,
'Twill pay my passage till the voyage ends.
And when I'm landed I will do my best,

And trust in Providence to do the rest.'
I left their presence, for the night was spent,
And to my chamber hied with heart content;
And while I sought for guidance on my knees,
I felt my father's mind was not at ease,
And I implored that he some day might see
The grievous wrong that he had done to me ;
And further, that his heart, and mother's too,
Might feel contrition for the wrong to you.
And now, my love," he cried, " a week from hence
I'll tread the path marked out by Providence.
The *Campbell* sails from Bathurst Basin near,
For Liverpool, where I intend to steer ;
And soon from thence on other steamer go
For Melbourne City, with my heart aglow.
You'll not upbraid me for my soul's incline,
'Tis for my Marion's good, as well as mine.
I'll write as soon as I am landed there,
And you keep heart, don't yield to grim despair.
I'll make my way at something, you rely,
And you will help me in sweet by-and-bye.
You'll not be left, my Marion, alone,
Your brother will protect you when I'm gone ;
And he, perchance, will bring you o'er the sea,
When I have found a home for you and me.
He has no earthly ties to hold him here,
And he may find when there some useful sphere ;
A path may open o'er the ocean wave
For him, while he is young and strong and brave.
And now, my love," he said, " I've told you all,
We must away, the dew begins to fall ;
The night-shades creep upon the craggy height,
And old Leigh Woods are fading from our sight.
I'll see you home, and Ethelred will wait
To give you greeting at the garden gate.

Then, in a week at most, both you and I
Will have to breathe for years a fond Good-bye.
Yet, though we part awhile, again shall meet,
And our next meeting will be doubly sweet.
When I am landed I will write to you,
And tell you more what I intend to do ;
Then, if you hear not for some time to come
What I am doing, or where is my home,
Be sure of this, that I shall do my best
To let you know, and keep your mind at rest.
Have faith in me, as I have faith in you,
Though distant, let our love keep strong and true ;
And having faith in God will yield delight,
For He will guide us in the path of right.
On His direction let us e'er rely,
For He hath pledged to guide us with His eye ;
We shall not err, for He is our defence,
While walking in the path of Providence."

PART II.

A WEEK rolled on, and quickly passed away,
Yet at the closing of each numbered day
Did Ernest and his Marion meet awhile,
The passing moments sweetly to beguile ;
They planned the future with a purpose true,
And made arrangements just as lovers do,
Until the last day came, when they must part,
As lovers do too oft with heavy heart.
Yet on the morn when Ernest sailed she stood
To watch the steamer from the famed Leigh Wood,
Where they so oft had seen the vessels pass,
While standing on the richly-tinted grass ;
And though the tear-drop started from her eye,
She waved her 'kerchief for a fond Good-bye ;

While he upon the deck was seen to stand,
And waving back Adieu with his strong hand,
While his strong heart was throbbing with delight,
Until the vessel took him from her sight.
For six long months did patient Marion wait,
Though oft came peering to the garden gate
To watch the postman's form as he drew nigh,
And when no letter came she heav'd a sigh,
And thought it long before her Ernest sent,
While there much time all anxiously she spent.
At length one morn, while watching the old clock,
She heard the well-known feet and postman's knock.
And he held out the letter with a smile
Poor Marion had waited for awhile.
She closed the door, then op'd the letter wide,
And Ethelred came smiling to her side ;
He wished to know the contents in review,
Just as the sisters' loving brothers do ;
Then joyful Marion the letter read,
She had no secrets from dear Ethelred.
It told of Ernest, safely landed there,
Who bade his Marion then be of good cheer ;
The voyage had been good, the sea was calm,
All free from danger, he had no alarm ;
While on the ocean he had been o'erjoyed,
And on the whole been usefully employed ;
He'd gained some information from a friend,
On whose veracity he could depend ;
A gentleman, who came from Bristol's port,
A Christian man, and one of the right sort ;—
Not one of those who did not care a pin
To ape the Christian, just to take you in ;
But one whose life for many years, at Knowle,
Proclaimed he had a noble heart and soul.
" He knew your father when he was a boy,

And when I told him all it gave him joy.
For he has promised me with heart delight,
If I will go with him, to set me right ;
He has a home and acres of rich land
That he has gained by diligence of hand—
A thousand miles from Melbourne, near a wood,
But all the soil near it was very good.
He'd lived on it for years, and had been o'er
To see his friends in Bristol just once more.
Would I go with him home and stay awhile,
'Twould give him pleasure, and the time beguile ;
I could then for myself see what he'd done,
Although to heir it he had not a son.
His boy was dead ; and he no daughter had,
And oft the thought of this had made him sad.
And while he of his long-dead boy did speak,
I saw some large tears rolling down his cheek.
' But,' he continued, ' I have yet a wife,
As good as e'er a man can have in life.
But she, like me, is turning rather grey,
Our time, we feel, is ebbing fast away ;
But she would have me to come to Knowle again,
And 'twas through her I ventured o'er the main.
Yet I've had joy, and more than tongue can tell,
But to old Bristol I have said, " Farewell."
We have good servants in our homestead now,
Whom I can trust with anything, I vow.
And so I left my home without a fear,
For all will be kept right while they are there.
And yet I often feel that I want one
Whose judgment I can well depend upon,
To do those things which servants cannot do,
Attend to my accounts, and look them through ;
And see to all expenses, and beside,
All business matters keep on the rightside.

'I think,' he said, while giving me a smile,
'If you will go it will be worth your while;
Young Marion Somerton I never knew,
But both her parents, they were brave and true;
And I am sure their child would never love
A man she thought would e'er unworthy prove,
If, like her mother, she could judge, I know,
The one through life with whom she wished to go.
And there is much that I esteem in you,
I now must tell you, for I feel it's due;
I've watched you from the day that we set sail;
And once when we were threatened by a gale
You did not flee for solace where, alas!
So many fled, to the all tempting glass.
Then at the table, when each meal was spread,
All glad and thankfully you bow'd the head;
Reminded that those gifts were all bestowed—
From the all good and great Provider flowed;
And to show gratitude for mercies given
Was not the least requirement of heaven.
And when the Sabbath's calm came on the sea,
You did not join in scenes of revelry,
But tried to make the Sabbath hallowed, blest—
A day of worship, and a day of rest;
You sang sweet hymns of praise with soul sincere,
And felt it good to join in worship there.
Don't blame me that I watched with such intent
Your movements daily—it was all well meant;
And if you will decide to go with me,
I think in all that's good we shall agree.'
I heard this stranger thus address me, love,
He was to me a herald from above.
I drank in every word he spake with glee,
They seemed like honey-drops to comfort me.
And then I promised, when we reach'd the land,

That I should be at his entire command ;
I felt that Providence, who shapes our ends,
And for whose guidance right-trained man depends,
Had been at work for you, though in Leigh Wood,
And all things now were working for our good.
Well, after many days we sighted land,
With joy and gladness, you may understand.
And when we landed on the waiting shore,
I felt so thankful with the voyage o'er ;
And to a good hotel we went that night
With feelings of unspeakable delight.
And ere, my love, I there retired to rest,
I wrote this letter, may it find you blest.
To-morrow we shall start, for where I'm told
There have been diggings with abundant gold ;
But we shall pass them with our mind at ease,
To where the honey flows from waving trees ;
Where pastures rich on many a mountain steep
Find food abundant for his flocks of sheep ;
And where the soil-refreshing, falling rain,
Prepares the earth for yielding golden grain ;
And vineyards cluster with abundant store
Of luscious grapes, to well repay the grower.
And now, my love, this letter I must close,
I feel that I have need of some repose ;
When we have reached our home, you may depend
Another letter I shall gladly send,
When I have seen the place that's now afar—
Yes ! far from that, my love, where you now are—
And made my observations for a time
On its surroundings, seasons, and the clime.
Keep up your spirits, let your home be bright,
I feel I'm walking in the path of right.
Then give my love to Ethelred, and say,
I hope to meet you both again some day

In this fair land, with all it has to give,
And where we may in peace and plenty live.
And tell him, while we meet, he is to be
The guardian of my love across the sea.
And then some day, when we are safely met,
For his attention I will pay the debt.
And until the next letter you receive,
I of you both, with love, must take my leave."
When Marion thus had read the contents o'er
Young Ethelred was glad, but Marion more ;
For joy-tears fell like rain from both her eyes,
This letter was to her a sweet surprise ;
And golden visions floated in her brain
Of her own Ernest, and the meet again.
And until night-shades gathered round the door,
Did she with Ethelred in fancy pore
O'er joys to come beneath a distant sky,
At home, sweet home, in coming by-and-bye.

PART III.

SIX months had passed, and near the garden gate
Expectantly one morn did Marion wait ;
She saw the rural postman cross the stile,
And coming nearer, with a knowing smile
He held a letter out, he thought was due,
And said, " Miss Somerton, this is for you ! "
Poor Marion's heart was thrilled with new delight
When the handwriting met her waiting sight.
She knew it was from Ernest's loving hand,
And written from Australia's distant land.
Her brother Ethelred was not at home,
He'd gone awhile in fair Leigh Woods to roam,
To gather ferns and cowslips by the way,
And nice primroses for a sweet nosegay,

That he might give his sister in their bloom
The wild sweet flowers to adorn her room.
So Marion went within the arbour's shade,
Where she and Ernest had the love-vow made ;
And spreading out the letter in her hand,
She read, while she the balmy zephyrs fanned :
" My own true love, I write again with glee,
To give you pleasure o'er the bright blue sea.
I daresay you have thought this letter long
Before it came,—but there is nothing wrong.
I told you in my last to patient be,
And also wished you to have faith in me ;
For I should like to look around me well,
That I the better might to Marion tell
What I had seen, and how I liked the place
To where I journeyed with a stranger's face.
Now I will tell you what did me betide,
And on the whole I am well satisfied.
It took us just a month to reach the farm
Where my friend lives ; but it has such a charm,
When you are there, you all exultant say
You think no more of dangers by the way.
For travelling, my love, doth comfort lack,
There was no railway with its iron track ;
We had to coach it with no well-made road,
But one all rough, that nature had bestowed.
We'd many ups and downs, but ne'er o'erthrown,
O'er lengthy grass that needed to be mown.
But we arrived all safe, I joy to tell,
And found my friend's own friends at home all well.
His treasured wife, with heart too full to speak,
Came to his arms for kisses on her cheek ;
And treasured servants, who now till'd his land,
Came in to have a shaking of the hand ;
And while the servants were preparing tea,

Why then, of course, all eyes were fixed on me.
But they were soon acquainted with my name,
And also of the hamlet's, whence I came.
Then his good wife came to me in surprise,
And, looking full in my bright hazel eyes,
Said—'Tell me, pray, what was your mother's name
Before she married—was it Blanche Meldame?'
I said it was, and then she cried with joy,
'I am your mother's sister, darling boy:
An aunt from Leigh Woods green you never knew,
For I was known while there to very few.
I oft had wondered whether she was dead,
Since we were to this land of plenty led.
I've written more than once, and often mourned,
For all the letters written were returned;
So we concluded that your parents died,
And you, perchance, was lying by their side.
How strange to meet you in this distant land,'
And then she took me kindly by the hand.
And when this work of greeting me was done,
She said, 'From henceforth you shall be my son!
Our only boy is dead some years ago,
And in yon silent valley lieth low.
He was a treasured son, so true and brave,
And we have planted rose trees round his grave,
To e'er remind us in their springtide bloom
That he is only sleeping in the tomb,
And that one day he will come forth with joy,
And live where death can never more destroy;
Where we shall join him, and the joy-bells ring,
In presence of the world's redeeming King.'
You may be sure, my love, this great surprise
Brought tears from mine and many listeners' eyes;
While he who brought me here, I felt with pride,
Was uncle now, and I was satisfied.

Thus days and weeks pass'd o'er, and we were sat
One eventide at home in friendly chat,
When aunt and uncle smiling, look'd on me,
For I was musing, they could plainly see.
Then uncle said, ' What think you, Ernest, boy,
Would Marion like to come and share your joy ?
I've told your aunt the news that you had come
To find good Marion Somerton a home.
And when I told her this with heart sincere,
She said, ' A home, of course ; and why not here !
We both are growing older day by day,
And she must come, thus both can with us stay ;
And as they love so true let them be one,
Then we shall have a daughter and a son ;
They'll take some care from us, and this is right,
That doing this may bring to all delight ;
For they will share alike—they'll understand—
When we are gone, the farmhouse and the land."
Do these suggestions, Ernest, meet your views ?
You have your choice, for it is yours to choose.'
I then told them, with loving heart sincere,
That you would come at once, I had no fear.
I thought it very kind for them to make
Such wise provision for my Marion's sake ;
And said I'd serve them like a faithful son,
For all the good things they to me had done.
And then I mentioned Ethelred by name,
That you would lonely feel unless he came.
And when I told them of his love for you,
My aunt exclaimed, ' Of course, let him come too.
There are openings here for all who will but try,
And they'll succeed, if bent on industry.'
So now, my love, you keep your mind at ease,
I think this news my Marion will please ;
And I should be so glad if you would send

To my own parents, by some trusty friend,
The tidings that my mother's sister 's here,
Whom she had long thought dead, with husband dear.
They are so happy with a new-made joy,
And have adopted me for their own boy.
Send them this letter by your friend to see,
And with it send unchanging love from me.
And now, my Marion, while the coast is clear,
Prepare at once, I long to greet you here ;
I send you an enclosure from my friend,
And one from him that's more, you may depend."

PART IV.

JUST as this letter's contents were read o'er,
Her brother Ethelred looked through the door
That formed protection for the arbour's shade—
It was a lattice door himself had made.
And when she saw his welcome form at home,
She smiled, and said, " My Ernest's letter 's come ! "
And then she let him read it where he stood,
And he pronounced its contents very good.
Then to the house they both at once retired,
While with true gratitude they were inspired.
And e'er that night they both retired to rest,
They made arrangements they then thought the best :
To leave Leigh Woods, with all its treasured store,
And go to Ernest on Australian shore.
When morning dawned, they did the letter send
To Ernest's parents by a well-known friend.
And when this letter met their waiting sight,
It gave them both unspeakable delight ;
For they had felt, since Ernest left his home,
They had done wrong in forcing him to roam ;
And they had had remorse for what they'd done

In giving needless pain to such a son ;
And also for the wrong that they had done
To Ernest's lover, Marion Somerton.
And then they hoped that both alike would thrive
With Ernest's aunt, as she was yet alive.
And this glad news to them was sweet surprise,
It brought the tear-drops from these parents' eyes.
Then they resolved at once to go and see
Both Marion and Ethelred at home in Leigh.
And these were more than glad to see them come,
They gave them welcome to their peaceful home.
Then Ernest's parents frankly owned the wrong
They'd done to Marion, it had grieved them long.
And Marion there performed the Christian's part,
By granting both forgiveness from her heart.
And then they pressed her, to their Ernest tell,
They sent their love, and even wished him well.
And it might be some day themselves might come
To visit both in their now distant home.
And they prevailed with Marion on that day
To let them, as her friends, their passage pay ;
Her brother would be guardian, and for life,
To her who was to be their Ernest's wife ;
And they might on their future aid rely.
And then there came at last the long Good-bye.

PART V.

A MONTH from hence a steamer from the docks,
All newly fitted, passed St. Vincent's rocks ;
And on its deck there stood, with lifted head,
Loved Marion Somerton and Ethelred ;
While waving 'kerchiefs from kind hands were seen,
From friends who knew them while at Leigh Woods green ;
And loud " Good-byes " were heard as on they went,

Until the voices were all nearly spent ;
'Till last farewell came floating on the breeze,
And lost its echo 'mid the Leigh Wood trees.
The steamer passed " Cook's Folly " on its way,
Behind the tug-boat, on that noted day.
And then when Ethelred the tower descried
In which Sir Walter's heir so strangely died,
He told the passengers, just off to sea,
The whole of its all-thrilling history ;
The Gipsy's prophecy he gave with bated breath,
And its fulfilment in Sir Walter's death ;
When he fell victim to a viper's power,
In that dark, ivied, antiquated tower.
The vessel's speed now quickened, and she sped
Soon by the new docks rear'd at Portishead.
And while the wind was veering to the south,
They took a last long look at Avonmouth ;
For their trim steamboat, 'mid some falling rain,
Was dashing onward to the surging main.
Their voyage o'er was not from danger free,
Some storms they had upon the roaring sea ;
And one dark night, while on the billows tossed,
The captain thought the steamer would be lost ;
A stiff nor'-wester came to them defy,
And billows soon were rolling mountains high ;
The lightning flashed, the thunders pealing came,
'Till all the water seemed a sheet of flame ;
Then all below were ordered on the deck,
For fears were high the ship would be a wreck.
The boats were mann'd, and ready for the sea,
When, lo ! the sea grew calm, as calm could be ;
And then the steamboat did without the breeze.
The gallant vessel glided on with ease,
While passengers were glad, as on they sped,
In company with Marion and Ethelred ;

For all were going with a firm rely,
Their fortunes in the rich new world to try.
One early morn, before they rose from bed,
They heard a welcome cry of " Land ahead ! "
And so it was—the night watch on the deck
Discovered in the distance just a speck
Of something shaping like a human hand,
And by-and-by he saw that it was land.
For he had crossed the saline sea before,
And knew it to be Melbourne's waiting shore ;
And then the passengers with frenzy cheered,
When the welcome waiting shore appeared.
Then long " Good-byes " were wished, and hands were shook,
While friends there met were taking the last look ;
And " Much success " was wished in sweet refrain,
'Till many parted, ne'er to meet again.
But Ethelred and Marion stayed that day
In Melbourne City, with its grand array ;
And while they passed through many a busy street,
It gave surprise to find them so complete ;
Until they found a rest with great delight,
In that hotel where Ernest stayed the night.
They had some converse with the host as well,
Who told them something he was pleased to tell ;
That he knew Ernest's friend, and his good wife,
They had been friends to him in his past life ;
It was through them he settled in that home,
And he was glad that he to it had come ;
The emigrants to him had come from far,—
He kept no drink-polluting liquor bar.
With perseverance he had made his way,
And found that doing right would always pay ;
Then ere they all that night retired to bed,
The host before them good refreshment spread,
And kept the rule made on his opening day,

Gave thanks to heaven for mercies of the way,
And with these thanks he urged the Source of light,
To grant them all protection through the night.
The morning came, and waiting Ethelred
With Marion on their journey further sped ;
Their track had been marked out by their kind host,
Who is to emigrants a pride and boast ;
And by his wise direction they went on,
Till Eden Grove at length they looked upon.
The vale they entered was beyond compare,
For golden corn was ripening in the ear ;
While sheep were browsing on the distant hills,
And water flowing from the crystal rills ;
The zephyr wind was singing 'mid the trees,
And joined in chorus by the humming bees.
'Twas like a paradise, they both did prove,
Where everything was breathing, " God is love ! "
A shrill blast from the coachman's horn was sent,
And many knew not what was its intent,
Until, on turning down the sloping land,
They saw a large farmhouse majestic stand ;
And people came from out its opened door,—
Yes ; some whom Marion never saw before.
But there was one among that moving throng
Who for his Marion had waited long.
And soon he saw her, with her many charms,
And quickly held her in his loving arms ;
Then breath'd to her, while thinking o'er the past,
" Safe, love, at home ; yes ! safe, my love, at last."
While she exclaimed, with joy no tongue can tell,
" Yes, Ernest, safe ; thank heaven, all is well."
And then there came two new friends just at hand,
To give her welcome to that distant land ;
The grand old settler, and his honour'd wife,
Gave her true greeting to their home for life.

And Ethelred was welcome, both did say,
To their bright homestead, as the flowers in May.
Then soon they found, in that sweet home of glee,
Themselves all seated at a cosy tea ;
And o'er it they long told of dangers past,
And how life's bitters brought sweet joy at last.
Thus hours they spent on that glad meeting night.
In pleasant converse and untold delight.

CONCLUSION.

A few weeks hence a wedding party met
Within that home, without one heart regret.
Yes ; Ernest had his own lov'd Marion won !
And in the old church near they were made one.
The sweet bells rang that day a merry peal,
While friends and neighbours shar'd the wedding meal.
Much joy was wished by many an earnest tongue,
And then the day was crowned with thankful song.
There Ernest and his Marion dwell in peace,
And find their joy abundantly increase ;
They share the burden, while they shun the strife
That often mars the joy of married life.
And 'neath their vine and fig-tree with delight
They now can sit on lovely summer's night,
And read that welcome letter in their glee,
That brought such news, good news, from o'er the sea.
They feel the praise is due to One above,
Who kept them faithful in the path of love ;
While each feels thankful they have done their best,
And trust in Providence had done the rest.

IN MEMORIAM.

JAMES ABRAM GARFIELD,

President of the United States. Died September 19th, 1881 (aged 50 years), from the effects of two pistol shots from the hand of an assassin, Charles Guiteau, July 2nd, at Washington.

T o-day there comes, on wings of lightning sped,
H eartrending news athwart the ocean bed :
E mblazoned message—noble Garfield's dead !

P eace to thy ashes, mourned Columbia's son ;
R est, earnest toiler, for thy work is done :
E steem'd by all who loved the truly brave,
S weet sleeper, rest within thy martyr's grave.
I n life's great battle thou, a son of toil,
D id'st live the crafty and the base to foil ;
E nnobled hero, with a soul sincere,
N ow thou hast done with faithful service here,
T hy Mother country sends this garland for thy bier !

G *arfield*, thy name will live, thy virtues shine :
A *ssiduous* statesman while at duty's shrine :
R *enowned* for valour, with thy honour bright ;
F *earless*, e'er walking in the path of right ;
I *ndustrious*, kind, and prized when understood ;
E *nduring* all things for thy country's good.
L *oved* Garfield, rest ; " the good can never die "—
D *eath* has but borne *thee* to the home on high !

"THE REASON WHY."

SOME men have ask'd, "Why not employ
　　Your time at working wood?"
　I answer all such men with joy,
Because I'm doing good.
I've done with making doors, I trow,
　And window sashes too;
I've made my share of these, and now
　I've something else to do.

I toil'd and made in younger days
　Drags, harrows, carts, and ploughs,
Near where Lord Byron sang his lays,
　And penn'd his lover vows.
I've work'd in woods he owned, I know,
　While making hurdles new;
Of this I'm not asham'd, but now
　I've something else to do.

I then could rise in summertide
　At breaking of the day,
And to my labour haste with pride
　Though it was far away.
I go to work much sooner now,
　When my loved muse doth woo;
But not to making gates, I vow:
　I've something else to do.

"A man's a man," said poet Burns,
　And feeling this, I dare
To build when twilight's shade returns
　New castles in the air.
I'll try to build them like a man,
　And not to make me rue;
But show, throughout my life's brief span,
　I've something else to do.

A REMINISCENCE.

ES, it is a year to-day,
  I was seated by the side
  Of a loved one blest for aye ;
One who was her parent's pride.
She was drooping, sinking fast,
  As the lily fades away,
From consumption's deathly blast ;
  Yes, it is a year to-day.

She was sitting on her bed,
  Leaning on her father's breast,
It was a pillow for her head,
  For her mother's was at rest ;
And she soon would greet her, where
  Myriad ransom'd spirits stay,
In the " sweet home " over there ;
  Yes, it is a year to-day.

I remember her last look,
  While she near'd the better land,
How she prized the "good old book,"
  How she waved her little hand,—
When she said with spirit brave,
  As the good can only say,
" I fear not the waiting grave ! "
  Yes, it is a year to-day.

Oh, this day has marr'd my mirth
  With the memories it has given,
For it left less joy on earth,
  When it took my joy to heaven.
Yet I will not dare complain
  In this reminiscent lay,
For my loss has been her gain,
  Though it is a year to-day.

June 16th, 1881.

HOLD THOU MY HAND.

Written for Mattie in her last illness.

MY Father, I am Thine, though in distress,
Hold Thou my hand, leave me not comfortless;
Now let my wavering faith's capacity
Behold its Lord, and loving Saviour see;
Then let His well-known whisper in my ear
Dispel the gloom, and banish all my fear,
While in the chamber calm I bow the knee,
And bring me nearer—yes, my God, to Thee.

My Father, I am toss'd on life's rough main,
Hold Thou my hand, the breakers give me pain;
Strange storms arise, for waves run mountains high,
While billows roar, and cloudy is the sky;
Fell lightnings flash, the pealing thunders roll,
And threatening horrors fain would sink my soul.
Be Thou my helper in this raging sea,
And bring me nearer—yes, my God, to Thee.

My Father, I am tried as in the fire,
Hold Thou my hand, my joy, my own desire;
Though fierce the furnace, let it burn the dross,
And bring me nearer to my Loved One's cross,—
That I like Him may bear the scorching sun,
And 'mid the trial say, "Thy will be done."
So shall this crucible a magnet be
To bring me nearer—yes, my God, to Thee.

My Father, I am weak, but Thou art strong,
Hold Thou my hand—the time will not be long:
I fain would trust Thee through the Jordan flood,
Thou great unchanging and eternal Good;
My fragile bark, if Thy hand guide the helm,
Shall glide where sin nor sickness overwhelm,
To where there is a peaceful, glassy sea,
And bring me nearer—yes, my God, to Thee.

EVA DEAR, AND WILLIE.

YONDER, where the strong hearts quail,
At the churchyard in the vale,
There are two no skill could save,
In a little turfy grave—
   Eva dear, and Willie.

Loving hands have laid them low,
And upon the fallen snow
Placed two wreaths of ivy-green,
Just to show they loved, I ween—
   Eva dear, and Willie.

Fever came that wintertide,
Touch'd them till they droop'd and died ;
Now they bloom in fairer bowers,
Like two never dying flowers—
   Eva dear, and Willie.

They were little jewels fair,
Priceless, and beyond compare :
And they shine with lustre bright
In the city out of sight—
   Eva dear, and Willie.

They were little lambs at play,
The Good Shepherd came that way ;
One was on its mother's knee—
" Give the lambs," He said, " to Me "-
   Eva dear, and Willie.

" They shall on My bosom lean,
And shall feed in pastures green ;
Let the little lambkins go
Where the living waters flow "—
　　　　　　Eva dear, and Willie.

But the sire and mother's heart,
Seem'd all loth with them to part ;
They esteem'd them blessings come,
Just to cheer their cottage home—
　　　　　　Eva dear, and Willie.

Then fell kisses on their cheek ;
But those love ties had to break,
When they heard the Shepherd say,
" Let Me take them home to-day—
　　　　　　Eva dear, and Willie.

I will give them joy untold
When we reach the heavenly fold ;
They shall shelter in My breast,
Where no wolf can them molest "—
　　　　　　Eva dear, and Willie.

Then two hearts of love were one,
And they breathed, " Thy will be done."
The Good Shepherd heard that prayer,
And He took them " over there "—
　　　　　　Eva dear, and Willie.

Now they're safe from fear and sin ;
Reach'd the fold and safe shut in ;
In the land of no more night,
Angels give them pure delight—
　　　　　　Eva dear, and Willie.

They have joined the seraph throng,
Sing the sweet redemption song ;
And have found eternal gain,
In the home of no more pain—
                    Eva dear, and Willie.

Death can never reach them there,—
They are in the regions fair ;
Just a season gone before,—
To the bright and peaceful shore—
                    Eva dear, and Willie.

Now they beckon friends away ;
Could we hear them, they would say,
" Come to our sweet home above,
To the little ones you love "—
                    Eva dear, and Willie.

THE TRUE FRIEND.

TO-DAY and for ever there is One watching,
    Watching and caring for you ;
Though men frown on you, He is a Brother—
    One who is faithful and true.

Look to Him ever—He is unchanging
    Both in His love and His care ;
He will befriend you, if you in earnest
    Go to Him often in prayer.

"UNDER THE OLD OAK TREE."

NEW SONG.

COME to my heart on memory's train,
 And contemplation's wing ;
  Sweet thoughts to cheer me once again
While here I sit and sing
On hours I spent in Auld Lang Syne,
 With one all dear to me ;
A heart that beat all true to mine,
 Beneath the old oak tree.

CHORUS—Under the old oak tree,
   Under the old oak tree ;
    On that known seat, our love's retreat,
    Beneath the old oak tree.

We woo'd there 'neath its branches long,
 Until we two were wed ;
And then we sang our bridal song
 In its refreshing shade.
There many a long, long year we went,
 In twilight hour to chat,
While near us, blest with sweet content,
 Loved olive branches sat.
     Under the old oak tree.

But joys of yore are wither'd now,
 My olive branches gone ;
And my first love's death hush'd, I vow,
 And I am left alone ;
But yet there stealeth over me,
 While here I calmly sit,—
The memories of the old oak tree,—
 These have not left me yet.
     Under the old oak tree.

FIFTY-NINE TO-DAY.

HE midnight hour had swiftly gone,
  And I retired to bed ;
Yet when the college clock struck one
  I could not rest my head.
Strange thoughts came to me, such a host
  For many a coming lay ;
But this one kept the uppermost,
  I'm fifty-nine to-day.

And this was true. Then I look'd back
  To days of yore, forsooth,
When I went nimbly on the track
  From childhood days to youth,
And then to early manhood years ;—
  But these have passed away
'Mid varied hopes and many fears,
  I'm fifty-nine to-day.

I will not write as poor Tom Hood,
  Who told, in accents wild,
That he was not so near to heaven
  As when he was a child.
I feel that I am nearer come,
  Than when in childhood's way—
Yes ; nearer to my Father's home,
  I'm fifty-nine to-day.

My good old mother's living yet,
  I love her more and more ;
Don't blame my heart, 'tis on her set,
  For she is eighty-four.
And I know on this morn all glad
  She to her friends will say,
While thinking of her distant lad,
  " He's fifty-nine to-day ! "

December 27th, 1881.

THE LIFEBOAT.

[FOR SETTING TO MUSIC.]

THE wild sea waves are roaring,
   And vivid lightnings flash,
   Loud voices are imploring,
  'Mid pealing thunder's crash ;
Ahoy ! ye brave lifeboat's men.
  To yonder signal press,
A gallant barque is on the rocks,
  The ship is in distress.

CHORUS—Kind heaven send a lifeboat
      In every storm at sea,
      And keep her noble crew afloat,
      Where'er their duty be.

The lifeboat crew soon mann'd her,
  Nor feared the dashing spray,
And with her bold commander
  She plough'd the ocean way ;
Though madden'd surfs behind her,
  And raging winds before,
Her strong brave hands remind her
  True Britons ply the oar.

On, on she rides victorious,
  Nor dreads the ocean grave,
Down, down she glides all glorious,
  Then tops the mountain wave ;
And soon 'mid shouts of gladness
  From every boatman's lip,
Despite loud wails of sadness,
  She nears the sinking ship.

Hurrah !   A living cargo
  Soon fills the waiting deck,
Sad bleeding hearts in thrilling woe
  Are rescued from the wreck.
" They're safe ! all safe!" re-echoes
  From men with skilful oar,
And then 'mid ringing cheers they come
  Back to the welcome shore.

NEW SONG.

SHE SWEETLY WHISPERED "YES."

Y love and I were seated
      One summer's twilight hour,
    Where we had many pleasant dreams
  In true love's shady bower ;
And soon I breath'd, " Dear Lillie,
  May I to you confess
A secret I can hold no more ?"
  She sweetly whispered, " Yes ! "

" Then, Lillie, I will tell you,
  I wish you for a wife :
Oh ! will you be my angel, dear,
  The solace of my life ?
I am in earnest, Lillie,
  The question home I press,—
Now will you name the happy day ? "
  She sweetly whispered, " Yes ! "

Long years have gone since Lillie
  Breath'd this glad word to me,
While we, all joyful, sat beneath
  The village " Old Oak tree."
And now, in sweet home's quiet,
  We oft united bless
That golden summer's twilight hour
  She sweetly whispered " Yes ! "

A PASTORAL.

Written on Clifton Down, 1881.

WHITE sheep are browsing on the Down,
　　Their shepherd 's near, in russet brown ;
　　His faithful dog is standing by,
While on him rests the shepherd's eye.
Old Rover's watching on the hill,
Intent upon his master's will,
And at a given signal flies
Some woolly lambkin to surprise.
The shepherd's crook is raised to show
His faithful dog the way to go,
And he brings back the wanderer bold
To where he finds a shelter fold.
These faithful acts the shepherd please
While standing underneath the trees,
And then, the moments to beguile,
He gives his canine friend a smile ;
While Rover seems at his known call
To fully understand it all.
How peaceful is that shepherd's life,
Away from all the city strife ;
He seems to be a monarch grand,
With subjects all at his command.
Who dare his treasur'd flock molest,
While he is there to give them rest ?
They seem in woodland pastures fair
All safe beneath their shepherd's care ;
But, lo ! a stray hound comes to chase

1

His fleecy flock before his face,
And then his voice is quickly rais'd,—
While Rover, who is sore amazed,
Speeds forth to where the cur doth lie,
To make the fell intruder fly ;
And loud his barking doth resound
Until the foe has left the ground.

MORAL—O faithful dog ; O shepherd rare,
   With watchful eye and earnest care ;
   May I like you my calling grace,
   And faithful be in every place.

HAVE A SOUL.

IN the purposes of life,
     Have a soul!
You will need one 'mid the strife—
     Have a soul!
And let it have this great aim,
Not to merely find a name,
But to win immortal fame
     For your soul!

H O P E.

SWEET angel, were it not for thee,
 The soul would have no rest ;
  And man, while crossing time's rough sea,
Each storm refuse to breast.
But having thee to cheer him on,
He can with danger cope ;
For thou art his soul's benison,
Thou blessed angel, Hope !

CONFESSION.

I MUST make a full confession,
  For I cannot rest
Until for a strange trangression
  I have all confessed.
Heed the secret of this lyric
  Under your control ;
Hear me, without panegyric,
  Open out my soul.

Strange that I, who preach to others
  About doing right,
Urging men to live like brothers,
  Should in theft delight.
Yet it 's true I'm often guilty,
  And I'll make it known ;
For 'tis best, I find, when erring,
  All the wrong to own.

I was tempted in a moment,
  And thus it came to pass :
One May morning in the sunshine,
  On the welcome grass,
I was musing in my station
  O'er what some will please,
When this object of temptation
  Came beneath the trees.

And I went without compunction
  Where some daisies grew ;
Stole my heart a priceless unction,
  Welcome as the dew.
Will you grant me absolution
  When I state with joy,
That I stole *a kiss*—a sweet one—
  From a *baby boy ?*

"I WILL COME AGAIN, LOVE, TO THEE."

A MAIDEN fair was seen to stand
  On the wild sea's beaten shore
With her sailor love, in their native land,
  Where she ne'er might see him more.
So he sang sweet strains to cheer her heart,
  And as sweet as sweet could be ;
For his song was this—"Though we must part,
  I will come again, love, to thee ! "

His gallant barque's white sails were set,
  And a boat was waiting nigh ;
Then he kiss'd his Maude where they had met,
  And they breathed their fond " Good-bye ! "
Yet she heard him sing with cheering voice,
  As he went to the roaring sea,
And his strains were these—" Sweet Maude, rejoice,
  I will come again, love, to thee ! "

A year pass'd by with leaden pace,
  And, lo ! with a true love charms,
Two lovers stood in a firm embrace,
  Locked safe in each other's arms ;
They had met again, on the seashore where
  One sang with a raptur'd glee,
Those strains so sweet, in a waiting ear—
  " I will come again, love, to thee ! "

YOU NEVER NURSE ME NOW.

" HOW is it, John, you're strange to me
 Since we have married been ?
 You used to nurse me 'neath the tree
Upon the village green.
The lovers' oak has seen you, John,
 And heard your plighted vow,
That me you'd always nurse, and yet
 You never nurse me now !

" Have I not been a faithful wife
 Since we two first were wed,
And kept our homestead free from strife
 While you were earning bread ?
Then in our cot, at your return,
 To every wish I bow ;
And yet you don't do as you did,
 You never nurse me now !

" The thought of this has brought me fear,
 While passing on life's way,
And so I felt with love sincere
 I'd mention it to-day ;
I will be frank in married life
 With him who heard my vow ;
Then hear me as your own true wife,
 You never nurse me now ! "

Soon two strong arms embraced a form
 They'd held in days of yore,
And tear-drops soon began to fall
 Where smiles were seen before.
" Forgive me, love ! " John softly breathed.
 She cried, " 'Tis done, I vow ! "
And now she never has to say,
 " You never nurse me now ! "

GREETING ODE.

[BY REQUEST.]

Respectfully and affectionately inscribed to Mrs. R——, Glandare House, late
Miss P——, Hirwain, on returning from her bridal tour, June, 1881.

Air—" The Men of Harlech."

BRIDE of Glandare ! here we meet thee !
Rose of Hirwain ! now we greet thee !
And to nuptial song we treat thee—
 Thee, our village pride.
Young and old bring welcome treasures,
Pleasant notes, harmonic measures,
To enhance hymeneal pleasures
 Of a treasured bride !
Many tongues are singing, while joy-bells are ringing,
Till the strains, in sweet refrains, are purest pleasures bringing.
 Loved friends on every hand unceasing
 Welcome thee with joy increasing ;
 Pouring on thee richest blessing,
 Glandare's bridal queen.

 Pride of Hirwain, hark ! we sing thee,
 And love garlands gladly fling thee,
 While our meed of praise we bring thee,
  Near thy own sweet home.
 Thou hast left a land inviting,
 'Mid Italian scenes exciting,
 With the one thou dost delight in,
  To thy loved ones come.
Welcome we are singing, and the welkin's ringing,
Till the sound spreads wide around, two fond hearts pleasure bringing.

Friends now on every side are pressing,
Onward come with love's caressing,
Wishing joy and every blessing
Glandare's bridal queen.

Joy of Hirwain! bliss attend thee,
All that's good in heart we send thee,
Pray that heaven may defend thee,
    Lady that we love.
May thy path be strewn with flowers,
All thy days have peaceful hours,
Welcome as the summer showers,
    Where thy feet may rove.
Welcomes now are waking ! hill and valley shaking !
Greet thy ear, from hearts sincere, with blessings o'er thee breaking.
While silvery bells are gladsome ringing,
And true friends of thine are bringing
Flowerets sweet to cheer thee, singing,
" Welcome, bridal queen !"

In Memoriam.

FRED GRACE.

The youngest of three brothers, who died September 22nd, 1880.
Aged 29 years.

ONE Grace is dead, of Graces three—
    Fred Grace his name, all graceful he ;
    Good graces won this Grace renown,
Young Grace found grace in every town.
But now this Grace is Grace no more—
To grace the bat, the ball, the score,
For he with grace has bow'd his head,
And Grace's body's with the dead ;
But Grace's spirit lives, we trust,
Through grace rejoicing with the just.

POOR ROBIN'S DINNER PLEA.

A new Christmastide Ballad and Prize Poem.

THE howling wind was sweeping o'er the moor,
    And beating wildly on a cotter's door,
    While winter's rain was pattering loud and fast,
As though in concert with the stormy blast.
An old man sat on this remembered night
Within that cot—in evident delight ;
His pen in hand, that cannot slothful be
To write this ballad—Robin's Dinner Plea.
Poor robins ! These are found where'er we roam
In want and suffering—some without a home.
The hamlet, town and city have their share
Of robins, helpless—robins in despair.
From whence they came, or what produced their woe,
We know not now, nor do we ask to know ;
But be it ours who can to soothe their grief,
And send these robins poor some true relief ;
It may be, some were born in haunts of shame,—
In places vile, that are not fit to name ;
But they are born, and must not helpless lie,
Forlorn and friendless, and—from want—to die.
The fault 's not their's, and they must not be left
With downcast faces, and of hope bereft ;
These robins sad must have some Christmas cheer—
Send them a dinner, if but once a year.
Poor robins ! Some were born in homes of wealth,
With bright surroundings, and in glowing health ;
But from misfortune's dire relentless sway,
Their home and friends, alas ! are swept away ;

And these are wanderers through the silent night,
Or sleep in cellars till the morning light :
No friend to cheer them in their dark abode,
Or guide them safely on life's thorny road.
The stranger's eye looks on them in amaze,
And oft they cringe beneath the vulgar gaze,
While their poor throbbing heart would urge this plea
To every passer by— Oh, pity me !
Remember these poor robins in despair—
Send them a dinner, if but once a year.
And then there are poor robins in the land—
Lone orphans, made by death's unsparing hand;
The fever's touch prevailed one evil day,
And bore their loving parents both away.
And now they're left to mourn with heavy heart
The day they had with their loved friends to part.
Lone robins now.   Oh ! how they daily miss
The father's blessing, and a mother's kiss ;
But they have been bereft who once were glad—
Poor robins now in need, alone and sad ;
Without a homestead, and without a friend,
These robins poor, on charity depend.
To-day are brothers, sisters, robins poor,
Found begging somewhere,—oft from door to door.
Oh ! think of these this coming Christmastide,
And be the friends of those whose friends have died—
God bless these robins, pray, and be sincere
By sending robins also Christmas cheer.
Some robins there are seen in city's street—
Poor gutter children, with their shoeless feet—
With parents living, but who from them shrink,
Because those parents are the slaves of drink.
All comfortless they live, and have to roam
To seek a pittance from their drink-curst home.
These stand with anxious look and tearful eye,

To beg a copper from the stranger nigh.
Keen hunger pinches, and they have to crave
As robins do for crumbs, their life to save
Poor robins are the drunkard's children here,
These suffer want and overwhelming fear ;
And these must have true sympathy and love ;
The drunkard's child all Christian hearts should move,
And lead them all to labour, and to pray
That drunkard's drink may all be swept away,
And brighter homes be found on every hand,
The hope and glory of our Christian land.

CHARITY.

H ! angel of love, sent down from above,
Thy form is surpassing compare ;
The world thou would'st bless with thy loving caress,
And every heart's burden would bear.
Of graces thou art, in thy every part,
The greatest, the purest, and best :
For while thou art nigh, mankind may rely,
The world will have quiet and rest.

INGRATITUDE.

HERE is a thing beneath the sun
That never seems its course to run ;
'Tis ever in its manners rude,
It's name is base ingratitude.
When shown to man—if he's a friend—
Is scandalous, we may depend ;
But shown to God, we may descry
'Tis sinful, and on this rely.

KISS ME, MOTHER, SWEET "GOOD-NIGHT."

" OH, mother, I am weary now,
　　Place your soft hand upon my head,
The cold death-chill is on my brow,
　　Your ' Nellie dear ' will soon be dead.
Bright angels they are coming here
　　To take me, mother, from your sight ;
Then, mother, dry your every tear,
　　And kiss me now a sweet ' Good-night.'

" Dear mother, though I have to die,
　　When I am gone you must not weep ;
Don't, mother, after Nellie sigh,
　　Or at my grave a vigil keep :
My little casket needs no care,
　　For I shall be a jewel bright,
In the sweet home that's ' over there,'
　　Then kiss me now a sweet ' Good-night.'

" Lov'd mother, won't my father dear
　　Soon greet me in that home above ?
You told me he had entered where
　　The golden harpers sing above ;
And baby, that you held so high
　　To kiss and fondle with delight,
Will smile to meet me in the sky,
　　Then kiss me, mother, sweet ' Good-night.'

" My mother, I am dying fast,
　　Now hold me gently by the hand ;
Lov'd angels they are come at last
　　To take me to the peaceful land.
Yes ! in the room with golden wings
　　I see them, mother, clad in white ;
They'll bear me to the King of kings,
　　Then kiss me, mother, sweet ' Good-night.'"

DOWN BY THE FOUNTAIN SIDE.

OWN by the fountain side I go
    Whene'er I feel distress'd,
      Down where the crystal waters flow,
  To give my spirit rest.
Beside that stream a lov'd One stands,
  And offers since He died
Pure living water from His hands,
  Down by the fountain side.

I there have gladly quenched my thirst
  On many a sultry day,
And from the time I went at first,
  I ne'er was turned away.
My Father bids me welcome there,
  And all the world beside ;
This water is so rich and rare,
  Down by the fountain side.

While crossing o'er life's desert sand,
  And Time's uneven way,
With weary feet and trembling hand
  I oft a visit pay.
This water my refreshment is,
  All freely 'tis supplied,
And while I drink I find new bliss,
  Down by the fountain side.

Oh, living stream ! Flow on, flow on :
  This living water give,
Till every dying Adam's son
  Shall drink—and, drinking, live.
Then in the better land all blest,
  With myriad hosts supplied,
Sing to the One who gave them rest,
  Down by the fountain side.

CHRISTMAS EVE, 1881.

LONE, yet not alone, I sat,
  And bade farewell to gloom ;
  The fire burnt brightly in my grate,
Within a cosy room.
So I resolved of carking care
  Awhile to take my leave ;
And with a poet's mind to share
  The welcome Christmas Eve.

I thought on days of long ago,
  When loved ones at my side
Sang me sweet songs with heart aglow
  Throughout the Christmas-tide.
Yet for these back I dare not crave,
  Nor yield to grim despair ;
I felt the loved ones gone were safe,
  And singing over there.

And then I thought while Christmas wanes
  That I would just be glad,
And try to write some grateful strains
  For mercies that I had.
I'd health and strength and reason left,
  I hoped for years to come,
And though of loved ones was bereft,
  I yet had life and home.

This made me feel that festal night
  I ought no more to grieve ;
And I spent then 'mid new delight
  A happy Christmas Eve.
And when the midnight hour drew nigh
  I went to rest away ;
For I had more important work
  To do on Christmas Day.

EXCELSIOR!

A Day Dream in Autumn on St. Vincent's Rocks.

THE skies were glad one sunny morn,
　　When fields were clad with golden corn,
　　And feather'd songsters pure and good
Sang out from sylvan fam'd Leigh Wood,
　　　　Excelsior !

A listening bard was near the spot,
He heard their sweet forget-me-not ;
Far from the din of city's mart
It echo'd in his throbbing heart,
　　　　Excelsior !

And then he sat beneath a tree
That whispered, sweet as sweet could be,
" I long for thee to come and dream
On one all-good, entrancing theme,
　　　　Excelsior !

The night is past, thou hast not slept,
Thine eyes have wakeful vigil kept ;
Here rest awhile this autumn day,
And let thy spirit soar away—
　　　　Excelsior ! "

He heard this whisper in the breeze,
Like harp notes 'mid Æolian trees :
It seem'd to come from angel sphere,
Intently chiming in his ear,
　　　　Excelsior !

And then this dreamer sought repose
Near where the winding Avon flows ;
But to that fairyland there came
A seraph, singing notes the same,
    Excelsior !

This angel gave the bard to know
That from the scenes of " long ago "
A baby boy's lov'd form had sprang,
Whose mother o'er his cradle sang,
    Excelsior !

And he must guard this slender child
Lest he should early be beguil'd ;
Protect him with an outstretch'd arm,
And cry, 'mid ambush'd foes' alarm,
    Excelsior !

This dreamer then long watch'd the boy
'Mid changing scenes of grief and joy ;
And found that as he older grew
He had this motto e'er in view,
    Excelsior !

For near a charming woodland dell
He heard him breathe a long farewell
To friends and home : stern duty cries
Had rang within his bosom—Rise !
    Excelsior !

And then were tear drops on a cheek,
As though his mother's heart would break,
While the last kiss her boy she gave,
And parting words—Be true, be brave ;
    Excelsior !

Then in his dream he saw the lad
Dry up those tears that made him sad ;
For earnest toil his spirit stirr'd,
Near Byron's home, where Byron heard—
     Excelsior !

And there he wrought, from day to day,
Till youth's bright season passed away,
When some lov'd voice he understood
Exclaim'd, while he was shaping wood.
     Excelsior !

He heard this message and obeyed,
From Sherwood's charming scenes he strayed,
To seek within his native town
What was his glory—Right's renown,
     Excelsior !

And for a time the skies were clear,
His mind and heart were free from fear ;
For everything around him cried,
Despite the tempest that defied,
     Excelsior !

But, ah ! there came an evil day,
When home and friends were swept away ;
A too confiding heart betray'd,
That long had sang, all undismay'd—
     Excelsior !

This dreamer saw this sad one thrust,
By one base hand, low in the dust ;
Until his Master from the skies
Said to that stricken one—" Arise !
     Excelsior !

There's work for me will make thee blest,
In an old city of the West ;
My banner take, it will suffice,
And hold it up, with this device,
     Excelsior !"

Then on he went with spirit brave,
And bannerol his Master gave,
For with his angel Hope that day
He sang rejoicing by the way,
     Excelsior !

And many years, all strong and hale,
He toiled within that city's pale ;
But kept within his heart and tongue
This key-note for his coming song,
     Excelsior !

Until one lovely summer time
He sat upon a mount sublime,
Where grand St. Vincent's Rocks in pride
And glory to his spirit cried,
     Excelsior !

'Twas then came rushing from his brain
Effusions in a lengthy train ;
And while these deck'd a poem stall,
The latest to the first would call,
     Excelsior !

And there he wrote from year to year,
Despite the knowing cynic's sneer :
For something he could not control
Was ever singing in his soul,
     Excelsior !

K

High-minded priests long passed him by,
With no good lurking in their eye ;
And though his sentient soul was stirr'd,
These cadent notes from heaven were heard,
    Excelsior !

Some said, by looks as cold as death,
" Can good come out of Nazareth ?"
And then his whispering aspen tree
Said to the wise ones, " Come and see."
    Excelsior !

There many a Levite turned his head,
As though he wished the bard were dead ;
But something whisper'd from the sky,
" Thou must not upon these rely"—
    Excelsior !

But true Samaritans soon came,
With words of cheer and worthy fame ;
True kindness brought the love well tim'd,
And then his soul with joy bells chimed,
    Excelsior !

Again he seized his waiting harp,
Nor heeded more the sneerer's carp ;
Resolved his future strains should be
For Truth, and Right, and Liberty,
    Excelsior !

And while he tuned his lyre anew,
This dreamer found he wiser grew,—
While aiding others he was blest,
For love sat singing in his breast,
    Excelsior !

Then many years, for old and young,
He trillèd strains of purest song :
To give the world a better fame,
He sang to rich and poor the same,
    Excelsior !

And distant lands have had and prized
What some strange knowing ones despised :
Good words from noble men have come
That echo in his heart and home—
    Excelsior !

This dreamer saw all this and more
Was coming from a furnished store,
When lo! his dream was put to rout,
For merry Christ Church bells rang out,
    Excelsior !

And then he woke, in strange delight—
The skies had hailed the lamp of night,
While glittering stars sang out with glee,
Above the whispering aspen tree,
    Excelsior !

His smiling tree heard this, and said :
" This dream will live when thou art dead
I will interpret it, my son,—
That baby boy and thee are one ! "
    Excelsior !

TRUE NOBILITY.

TRUE nobility is this: every doubtful action scorning,
    Hailing with unmix'd delight every law of right's first
       dawning;
Holding with determin'd grasp faithful truth's strong, potent lever;
Dauntless, forcing error's wrongs from this grand old world for ever.

True nobility is this: when the tyrants' hands are pushing
Down to earth the honest poor, and beneath their high heel crushing—
Then, defiant of their rage, true love's welcome banner bearing,
Gladly bleeding hearts assuage, and their life's deep sorrow sharing.

True nobility is this: while the grasping world is striving,
Risking souls for sordid pelf, and have falsely call'd it thriving,—
Shows by deeds of priceless worth that our life's a fleeting measure,
Far too short to spend on self, and but wasting golden treasure.

True nobility is this: when the rich and proud are flattered
For their bags of glittering ore, with true sense of honour scatter'd,—
Fearless cries, despite the clang of fawning sycophant and faction,
They are only rich and great who are men of honest action.

True nobility is this: while the noisy crowd is raving
On the rights of capital, and the wrongs of labour-saving,—
Then it states with wisdom great, and well worthy of the sages,
You shall have a fair day's wage, give a fair day's work for wages.

True nobility is this: and 'tis worthy of embracing,
Happy they who hold the pearl: ever from their bosom chasing
All that's sordid, mean and wrong, nobly aiming to be living
For the weal of human kind, fleeting time's best moments giving.

True nobility is this: would you find the priceless treasure?
Seek it from the Book of Life, this reveals its standard measure;
Yes, its noble charter lies there with virtue's graces blending—
All who seek may find this prize in a life of joy unending.

A CALL TO THE SPIRITUAL LABOURER.

GO, work to-day. My vineyard needs thy care :
   The labourers are few—no more delay.
   Let earnest toil be thine, with faith and prayer,
To train My plants ; I will thy wages pay.
When death's dark night is setting in apace,
   Thy life's work finish'd, thou shalt have a prize—
My lasting guerdon, and a worthy place
   In Canaan's fruitful vineyard of the skies !

NEW SONG.

MY MOTHER.

OH, bring me my harp—I am weary,
      Beneath the lov'd shade of my tree ;
   I will sing a sweet song for my mother,
      For she has been loving to me :
'Mid the billows of time's troubled ocean,
      When sorrow has threaten'd my breast,
I have found in her heart of devotion
   A pillow on which I could rest.
         My mother, dear mother,
         The boy is now thinking of thee :
      For thou hast e'er been
      In life's changing scene
      A true-hearted mother to me.

They tell me thy brow is now wrinkled,
   That age hath beclouded thy sight ;
Yet dearer to me thou art growing
   Than springtide or summer's delight.
Thy name brings a charm to my spirit
   More welcome than jewels or gold,
It gives a sweet tone to my harp strings
   That fills me with rapture untold.
       My mother, &c.

I think of thy love, treasur'd mother,
   When night throws its shadows o'er me,
Of care in the days of my childhood,
   When cradled or sat on thy knee.
And when the old homestead I quitted,
   Saw vacant my father's arm chair,
Thou didst not forget or neglect me—
   Thy love, darling mother, was near.
       My mother, &c.

I'll sing then to thee, my loved mother,
   A pure though a parting refrain,—
For in this cold world, with its changes,
   I never may see thee again.
Yet hope brings a calm to my spirit,
   The angel on whom I rely ;
If not in time's vale, I shall meet thee
   In the home of the sweet by-and-by.
       My mother, &c.

MINNIE WRAY.

INNIE WRAY and I were walking
  In a shady nook,
  Where we oft had pleasant talking
By the " silver brook."
And I whispered, " Minnie, darling,
  Tell me here, I pray,
Can you, will you love me, Minnie,
  When my locks are grey ?

" Minnie, dear ! you know 'tis whispered,
  When the man is old,
Then there is a change in woman,
  Woman's love grows cold.
Is it true, my angel Minnie,
  What the people say ?
Can you, will you love me, Minnie,
  When my locks are grey ? "

Minnie look'd at me in earnest,
  With a searching look,
Then she whispered, sweetly, softly,
  By the " silver brook : "
" All are not unfaithful, Willie,
  Trust your Minnie Wray ;
She will love and she will cheer you
  When your locks are grey."

Many years have gone since Minnie
  Breath'd these words to me,
In fair Clifton's shady bower,
  Near the woods of Leigh ;—
Where I love to stroll with Minnie
  In life's closing day,
For her love to me is stronger,
  Now my locks are grey.

MY ANGEL BOY.

'TIS more than twenty years ago,
    And very many miles away,
    Beneath a silent portico
A little oaken coffin lay.

It held one treasure of my heart,
    A babe I oft had clasped in joy ;
But now, alas ! I had to part
    With him—my darling angel boy.

His mother dear had passed away,
    And but a few short months before ;
One summertide's calm, closing day,
    She glided to the peaceful shore.

Her once fair form is earth to earth,
    And dust to dust, beneath a tree
Where sleeps a man of noble worth—
    The Christian bard Montgomery.

And I had named my angel boy
    The same as he, with joyful tongue :
And thought, perchance my Walter James
    Some day might be a son of song.

Alas ! how vain are human hopes !
    Another hand has claimed my prize ;
For he is with his mother now,
    And that sweet singer in the skies.

Yet in the silent twilight's wane
    I think of each with raptur'd joy ;
And that glad hour, when I again
    Shall clasp my darling angel boy.

MORNING.

WELCOME, Sol! Thy beams are shining
   Gladsome from the eastern sky;
   Spirit cheering, joy divining,
All is fair with love's entwining;
Things on earth, in air, and sea,
Chanting pleasant minstrelsy.

Life again we start with pleasure,
Hope's bright sands in golden measure
Thou art carefully bestowing.
These we'll take with hearts o'erflowing;
Use them well—till, brighter dawning,
Comes the resurrection morning!

FAITH.

OH! were it not for thee in life,
   Life's purpose would be lost
   Amid its bustle and its strife,
   When we are tempest toss'd.
But with thy wonder-working power
We brace ourselves again;
And in thy strength to life's last hour
Defy the raging main.

MY FATHER.

In Memoriam.

AFTER a rapid flight of years,
Thy name comes ringing in my ears,
And fills my wakeful eyes with tears,
    My Father.

Past thoughts of thee will break my rest,
Ere sunlight gilds the mountain crest,
Like busy workers in my breast,
    My Father.

E'en 'mid the silence of the night
Some mystic spirit whispers, " Write :
For thy lov'd sire a lay indite "—
    My Father.

And now I take my priceless gem,
Worth more than earthly diadem,
To write thine In Memoriam,
    My Father.

Though fifty years have passed away
Since thou beheld my childhood's play,
To me it seemeth but a day.
    My Father.

And forty of these years have fled
Since I stood near thy turfy bed,
When thou wert numbered with the dead,
    My Father.

While to me clung, with anguish rife,
Our home-stay and support in life,
My mother and thy faithful wife,
    My Father.

Thrice hallow'd spot, thou sleepest near
A brother and two sisters dear,
Whose love to me was all sincere,
    My Father.

And near thee rests, all free from strife,
My loving, treasured, fair young wife,
Whom thou had'st never seen in life,
    My Father.

This cruel death, with icy brand,
The wily foe of every land,
Has brought me woes on every hand,
    My Father.

Yet memory comes on wings of light,
And brings some recollections bright
Of thee—though taken from my sight,
    My Father.

And on lov'd Clifton's bracing Down,
The fairy land of high renown,
I write these recollections down,
    My Father.

For they are ever dear to me,
And now methinks thy form I see
Beneath the whispering aspen tree,
    My Father.

I see thee as in days of yore,
When peace and plenty crown'd our store,
That no heart need to wish for more,
    My Father.

When in bright boyhood days I went
With thee all cheerful and content,
While on thy business duties bent,
    My Father.

And when I left our roof awhile,
To graduate in labour's pile,
I think I see thy farewell smile,
    My Father,—

While reaching me, with thoughtful care,
Thy parting gift—a watch to wear,
With my own name engraven there,
    My Father.

Then offer'd me with outstretch'd hand
One treasur'd book to understand—
Worth all the books in every land,
    My Father.

I have it on my table now,
The tribute of thy heart's endow,
And register of my heart's vow,
    My Father.

And what of clearer light I see
I owe it in entirety
To that good book thou gavest me,
  My Father.

Its teachings prompt this filial lay,
Though thou from me art gone away,
They bring me joy this autumn day,
  My Father.

For I remember years ago,
When thou wert tossed to and fro,
With long distressing pain and woe,
  My Father.

I saw thee on thy bed of pain,
And thought we ne'er should meet again,
Then whisper'd, as my heart's refrain,
  My Father—

"Is peace, true peace, within your breast?
Are hopes—all blooming and all blest—
Alluring you to heaven's sweet rest,
  My Father?

And then I heard thy feeble tongue,
Breathe forth these words like angels' song,
"When I am weak, then am I strong,"
  My Father.

Oh, precious words of worth untold,
To me they are more dear than gold,
Their echoes in my heart I hold,
  My Father.

For thee I never heard again,
Thy longing spirit burst its chain,
And found the land of no more pain,
  My Father.

Once more thy form, in my distress,
I saw when in its coffin dress,
With grief I never can express,
  My Father.

And when I could not hear thee speak,
I sobbing kiss'd thy cold, cold cheek,
And felt as though my heart would break,
  My Father.

But that is past ; and I am come
Some seasons nearer to the tomb,
And nearer to my better home,
  My Father.

There in fair mansions of the sky,
Where parents never more can die,
Thy son will meet thee by-and-by,
  My Father.

Sept., 1879.

AN IMPROMPTU.

Written by request, and in the presence of Will Carlton, a popular American poet, on back of the Author's Photo, under the Poet's Tree, as a reminiscence of his visit to Clifton, 1878.

MET on grand St. Vincent's height
    A stranger friend—with great delight ;
    He came from far Columbia's shore,
And I may never see Him more.
I wish him joy, with all my heart,
And now regret we have to part ;
Yet trust, when life's short journey's past,
We both shall meet in heaven at last !

THE NIGHT COMETH.

HE day is fast waning, the night is at hand,
    Hush, hush, no complaining ! Obey the command,
    Go forth for thy Master, be faithful and true,
The harvest is great, and the labourers few.

The valleys are white, and abundance will yield,
Oh, thrust in the sickle, this world is the field ;
Quickly gather the wheat, 'tis thy Master's desire,
But the chaff He will burn with unquenchable fire.

Oh, linger not, tarry not, night is at hand—
Away thy complaining ; obey the command ;
And let thy life-work be a labour of love,
To gather some sheaves for the garner above.

MY FATHER'S GRAVE.

'T is forty years to-day,
  I remember, in my woe,
I was standing far away
  By a mill-stream water's flow,—
Near an abbey church's dome,
  Where some elm tree branches wave,
Gazing on a new made tomb—
  On my father's open grave.

Near me stood, in sad surprise,
  Mother and two sisters dear,
With a little brother's eyes
  Swollen with the sorrow's tear.
We had early been bereft ;
  Lost a life no skill could save ;
And a coffin was let down
  In my father's open grave.

" Earth to earth," was softly said,
  Then there came a closing prayer
O'er the lov'd one—lately dead,
  While we stood in silence there.
But my mother's soul was crush'd,
  Though she had a spirit brave ;
And they led the bleeding heart
  From my father's open grave.

Yes ! 'tis forty years to-day,
  'Mid the scenes of long ago,
When in boyhood's golden way,
  That I had to feel this woe.
And I never can forget
  Sorrow that this parting gave,
Where so many mourners met
  At my father's open grave.

August 27th, 1879.

SYDNEY'S GREETING ODE.

AN ACROSTIC-WELCOME TO THE INTERNATIONAL EXHIBITION, SYDNEY,
NEW SOUTH WALES.

Opened September 17th, 1879.

W elcome, welcome to the nations.   Hark ! what myriad voices sing !

E arnest tongues, in loud ovation, make the very welkin ring.

L ist ! their pæan's crossed the ocean, o'er the mountains and the
vales—

C ome and see our Exhibition !   This the song of New South Wales.

O h, there's joy on ship and turret, bannerols are waving high,

M usic strains are sweetly blending, while the silver bells reply.

E arth is glad—'tis Sydney's anthem, Britain's Daughters' minstrelsy.

T rill the song with joy to heaven, sing to-day with raptured glee,

O n this brotherhood of nations—'tis the wide world's jubilee.

T rill the anthem louder, louder ; let its cheering notes increase,

H igher rise and consentaneous, until this world's discord cease,

E very heart becomes harmonious with the melody of peace.

I n our Exhibition's grandeur there is music for the soul ;—

N otes of unity inspiring, flowing in their sweet control ;

T reasures from the wide world's storehouse, bringing treasur'd friends
to meet—

E mpires, States, and large Dominions giving pleasures all complete.

R iches from the hives of labour, sent to cheer us o'er the main ;

N ew, yet wrought by toil incessant, alike by handicraft and brain.

A rt and Science here combining, give us thoughts of " Home, sweet
Home,"

T hrowing rays of matchless beauty 'neath fair Sydney's temple dome.

I nspiration we are feeling, and the people with a zest,

O n our soil of peace and plenty, in this land of Goshen blest,

N ow uplift their voice enraptur'd, with their ensigns all unfurl'd,

A nd this song comes pealing onward, as from a volcano hurl'd,

L ong success to Trade and Commerce, and good will to all the world.

L

E uropean Nations' models have been brought in rich supply,
X ylography's tasteful carving in its beauty meets the eye ;
H ome and foreign rare utensils from both cold and torrid zone,
I n a strange yet pleasing contrast, show a merit of their own.
B right and beautiful land tillers ready for the virgin soil,
I n their strong and marked perfection, waiting for the sons of toil.
T rophies from the mart and anvil, reapers for the golden grain ;
I ncidental things and useful, bringing their producers gain
O nward speed this Exhibition, International in name,
N oted may it be for growing International in fame.

S ing with us the joyful anthem. ye who hail from o'er the sea,
Y oung Australia's voice inviting, bids your hearts be full of glee ;
D istance must not friendship sever, though again we have to part,
N earer may we come together, until all are one in heart.
E nglar d's Daughter gives you greeting, Sydney hails you here to-day—
Y ou are welcome, welcome, welcome, as the virgin flowers in May.

N umberless and great the blessings that are falling on us now,
E arth, rejoicing, calls each nation, pledged by honour's sacred vow,
W orthily to breathe to heaven—speed the Press, the Loom, and Plough.

S ing ! oh, sing for joy in Sydney ; shout with hearty voice and soul ;
O nward for the world's true progress, onward let the tidings roll—
U ntil nation, bound to nation with the golden bond of love,
T rue in service for each other, in each treaty faithful prove,
H onour'd by a world-blest people, and the people's God above.

W elcome, then, to every nation, we will sing for our refrain ;
A nd, with twice ten thousand voices, louder yet prolong the strain.
L et the prince, the peer, and peasant from the hills and valleys green,
E very tongue and heart be gladsome for the Exhibition scene,
S hout with us in one grand chorus—loud and long,

"GOD SAVE THE QUEEN!"

SUMMERTIDE.

H, welcome, shining go'den leaves,
  Ye glitter on the Poet's tree ;
I view you with untold delight,
  For ye are beautiful to me.
Bright sunlight from the Orient sky
  Hath made you pleasing to behold,
With rays of lucent rarity—
  Oh, welcome, leaves of shining gold.

Oh, whispering, waving, golden leaves,
  Ye tell me it is summertide ;
And I look up to you in joy,
  With all a lover's latent pride.
I saw you early budding forth,
  With bliss that never can be told ;
To me ye are of priceless worth—
  Oh, welcome, leaves of shining gold.

Oh, shining, welcome, golden leaves,
  Ye whisper on this summer day,
That here ye only shine awhile,
  And only for a season stay ;
Ye wave and tremble in the wind,
  To purposes divine unfold,
That lessons ye may teach mankind—
  Oh, welcome, leaves of shining gold.

Oh, whispering, shining, golden leaves,
  Ye say that Winter winds will come ;
That in this world are sad bereaves,
  And this is not man's lasting home.
The years and golden hours of time
  He spends just as " a tale that's told ; "
Yet there 's a more congenial clime—
  Oh, welcome, whispering leaves of gold.

Oh, welcome, whispering golden leaves,
  Ye bid me work without delay :
For golden moments quickly fly,
  And golden time will pass away.
But they who toil for doing good
  Will shine as stars in bliss untold,
Beyond the surging Jordan flood—
  Thrice welcome, leaves of shining gold.

TO MY WIFE.

KATE, my love ! nay, sweetly smile,
    Let not clouds of gloomy sadness
    Gather round thy brow awhile,
      Or they'll shade my sun of gladness.
Spots will come on life's horizon,
  Yet kind heaven can these remove ;
Our kind Father's e'er devising
  Joys for those who dwell in love ;
He can cheer in every sorrow,
  Heal the wounds His hand hath given,
And will gild our bright to-morrow
  With the sunlit rays of heaven.

WILLIE'S ONLY LEFT ME AWHILE.

SING to my love in a rapture of bliss,
  A lay he will greet with a smile ;
'Tis Lizzie's heart song, and the chorus is this —
  Willie's only left me awhile.

I will not complain at his going away,
  To sail by the banks of the Nile ;
I know he'll be true to his darling each day—
  Willie's only left me awhile.

I could not believe, when we had to part,
  That he would his Lizzie beguile ;
He took with him trust from one doting heart—
  Willie's only left me awhile.

The time it doth pass all sweetly away,
  And free from the shadow of guile :
For I am e'er trilling this welcome heart song,
  Willie's only left me awhile.

I think of my love in the silence of night,
  With rapture and many a smile ;
My dreams are all pleasant with purest delight—
  Willie's only left me awhile.

I'll write to him oft, and bid him be strong,
  And for him sweet stanzas compile ; .
My strains shall be these—it will not be long--
  Willie's only left me awhile.

Adieu, then, to Willie, a season at least :
  We shall meet near the old meadow stile ;
And this brings my heart a continual feast—
  Willie's only left me awhile.

OUR PRINCESS ALICE.

By *MATTIE GABBITASS.*

THE white snow of December
  Was falling 'mid the rain,
And bells were softly pealing
  A requiem refrain.
For gloom hung o'er the nation,
  While knees were bow'd in prayer
As we thought of Hesse Darmstadt,
  And lov'd ones weeping there.

When wintry winds were sighing
  Amid the palace trees,
And feathery flakes were flying
  By myriads on the breeze,
Disease came—unexpected—
  With his contagious breath,
And close behind his shadow—
  The messenger of Death.

He touch'd the eldest daughter,
  And like a fragile flower
Bends to the keen and angry blast,
  She sank beneath his power.
Then all the royal children
  Were smitten by the blow,
And that once joyful palace
  Became a scene of woe.

The little Princess Marie
  Lay on her couch serene ;
For in the early hour of morn
  A white robed throng had been.
They bore her spirit gently
  Upon their snowy wings,
And lodg'd it on the waiting breast
  Of Jesus, King of kings !

Within the palace chamber
   A Prince was on his bed,
And though appearing stronger,
   Disease had not yet fled.
He ask'd for little Sister,
   That he might have her near ;
His tender heart had missed her
   Since death had entered there.

His mother told him gently,
   Though smarting with the pain,
That in a brighter world one day
   They soon would meet again.
Then tears came quickly falling,
   With grief so strong express'd,
And with her heart's affection
   She clasp'd him to her breast.

That mother's strong devotion
   And love was wondrous deep,
But when we mused upon the cost,
   Our eyes could only weep,—
To see the pride of nations,
   In life serenely mild,
Fall like a stricken lily
   From death kiss of her child.

Thus died our noble Princess,
   Whom England mourns to-day ;
And now for Hesse Darmstadt
   We would most humbly pray
The God of consolation,
   Too good to be unkind,
To bless the sorrow-stricken Duke
   And loved ones left behind.

SLAVERY'S DEATH KNELL.

A reply to Mr. Bennett's Poem in the London Illustrated Paper.

WHAT is it? asks this Poet brave,
For which so many idly rave,
E'en over freedom's gory grave?
What hath convulsed a continent,
United States asunder rent,
And millions upon millions spent?
    'Tis Abolition.

'Tis easy said,—not so the proof
To thinking men who stand aloof
Far from the iron despot's hoof.
Those know too well, and had foretold
'Twas Britain's eager love for gold
That brought the woes we now behold,
    Not Abolition.

Had she been faithful to her trust,
And risen from her selfish dust,
Shaken her soul from wealth's keen lust,
Ere this, yon States across the sea,
America, misnamed the Free,
Might long ere this have ceased their plea
    For Abolition.

Had England's sons and daughters fair,
Whose hearts are touch'd with bondsmen's prayer.
When slavery's produce entered here,
Arisen in mighty phalanx bold,
And to the crafty merchant told
He should not have their English gold,
    But Abolition,—

Who knows but these sharp words of fire,
Sent forth as England's one desire
To free the slave from evils dire,
Would not ere this have freed from pain
The sons of Ham, and snapt their chain,
While led to freedom's fold again
　　　By Abolition.

And shall a man this work ignore,
Which would true consolation pour,
Like healing balm, for slavery's sore?
Would save at dreaded auction block
Each wife and child from parting shock,
And placed lov'd sires on freedom's rock,
　　　Through Abolition.

This welcome angel seeks to save,
Though greedy gain and priests may rave;
She's cheering now the fetter'd slave.
In them she doth God's image scan,
And cries, " Behold me, brother man ;
I'll free thee from the tyrant's ban,
　　　I'm Abolition."

And who dare strive her work to stay,
Or try to block her opening way,
That augurs soon a brighter day ?—
When black men shall as white be free,
Safe sheltered 'neath a storm-proof tree,
Of deathless, endless liberty,
　　　And Abolition.

Shall England's sons, with purpose rife,
Try to extract true freedom's life ;
Support, sustain this gory strife
By finding means, according aid,
That despots may not be afraid,
While British gold is freely paid
　　　'Gainst Abolition ?

Shame on my country, banish far
Friends of this fratricidal war,
That would earth's beauty further mar,
By helping those who are not good
To keep their nation stain'd with blood,
Now writhing 'neath the curse of God,—
    Oh ! Abolition.

Their reckoning day approacheth fast,
They cannot 'scape the looming blast ;
No ! it shall surely come at last.
In vain they try the storm to brave,
Despite their greedy Mammon's rave,
Strong hands shall dig their unwept grave
    For Abolition.

Until that day auspicious comes,
When light shall beam in darkened homes,
And myriad minds shall burst their tombs;
Till then, ye Friends of Freedom, fight
And cry, with heart and soul and might,
"Onward, for God will help the right,
    And Abolition."

MOTIVES.

A LYRIC.

DO not be impatient, brothers,
    To be judges ; you may read,
    It is wrong, this judging others—
Yes, 'tis very wrong indeed.
Leave this judgment to the Master,
    For He knows the right and wrong ;
It will save you much disaster—
    That's the sequel to my song.

THE APPOINTED WEEKS OF HARVEST.

YES ; they shall come !   The word of truth declares,
    Despite the tempest and the cloudy sky ;
    Earth's fruits shall yet be gather'd, He who cares
For man hath spoken, and He cannot lie.

Yes ; they shall come !   Our Father gives His word—
  His sorrowing children then may banish fear :
For He is yet our world's all-sovereign Lord,
  And every suppliant cry will reach His ear.

Yes ; they shall come !   As soon shall heaven and earth
  On their huge pillars strong all trembling quail,
As His sure word, which gave creation birth,
  Be broken now, or His grand promise fail.

Yes ; they shall come !   The golden grain, that waves
  Luxuriantly in fields with drooping head,
Shall bend beneath the reaper's sharpened blades,
  And help to feed earth's toiling sons with bread.

Yes ; they shall come !   Though man a bruised reed,
  And full of unbelief to fear gives way ;
Forgetting He whose hand the sparrows feed,
  And clothes the grass, which fadeth in a day.

Yes ; they shall come !   His mercy loudly cries,
  'Mid much abundance,—for the fields are white ;
These all are burdened with their rich supplies,
  Yet sing all cheering with a golden freight.

Yes ; they shall come !   Obeying God's command,
  And bring true blessings to each waiting home ;
God's promises are sure, and firmly stand,
  The appointed weeks of harvest, they shall come.

IN MEMORIAM.

Frances Ridley Havergal, one of our most gifted Christian Poets ; Daughter of Canon Havergal, Astley Rectory, Worcestershire ; died January 3rd, 1879. Her last words were, " How splendid to be so near to the gates of heaven."

I   n the land of no more dying, where the heavenly arches ring,
N   ow, sweet warbler, thou art singing anthems to redemption's King.

M   ingling with yon happy spirits, where the seraph hosts adore,
E   ntered where the good are welcome, and the parting is no more.
M   ourning friends have laid thy casket in its silent, narrow bed,
O   'er it breath'd love's valediction, in " God's Acre," with the dead.
R   esting there it sleepeth sweetly, as His precious numbered dust,
I   n the certain hope of rising at the rising of the just ;
A   nd thy spirit, all triumphant, in Mount Sion's temple sings,
M   eets the choirs of ransomed songsters, worshipping the King of kings.

F   riend to all that life ennobles, helper of the human kind,
R   eady with thy hand of mercy, and thy ready-furnished mind,—
A   ll who came to thee for succour ever found a friend indeed,
N   urture, guidance, e'er bestowing to the stricken ones in need.
C   hrist thy Master and Redeemer was thy treasur'd, welcome guest,
E   mulating His example, made thee blessing and all blest,
S   aved by Him, for Him thou liv'dst, in thy mission noble, true ;

R   esting on Him for salvation, gave the glory as His due.
I   n the summertide of beauty thou art taken from us here,
D   eath immortelles have been witnessed, lain upon thy coffin bier,
L   ov'd ones round thy grave have gathered, where affection's tears
        were shed,
E   xtemporal wailings, uttered by the friends who thought thee dead.
Y   et thou livest, Zion's singer, in thy cheering " wayside chimes."

H onest hearts feel their vibration, while thou sing'st in fairer climes,
A nd in thy pure " life mosaic " many lov'd ones will be blest,
V alue more than earthly treasures words that give the mourner rest.
E very line of thy life penning now gives out a sweeter tone,
R edolent and consentaneous, with a merit of thine own,
G ently, softly thou hast glided home to tune a harp of gold,
A nd to hear the angels whisper of the joys to man untold.
L oved one, *au revoir* a season ; for a time we say " Good-bye,"
    Soon we'll meet thee in the mansion, in our Father's home on high.

ACROSTIC IN MEMORIAM.

HENRY WINTERBOTHAM, M P. FOR STROUD, INTERRED AT ROME,
DECEMBER, 1873.

Graciously accepted, with thanks, by the Right Hon. W. E. Gladstone, Premier.

H e has fallen ! Yes, the noble,—fallen in his manhood's prime,
E ngland's hope has drooped and faded in Italia's sunny clime ;
N ear the city of the Cæsars he has yielded up his breath,
R esting there from all his labours, in the cold embrace of death.
Y earning for his country's greatness, earnest for the people's good ;

W orking with a zeal untiring, every form of wrong withstood.
I n the midst of life's short journey he is from us passed away ;
N oontide sun, alas ! hath pierc'd him with its keen directer ray.
T ravel to the land of beauty, with its soft and balmy air,
E ntering for a brief reposing. 'mid those scenes all bright and fair,
R eck'd not ; these were unavailing nature's functions to restore,
B y all cruel death he's smitten breathless on a distant shore.
O n the annals of his country we will biograph his name,
T hese shall show to coming ages Henry Winterbotham's fame.
H e the wise, brave, good and honour'd, nobly hath his duty done,
A nd we trust has found reposing where the city needs no sun;
M ourn him not with hopeless sorrow, for there is a Hand above

M eeting out the best for ever, and its owner's name is Love ;
P erfect He in darkest night—righteous, for His ways are right.

ACROSTIC IN MEMORIAM.

R est, for thy toil is ended ; brave one, sweetly rest ;

I n thee pure virtue's blended ; thy memory is blest ;

C alled from a life of toiling. bright thy setting sun,

H ome to thy Father's mansion, life's great work is done.

A ll are thy loss bemoaning, thou wert wise and good,

R ipe for a brighter dawning ; over the Jordan's flood

D eath has but thee escorted, where thy name's enroll'd,

C alled thee to joys immortal, and to a harp of gold.

O ver the sea of sorrow, thy freed spirit sings,

B asks where there's no dying, near to the King of kings.

D ear to thy country living, true to her high behest,

E ngland its plaudits giving, writes thee for ever blest,

N ame on her heart engraven, immortal Cobden, rest.

LOVING-KINDNESS.

THERE is a something in the world
    At which some sneerers' lips are curl'd,
When it is unto others shown
Instead of unto them made known :
It may be own'd by one and all
That dwell on this terrestrial ball ;
Would you this loving-kindness know ?—
Then you must loving-kindness show.

THE HOLOCAUST OF SANTIAGO.

December 8th, 1863.

TWAS sunset, when the Jesuits' temple, high rearing
    Its awe-striking tower 'neath Santiago's fair sky,
    Look'd proudly defiant, denuded of fearing,
  Inspiring the homage of each passer by,
As though La Compania's foundations were sure,
And would as the pillars of heaven endure.

How futile the thought, and how sudden the changes
    That came o'er the vision of Spain's favour'd isle,
For He who the earth's varied motion arranges,
    Permitted to perish in one flaming pile ;
This boast of their country, Rome's votaries' trust,
Has crumbled to earth, and hath lickèd the dust.

But worse than all this hath the fierce desolation
    Rush'd fearlessly on in its chariot of fire,
And swept without pity the flower of the nation,
    As holocaust victims for dread funereal pyre ;
And hundreds of fair ones, whom man could not save,
In a Jesuit's dome found the devotee's grave.

In vain were some thousands of lamps brightly burning,
    A myriad tapers emitting their light,
While gorgeously deck'd was the ceiling, upturning
    Its cloud-like gauze folds, and its silver stars bright ;
Whose festooned oil lamps on the high altar meet—
A crescent and cross at the Madona's feet.

Alas ! these avail not ; for loud shrieks are rending
   The temple's high arch in a suppliant tone ;
Lov'd mothers and daughters to heaven are sending
   Loud, earnest appeals, with their life's latest moan ;
Then helplessly fall in the smouldering fire,
And in the fierce torture of heat they expire.

Some kind hearts were found near the dire conflagration,
   And heedless of danger rush'd forward to save.
Bold Nelson ! A son of America's nation,
   Shall have the world's guerdon as Nelson the brave ;
And Spain's fifty daughters a garland shall wreathe,
For him who has sav'd them from premature death.

Then one fair Orella's true love shall be told,
   Imploring, she knelt to the bystanders near,
And wooed, then besought them in language all bold
   To save from the flames her mother so dear ;
Then rising, she fled down the bright flaming road,
In her arms bringing back love's glorious load.

And Ugarte, a priest, will ne'er be forgotten
   By those who have lost their loved ones untold ;
Oh, no ! may they see such a system is rotten
   That clamours for crosses and candles and gold ;
And leaves there to perish from pitiless flame
Lov'd mothers and daughters, mementoes of shame.

Santiago, arise ! and learn a wise lesson,
   That God the Creator, Almighty and just,
Invites not display to secure His great blessing ;
   But all who would render pure worship, they must
Be sincere in heart to the guide of their youth,
And worship Him only in spirit and truth.

BEAUTIFUL WORLD.

OH, beautiful world! with carpet of green,
  In summer's gay herbage dressing,
    How cheering thou art when violets are seen,
  And primroses sweetly caressing ;
How rich is their fragrance, and leaves neatly curl'd,
To add to thy splendour, thou beautiful world !

Oh, beautiful world ! with thy orb of light
  In its noontide brightness shining,
Or deck'd with thy silvery queen of night
  On a cloudless sky reclining ;
When starlights irradiate as gold are unfurl'd,
Thy canopy gracing, thou beautiful world !

Oh, beautiful world ! with thy foaming seas
  And cataracts wilding rushing,
Entrancing the sound of each swelling breeze,
  Huge waves o'er thy steep rocks pushing.
On, on, down the rapids they go proudly hurl'd,
How grand, how majestic, thou beautiful world !

Oh, beautiful world ! thou art truly blest,
  Thy Maker is thee befriending.
A compassionate love from a Father's breast
  On thy children is ever descending ;
But, ah ! there is sorrow around thee now twirl'd,
And sin only mars thee, thou beautiful world !

HARVEST SONG.

1863.

MYRIADS of voices, raise
  Your grateful songs of praise,
  Let your aspirations bring
Heart thanksgiving to our King;
For His goodness hath increased
Fruits of earth for man and beast.

His wisdom hath again
Sent the refreshing rain,
Made the ridge and furrows seen
Shining with their blades of green;
And His sun, without alloy,
Fills the waving fields with joy.

Teeming with rich supplies,
This season far outvies
Some of yore : for golden grain,
Harvest home ! Oh, joyful strain ;
He who doth the ravens feed
Hath supplied our every need.

His eye omniscient saw
The hand of mercy draw
Freely from its hard earn'd store,
Feeding long His suffering poor ;
Now He pays what He foretold,
Gives it back a hundred-fold.

His word is ever true,
His mercies ever new ;
He has made the earth to yield
Increase in her widespread field ;
Shout aloud His praise on high,
Let it fill both earth and sky.

Young men and maidens, sing,
Loud let the welkin rlng ;
Parents, children, all unite,
Chant love strains of pure delight ;
Then a foretaste soon will come
Of the better harvest home.

UPWARD.

HIGHER up, my brother, don't be grovelling here ;
You must scale the mountains as they appear—
Higher and yet higher, nearer to the sun ;
Higher up, my brother, till your work is done.
Higher up, my brother, don't be looking down ;
There is One will help you, One of high renown.
Higher up, my brother, you must try to rise ;
Higher up, my brother, to your native skies.

HEART BREATHINGS TO LAURA.

A BIRTHDAY ODE—BY REQUEST.

WISH for thee, my treasur'd friend,
   On thy all-welcome natal day,
The purest bliss to sweetly blend
   This very cheering month of May ;
That life may full of gladness be—
I wish, dear Laura, this for thee.

Accept this tribute from a heart
   Rejoicing that it thine hath won ;
'Tis thy affection's counterpart,
   Love, greeting thee at twenty-one ;
Oh, may thy life all radiant be —
I wish, dear Laura, this for thee.

I pray that each returning year,
   No matter where thy lot be cast,
Will find thee glad when they appear,
   And each be better than the last ;
As crystal streamlets flowing free—
I wish, dear Laura, this for thee.

Then in the changing scenes of life,
   And one, I hope, will soon be thine,
To bear the honour'd name of wife,
   Be it my joy to call thee mine ;
May one true heart thy solace be—
I wish, dear Laura, this for thee.

Thus finding pure connubial joy,
   May it be thine when time is o'er,
To share the bliss without alloy
   Now waiting on a radiant shore :
Where lov'd ones cannot parted be—
I wish, dear Laura, this for thee.

FRATERNAL ACROSTIC.

TO MISS ALICE WILSON, CLIFTON.

T o you, Miss Alice, I present as many thanks as me befits,

O n my receiving at your hands, for mine, a pretty pair of mitts.

M uch pleased I am with such a boon, and more than my poor tongue can tell;

I n fact, my tongue is slow at thanks—I have to write them out as well.

S o in a pure acrostic lay, I now will tender with my pen

S ome grateful tribute for your gift to one of nature's gifted men.

A ssured be, I treasure much these mitts with their fraternal charm,

L ike ivy round the forest oak they cling to keep my fingers warm;

I n winter's night, when I have sat to guard our temple's outer door,

C onvinc'd I was these mitts were just what I had needed long before;

E nraptur'd I can see them now, for they are on my table new,—

W ith colours that I much admire—a lovely chocolate and blue.

I tender you my best of thanks, Miss Alice, and with heart delight—

L ong may your life on earth be spared to aid the noble and the right;

S weet peace attend you all your days, and give you joy in every sphere,

O n all that lovely woman can, may you be very useful here;

N ew pleasures with each opening day refresh you from the fount of love,

And when the last is pass'd away, unfailing ones in heaven above.

DECLINING SUMMER.

ES ! The Summer is declining—
　　For I see the golden sheaves
　　That the harvesters are binding
Near the Leigh Wood's changing leaves.
On the landscape in the distance
　　Men are busy as the bee :
And, though Summer is declining,
　　It is beautiful to me !

Now the Summer is declining,
　　For the sky begins to lower—
'Mid rare scenes of charming beauty—
　　By the well-known Dundry tower.
There are whitewash'd cottage homesteads,
　　Near which cattle feed in glee :
And, while Summer is declining,
　　This is beautiful to me !

Now the Summer is declining,
　　For the days creep in apace :
And the sun, though lustrous shining,
　　Sooner seems to hide his face.
For I often watch its setting,
　　As it gilds the woods of Leigh :
And, while Summer is declining,
　　It is beautiful to me !

Yes ! The Summer is declining,
　　And the leaves will soon be sere ;
Yet the clouds have silver lining
　　When the wintertide is here.
So I will not be despairing,
　　While I can such beauty see :
And, though Summer is declining,
　　It is beautiful to me !

EVANGELINE:

THE ANGEL FLOWER OF AVONDALE.

A BALLAD IN FIVE PARTS.

~~~~~~~~~~~~~~~~~~~~~~~~~~~~

PART I.

NEAR queenly Clifton's shady Promenade,
Sang her God-gifted and untiring bard :
There stands a mansion in majestic pride,
In close proximity to Avonside ;
Where Proctor's fountain sends, in sunlight's gleam,
Pure crystal water in abundant stream.
For young and old, from city's street or town,
Who seek refreshment on the bracing Down,
When summertide has called them to its bowers,
Amid the blooming hawthorn's virgin flowers.
Within this mansion lived, some years ago,
A merchant prince whose hair was white as snow ;
For.time, that leveller of human things,
Be they a race of peasants or of kings,
Had on his brow affixed the well-known brand,
Deep furrows from his own unsparing hand—
Reminders e'en to those who own a crest,
Whate'er man's greatness, this is not his rest.
This aged sire, for he was one in life,
Had years ago lost a true treasured wife ;

Yet had within his home, to make it blest,
One precious relic, for his spirit's rest,
Of her whom he had made his own true love,
Whose spirit mingled with the blest above,
Where all the good are gathered in delight
Whose faith was constant, and whose lives were right.
This relic rare he treasured and caressed,
Of earthly joys he deemed this one the best;
For it was a loved child, with instinct keen,
Whom he had named with joy, Evangeline;
As a reminder, in that stately place,
Of its loved mother, with her angel face,
Who then was singing with the seraph band,
Amid the ransomed, on the golden strand.
This treasured child was left him years ago,
And its own mother it did never know;
The smiles that fell on it in babyhood
From that young mother ne'er were understood:
For these had gone, with her departing breath,
To their reposing in the vault of death.
And he was left alone with only her—
A sad, bereaved, and lonely widower;
For consolation's source he'd not yet found,
He was a stranger to the joyful sound
A good Old Book declares is needful here
To bring heart-quiet in life's duty sphere.
Yes, he was stranger to that precious love
That comes to hearts in blessing from above,
When these have yielded to the force within
That bids men shun the luring paths of sin.
And wins them back, through life's uncertain lease,
To paths of right, of holiness and peace.
And yet he had in her whom he had laid
In death's cold chamber, 'neath the cypress shade,
Abundant proof that, through the vale of life,

The Christian faith had made her model wife;
For he could see, when trials to her came,
Distresses sore for which he was to blame,
How she with meekness bore his angered eye,
Without a murmur and without a sigh.
And when she glided through the vale of death,
He'd heard her breathe, with her expiring breath,
" I have Thy rod and staff to lean upon :
My Father, I am Thine ; Thy will be done !"
And these, her dying words, he ne'er forgot,
For he knew she had something he had not.
And oft when twilight's shade was hovering nigh
The tear of grief would trickle from his eye,
While musing o'er the scenes of long ago
That brought his wife such dire excess of woe.
And he the cause of that heartrending grief,
Because his soul was filled with unbelief ;
The good Old Book by him was deemed untrue—
His faith was pinned to notions that were new ;
Especially on those that make some weep,
That death to all is an eternal sleep,
And every man, when he resigns his breath,
Is like the beast that perisheth at death.
The thoughts of an hereafter he would spurn,
Though these opinions made his wife to mourn,
When he proclaimed them in her long-pained ear,
Without reflection and without a fear ;
He used to glory, and before her friends,
That He, whose blessing on the world descends,
Was just a something flickering in the brain
Of poor weak-minded mortals in the main ;
That fate ruled everything, he'd boldly state,
And then he'd argue everything was fate.
No wonder, then, that now he'd soul despair,
For he was a disciple of Voltaire.

When death took his loved wife from him below
True resignation he did never know ;
He would not bow submissive as a son,
And breathe the prayer, " Father, Thy will be done ! "
He had no Father-God to soothe his mind,
Or give him comfort, for his soul was blind ;
And yet within his breast at times would move
The doting spirit of parental love ;
And oft, while gazing on Evangeline,
He had the semblance of a joy serene.
For, though with his loved wife he had to part,
Her child and his had tendrils in his heart
That clung as only those can cling, 'tis said,
Whose loved one sleepeth with the silent dead ;
For he would hold her on his welcome knee,
And sit for hours in deepest reverie ;
Then many a kiss he planted on her cheek,
While his fond heart was full, too full to speak :
And then would come from him, without control,
Those silent gushings from his inmost soul.
And, though he had deep sank in unbelief,
He had dire sorrow pangs of inward grief
For her whom he had lost, with grief profound,
And her Evangeline whom he had found.
Yes, though a bold freethinker, he was man,
And loved his child as doting fathers can ;
The stores of wealth he had before his eyes
Were naught to be compared with this loved prize—
Though he had pleasure in his ships and gold,
What he had in his child could ne'er be told ;
For on her angel face, in his despair,
He looked and saw the mother's impress there.
And when her lisping tongue began to speak,
The tears of gladness sparkled on his cheek ;
'Twas then he vowed through life his child should be

His one sole thought for her felicity ;
Her training it should be to gild his name,
And through her life perpetuate his fame.
A guardian for this child was his next thought,
And for a right one he untiring sought.
He wanted one in education high—
A lady born, on whom he could rely ;
Proficient in the sciences and dress,
Au fait in music and the languages.
High culture for his child was his resolve,
That she might any knotty problem solve,
When at his table she should take her place,
With true politeness and becoming grace.
And yet he wished for one who would not press
Upon his child those questions that would bless,
If rightly instilled in the youthful mind,
And well adapted for all humankind,
On childlike faith in Him who rules above—
A wise Creator and the God of Love.
This was to him of course delusion vain,
The offspring of a weak, disordered brain,
Produced by teachers sowing varied seeds –
The formula of men who prate for creeds ;
Instead of doing what he'd taught of late,
Leave all our guidance in the hands of fate.
He soon found one of these ; she had been sent,
At his request, from off the continent.
She'd travelled much, and in her knowledge store
Had garnered much, she scarcely needed more—
In fact, had she known less, in her life's lease,
It would have added to her inward peace—
Less of the theories of men soul blind,
Whose tendency, alas ! oft warp the mind
From its true centre and safe guiding rod—
The World's Redeemer and Creation's God.

For she had mixed with those in her life's way
Who had no reverence for the Sabbath day—
The day of rest where she was wont to meet
In earlier years around the mercy seat;
And sing those hymns that gives the Christian joy,
Which bold freethinkers never will destroy.
Society to her was full of charms,
And she mixed in it without soul alarms;
The polished jest at sacred, serious things
She oft enjoyed, now it had gilded wings—
Divested of its plebeian common place,
She heard it, and then smiled with seeming grace,
Until the poison sank without control
Into the deep recesses of her soul.
And then she in her turn, with ready wit,
Would ridicule the truths of Holy Writ;
And pass through " Doubting Castle " on her way
To push the edifice of truth away—
The truth that's recorded for all who look
Within the precincts of the good Old Book.
And yet she was as polished as Rosseau,
Had fitting language, pleasant as Defoe;
She had acquired, while sitting at her ease,
In all she said a tendency to please.
No wonder, then, that such a " Fairy Queen "
Would please the father of Evangeline.
In their first interview she made him feel
That she was needful for his daughter's weal;
And she could guide with sure unerring hand,
By cultured shrewdness, kept at her command,
His true heart's treasure to a blest estate,
That through life's future he would estimate.
This pleased him well, her conduct was so brave,
And, for her frankness, this injunction gave—
To keep from his loved child, Evangeline,

Those Bible stories of a land unseen ;
On things eternal she must never dwell—
Must never speak to her of heaven or hell,
But try to lead his child by reason's light
On paths of science, which were only right.
" The bygone teaching of the schools," he said,
" Had filled the world with an unceasing dread
Of something that would be beyond the grave—
A theme on which the parsons love to rave,
And by their raving terrify John Bull,
To keep their stomachs and their pockets full."
This salient wit of course well pleased Madam,
Much better than the story of the Lamb,
That once was led to slaughter for mankind—
That thousands love to hear to heal the mind ;
And find in it a balm, like Gilead's, pure,
That ever healeth and will e'en endure.
These two did then arrange, with seeming skill,
The future of Evangeline at will ;
Forgetting, in their zeal, " Though man intends,
There is a Providence that shapes our ends."

PART II.

HE stately mansion's dome at Avondale
One winter's night was threatened by a gale,
That o'er the Atlantic swept with double force,
Like a bold charger on its onward course ;
And tore up trees that once in grandeur stood
Before this mansion, and in famed Leigh Wood.
This long remembered night was Madam sat
With young Evangeline, in varied chat ;
Until they heard the sweeping tempest roar.
And shake the portals of the mansion door ;

When, with her girlish voice, and all serene,
Spake out, inquiringly, Evangeline.
" What is it, tutor, dear, that howling makes ?
The very cave of old St. Vincent shakes ;
The sound vibrates and strikes upon the ear,
Enough to fill Cliftonia with fear."
" ' Tis but the elements," she deigned to say,
" Sometimes they're angry, as they are to day;
By their strange doings they are full of hate,
Fulfilling now the stern decrees of fate."
" And what is fate ? " inquired Evangeline.
" Can it be heard at all, be felt or seen ?
Is it a spirit with a wizard name,
Or is it something with a mortal frame ?
I wish to know it, for I've heard you say
So much about it in a passing way ;
And oft while you and father have conversed,
When I my evening lesson had rehearsed,
On varied subjects, in the twilight hour,
When we long sat within our woodbine bower,—
I've heard both he and you so oft relate
The wondrous doings of this wondrous fate.
Pray tell me, does it govern earthly things ?
The setter up and bringer down of kings ?
By it doth princes reign, and all things be,—
Is it the ruler of man's destiny ? "
" It is, Evangeline," the syren said ;
" What brings such thoughts in your young head ?"
" I'll tell you, then, if you will patient hear,
And won't hereafter be with me severe—
For I have found, a many months ago,
A treasure trove, if you would wish to know ;
But this rare treasure is not worldly pelf,
And I daren't keep the knowledge to myself.
One day, when you had left our mansion dear,

I found the key of mother's escritoire ;
And I unlocked it, in my girlish glee,
For I its contents oft had longed to see ;
To me it was a tributary shrine,
And though once mother's, I now felt it mine.
I looked it through, without the slightest fear,
And saw within it many a souvenir
Of fond affection, that the loved one sends
To give enjoyment to all dearest friends ;
But in one drawer I found a wondrous book,
And I was tempted much in it to look ;
So I unclasped it, and you won't me blame,
For on its title page I saw my name.
My mother's hand, ere she resigned her breath,
While gliding through the peaceful vale of death,
Had written there, and plainly to be seen,
' This book I leave to my Evangeline.
It is a Book, if prized, will make her blest—
The Book of books, all priceless and the best :
For in its pages she explained may find
The one Great Father's love to all mankind ;
How He in goodness made mankind upright
To be His glory and His great delight ;
And how they went, in a forbidden way,
From paths of right and rectitude astray ;
Until a scheme was planned by One above,
By He who is the source of perfect love.
And it was this -- He had an only Son,
That sat with Him on heaven's eternal throne,
The express image of His Father, He,
And full of love from all eternity.
And when no other means could be devised
To bring the wanderers back whom His love prized,
He'd send His Son from His blest courts above,
To show mankind the fulness of His love ;

And win them back to the safe, narrow way,
From whence in one fell hour they went astray—
The lost ones calling home to joys untold
That waited for them in His shelter fold.
This plan was well approved by His loved Son,
And He at once exclaimed, " Thy will be done ! "
And then He left the land of light and song,
The loudest praises of angelic throng,
And took a mortal's form to conquer sin—
A Babe was born in stable of an inn.
This wondrous Babe, the Infant but a span,
Soon grew in favour both with God and man ;
For on His mission He was all intent—
To do His Father's will He had been sent.
And He performed it wheresoe'er He stood ;
His life was well employed in doing good,
And all who saw Him toil could surely ken
He loved the bodies and the souls of men ;
Like the Good Shepherd from His Father's side,
He sought them long, until for them He died,—
For them He suffered grief and pain and loss
On Calvary's mountain, on a rugged Cross ;
Then He, the fruit of a fair virgin's womb,
Was laid within a deep-hewn rocky tomb,
Until the dawning of the third day came,
When death and the cold grave were put to shame,—
For from the gloomy sepulchre He rose
In triumph, to the terror of his foes ;
And soon ascended to His throne on high,
Above the vaulted, glittering, starry sky,
Whence one day He will come to earth again,
For myriads' pleasure, and for myriads' pain.
His mission then will be to judge the world,
" While mountains are in it on mountains hurl'd."
For in this precious Book 'tis surely said,

The sea and grave shall both give up their dead ;
And those who will abide that judgment day
Will be the good who walk'd in wisdom's way.
This way is pointed out in this blest Book ;
Each day, my child, then, in this Treasure look ;
Find comfort here, and on its truths rely,—
'Twill teach you how to live and how to die.'
" What think you of this Book, dear governess ? "
Evangeline inquired with firm address.
" Is it not wonderful in its detail ?
It is the Word of God that cannot fail.
I found these words upon its open page,
And they seem'd written by a very sage,—
One of those holy men with spirit fired,
That were with sacred truth from heaven inspired.
Its contents gave my heart a new delight,
And I was poring o'er them until night :
Yes—till I heard your well-known footsteps glide,
And then I put the treasured Book aside."
" You have surprised me, child," her tutor said,
While she abruptly toss'd her graceful head ;
And then, without preface, lest she should err,
Proceeded in this way to answer her—
"Evangeline, my dear, what notions crude
You have about a Book that will delude,
Unless experience and discretion guide
You while you read it, as you have, with pride :
'Tis so mysterious,—for its every page
Don't seem to me the product of the sage ;
But written just to keep mankind in dread
Of something that will happen when they're dead,
Instead of an employment that will give
Them stores of real pleasure while they live.
It may have had its use in ages back
To keep the minds of weaklings on the rack,

When ignorance rode rampant in the land,
And men its meaning could not understand ;
But in this age of culture and display,
Such books as this 'tis wise to put away.
We have rare works of science, you may see,
And books well filled with new philosophy ;
And from these you may gather, while you scan,
The true design and origin of man ;
Where reason lends its aid, though coming late,
To place our future in the hands of fate ;
'Tis best to leave it there, and comfort find,
Than having worry for the heart and mind."
" But will this give it ? " said Evangeline,
With mind and voice all cheerful and serene ;
" I dare not trust, I fearlessly relate,
My life and guidance to the hand of fate :
For in that Book my mother left behind
I did, while reading, this direction find—
' Acknowledge Me the Lord in all thy ways ;
I'll guide thee with Mine eye through all thy days.
Give Me thine heart, come, weary one, be blest ;
Come unto Me, and I will give thee rest.
Remember thy Creator in thy youth ;
Come unto Me—the Way, the Life, the Truth :
For all who seek Me early these shall find—
True consolation for the heart and mind ;
Come unto Me, and thou shalt have delight—
My yoke is easy and My burden light.
Come unto Me, My child, My mercy's free,
I now am waiting, and I wait for thee.'
I heard that voice of love while reading this,
And in that moment found an inward bliss ;
While I put out my hand, in deed and truth,
To Him who spoke for guidance in my youth.
With childlike faith, I then pledged every power

To Him who claimed me in that hallowed hour ;
I felt my heart no longer mine, but His—
And with that full surrender I had bliss.
And this increases, I can truly say,
Since I have trod the safe and narrow way ;
Because it leadeth to pure joys on high
That wait the Christian 'yond the starry sky.
I've lost all confidence in what you state,
That all things here are in the hands of fate.
I've learnt to exercise my common sense,
And see in all things here a Providence
That guides frail mortals when they seek its aid—
A Providence whose plans are wisely laid,
That numbers hairs of all its own—indeed,
That doth the ravens and the sparrows feed,
And clothes the lilies in their robes of white,
And saffron beauty, for the world's delight.
This Providence I own, with heart sincere,
And owning it, I have no cause to fear.
While reading that blest Book, I understood
That all things work together for our good.
When we love God with all our heart and soul—
The God that can the elements control—
He by a process of His own will give
His children true enjoyment while they live.
The bitter things and passing sweets of life
Will blend together without causing strife.
To bless His own, His purposes are one,
And while He works they pray 'Thy will be done.'
I feel 'tis best through life, and only right,
To let Him choose my path for true delight.
I know I'm safe while in the hands Divine ;
And love my mother's God, now He is mine.
In that good Book I found His will revealed,
And truth that had been long from me concealed ;

For His good Spirit opened to my mind
That when I thought I saw, I then was blind.
And while I read this, to my soul's surprise,
The scales of prejudice fell from mine eyes ;
And I went unto Him, the world's Great Light,
When He said unto me, ' Receive thy sight.'
And at His word, whom winds and seas obey,
Soul darkness fled, the night was turned to day !
And I found peace from Him who can it give,
I saw His face, and seeing it I live—
Not to myself alone, for earthly glee,
But unto Him who gave Himself for me.
I now can look to Him, without despair,
And to a sweet home, waiting ' over there,'
Where mother lives, all free from care and pain,
And I shall meet her ne'er to part again.
I've read of this sweet home on that blest page—
It has attractions that may well engage
The mind of all who wish for true delight
In that fair city that is out of sight ;
With pearly gates and streets of shining gold,
And joys unending that can ne'er be told.
Yes, tutor, and I now have righteous hate
For what freethinkers designate as fate.
I would not part with peace I now possess
For all freethinking guides to happiness.
But, hark ! I hear dear father's well-known tread,
He'll think 'tis time that I retired to bed ;
I'll go and kiss him, with a child's delight,
And wish him when I leave a sweet good-night."

PART III.

ONE springtide morning, in a breakfast chat,
A sire and tutor at their leisure sat ;
'Twas serious converse, you could plainly see,
For at that table there should have been three.
But one was missing then, 'twas truly seen,
And that now missed one was Evangeline.
Her parent made inquiry for his child,
As though he could not then be reconciled ;
For her instructor, with a voice composed,
Had told him she was slightly indisposed —
She would be better soon, did blandly say,
If she was kept in quiet through the day.
But this did not suffice her father then—
For he was one of those far-seeing men
That saw from little what was surely meant
To be a danger signal, shrewdly sent,
To warn him that the prize he held so dear
Would have to be relinquished even here.
And then he questioned her instructor long,
To ascertain what in his child was wrong,
And what distressing symptoms she had seen
To bring heart-grief to his Evangeline.
For he had noticed her, and very long,
Though oft in pain, her soul seemed full of song ;
" She seemed to him," he said, " in such a sphere
As though she sought not for her pleasure here ;
He'd watched her oft, while poring o'er a book,
Leave off at times and give an upward look,
As though she were in converse with a friend—
Though there was not one there, she might depend ;
And while she lingered in that mood awhile,
Upon her features there would play a smile.
And he had wondered, when he saw the sight,

What gave Evangeline such heart delight.
And one day he was tempted much to speak,
When he saw many blushes on her cheek ;
But seemed so bright and beautiful that day,
He could not utter what he wished to say.
'Twas strange she seemed to have such joy serene,
He could not understand Evangeline.
What was it made her differ from the throng
Of lady guests they had to mix among ? "
" I cannot tell," her tutor answered soon,
" But once, in autumn, she began to swoon ;
I felt somewhat alarmed, yet did my best
To bring her round and give her spirit rest.
You were not with us, you had gone from home
To spend the month with friends at Ilfracombe ;
Then she remained in an unconscious state
Much longer than to you I dare relate."
And then she told him, with a firm express,
What she knew well would give him much distress—
How she as well as he had noticed long
His loved Evangeline was far from strong.
The hectic flush that settled on her cheeks
Had been ill-omen, and for many weeks.
" But when she rallied from her swoon awhile
She gave me there a witching, winning smile ;
And said, ' I've been to such a joyful sphere,
And I have seen my own dear mother there.
I cannot tell you all I've heard and seen,
But I heard this, a voice call out, " Evangeline !"
It seemed as though I'd heard it long before,
Then a sweet angel form did near me soar,
And whispered, " I'm your mother, darling child ; "
And soon it looked me in the face and smiled.'
' Oh, hush ! Evangeline,' I kindly said,
And laid my soft cold hand upon her head ;

I feared she was delirious, and yet she
Was sensible and calm as she could be —
For she did then persistently declare
That she'd been to a sweet home 'over there;'
And this she tried to make me understand
By pointing upward with her little hand—
'Oh, sweet, sweet home,' she whispered, in delight,
''Tis in a city where there is no night.
I've read of it' she said, 'in that blest book
My mother left that I might in it look,
And find the treasure she had found before,
Ere she was gathered to the peaceful shore—.
Where all the pure in heart will find a place,
And see their loving Maker face to face.
I cannot tell you what I've seen to-day,'
She breathed, 'but this—we soared away,
Did I and mother, for a time alone,
Until we reached a beautiful white throne ;
And He who sat thereon, above our globe,
Was clad in brightness and a kingly robe ;
And while we neared Him, He complacent smiled,
When mother said to Him, " Behold my child! "
And He replied, " I know it, though 'tis thine
I've sealed it for the kingdom, it is mine ;
It is too pure for yon dark world below,
I'll clothe it soon in raiment white as snow ;
But it will have to go from hence again,
Awhile to suffer on a bed of pain—
For it is through much pain and conflict there
That all my ransomed ones find entrance here.
The mortal frame that clings with ruddy glow
Must be left yonder in the vale below—
' God's acre' must awhile this treasure keep,
But death will not be an abiding sleep—
The tomb is but a resting-place for all,

A silent chamber for the great and small,
Until the whole of my redeemed shall be
From earth's corruption and its evil free.
Thy loved one's casket there, though buried deep,
And he who mourns it may long o'er it weep,
'Twill be all safe in its own mother earth,
As safe as when its mother gave it birth ;
For it is in My keeping, never fear,
And I will watch it while 'tis sleeping there ;
Then in My own good time will bid it rise
To join the spirit gathered to the skies—
All glorious and beautiful 'twill be,
My fitting guest through all eternity."
My mother heard these words, and then, all blest,
She answered " Even so, Thou knowest the best."
And soon she beckoned me to come away,
While whispering " Darling child, thou canst not stay
Up here as yet, there's something else for thee
To do down yonder to give joy to me ;
Go tell thy father I now for him wait,
But he must give up faith in blinded fate,
And fix it upon Him who died to save
Mankind from sin and terror of the grave.
Go tell him this, or we shall never meet
With joy before the coming judgment seat ;
And tell thy tutor, loved Evangeline,
In heaven the scorner will be never seen." '
I heard her speak to this, and then I said,
While raising her a little in the bed,
' Hush, hush ! my child, you must no longer speak,'
For some large tears were standing on her cheek ;
And to compose her I did try my best
Until I gently hushed her off to rest."
" 'Tis strange," the father said, when he had heard
This long recital.   And he then averred

It must have been produced by nature's strain,
Or else it was delusion in the brain.
He'd see his child the first convenient day,
And try to drive these notions far away ;
Not thinking that the Power who gave him life
Could use that child to bring him to his wife ;
And use her first to lead his erring feet
From paths of error to the mercy seat.

PART IV.

HE famed Leigh Woods were just about to sing
Their sylvan welcome to returning spring,
When, lo ! another singer was found near,
And trilling notes harmoniously clear—
Not in the charming valley, Nightingale,
But in the well-known manse at Avondale.
And this sweet singer there was often seen ;
It was her father's joy, Evangeline.
These two were sitting in their splendid room,
Though twilight's hour was shrouding it with gloom ;
For she, all loving, though not feeling strong,
To her loved father had been singing long ;
And then she crept to rest a little while
Close to his side, and have a welcome smile :
He gave her one, then praised her pleasant touch :
Her music, it was sweet—he liked it much.
She had, indeed, a well-trained hand and ear—
Her notes were all so well arranged and clear ;
And he would like to hear from her sweet voice
Another treasured song of her own choice.
" What shall I sing," she whispered in delight,
" To give my father pleasure through the night ?
My treasured songs are now so very few ;

And father's always wanting something new :
Yet I have one he's never heard before—
I found it hid in mother's escritoire
One day, when I was looking in with joy
On its stored treasures ; and without annoy
I saw and read it, and I had a treat :
The words and music are so very sweet.
I think my father this would like to hear
From his Evangeline, to give him cheer.
I'll try to sing it o'er to him to-night,
When I have rested, and the room 's alight ;
But while the room is ready, may I ask,
If to my father 'twill not be a task
If he, some day, will tell me as a boon,
Why my loved mother had to die so soon ?—
For I was but a babe, I heard him say,
When from this world dear mother pass'd away.
I should have joy'd, had I but known her charms,
And felt myself sometimes in her loved arms ;
And even now, though father 's kind to me,
I ofttimes wish I could my mother see :
'Twould be so nice, and much enhance my bliss,
For her to cheer me with a mother's kiss ;
And then to have her give me, while I live,
That good advice which only mothers give.
'Tis said, a father's love 's worth more than gold,
But that a mother's love can ne'er be told ;
And I feel sure, from what I once did see,
That my loved mother had strong love for me —
For she has left me such a precious book ;
And I oft read it near the Leigh Woods brook
That floweth by the slope, when sweet wild flowers
Give such endearment to Cliftonia's bowers ;
But more of this to him some day I'll tell.
Now may I summon Mary with the bell ?

'Tis time to bring a light within the room—
It seems enshrouded in a pall of gloom ;
And then, when she doth here the taper bring,
To my dear father I will try to sing
The one sweet song I found when turning o'er
The treasures in loved mother's escritoire."
Her father pressed her hand—he could not speak—
For silent tears were chasing down his cheek.
His own loved daughter had, without intent,
Brought recollections as from heaven sent ;
For while he heard her he was filled with woe,
Reminded of the scenes of long ago.
Just at that moment to their drawing-room
The needed light was brought to cheer the gloom,
And loved Evangeline, in earnest thought,
Her grand pianoforte quickly sought,
And her loved song had found its fitting place,
For she looked on it with a glowing face,
And soon began to sing as sweet could be,
The welcome " Rock of Ages, cleft for me."
Her fingers seemed to glide with perfect ease,
While she was singing, o'er the ivory keys,
With very joy they seemed to move along,
As though her heart and soul were in the song ;
And then its sweet refrain brought inward glee—
Rock, " Cleft for me, let me hide myself in Thee."
Her father started as this caught his ear,
Until he trembled in his old arm-chair ;
For he was not at ease, 'twas plainly seen—
He had not pleasure or a mind serene ;
Though his Evangeline kept singing on
The one sweet song her heart was fixed upon ;
There she kept trilling with intention good—
" Now let the water, the water and the blood,
Be of sin, of sin the double cure,

Save now from wrath, from wrath, and make me pure."
The last sweet refrain fell upon his ear,
And through his soul there came a saddened fear
That he had not been where his child had been—
His treasured flower, his loved Evangeline :
She seemed to have a something in her mind
That gave her joy, while he, alas ! was blind ;
And then he muttered, in his anguish great,
" How strange. Can this be brought about by fate ? "
For his whole system had received a shock,
When he heard her sweetly singing of a Rock ;
" The Rock of Ages ; " what could that Rock mean ?
He had a mind to ask Evangeline ;
And yet he shuddered to be thought so wild,
With all his wisdom, to learn from a child.
He did not then the good Book understand :
" A little child shall lead them by the hand."
And by a way they know not, when they're sought,
The erring wanderers shall be homeward brought.
There was no knowing where his mind would stray,
Had not Evangeline then ceased to play ;
And coming to him with a witching smile,
She said, the passing moments to beguile,
" Dear father, do you like my mother's song ?
She must have sung it with a gladsome tongue ;
Its well-worn music is a proof to me
That it (for her) had sweet soul-harmony ;
And while I sang it in my rapture o'er,
I seemed to hear her from the heavenly shore
Exclaim, ' My child, sing on a little while,'
And then she gave me such a winning smile ;
And when she'd smiled she beckoned me away
To where the sweetest singers sing for aye.
Dear father, this is true, what I relate ;
Can such soul-rapture be produced by fate ?

I cannot think it—no, dear father, no.
But I am weary ; will you let me go ?
I want to rest a little on my bed ;
There is a strange sensation in my head ;
And on my cheeks the mirror doth disclose
The fading blushes of a dying rose.
Excuse me, father ; let me take the light.
Good-night, dear father ; kiss me sweet Good-night."

PART V.

THE summer flowers were sending, rich and rare,
    Their balmy fragrance on the ambient air,
    Just when the woodland scenes were at their best,
By fair Cliftonia's downs in beauty drest,—
When, lo ! there was one flower began to fade,
Near this lov'd spot the God of nature made ;
This treasur'd angel-flower was turning pale,
Within a room at queenly Avondale.
Yes ; it was filling hearts with anguish keen,
For this sweet floweret was Evangeline ;
She lay serenely on her downy bed.
With her loved father's arm beneath her head,
While near her side her tutor came to gaze
Upon her pupil, and in strange amaze.
For fell consumption's hand had nearly done
The work it had so rapidly begun ;
And she, her parent's hope, with failing breath,
Was gliding swiftly through the vale of death.
Her kind physician was within the room,
For he had long ago foretold her doom :
Had told her father to his mind prepare
To lose the darling he had deem'd so rare ;
He'd marked her sinking fast in months gone by,

And soon his angel-flower would have to die.
This message filled her parent's mind with dread,
And low and silently he bowed his head.
It was a stroke too much for him to bear,
And he was on the verge of dark despair :
For he'd no light to cheer him in the gloom ;
No hope to meet her when beyond the tomb.
His idol fate was absent with her wand,
And modern thought had no relief at hand :
And there he sat on this eventful day,
To watch his fond heart's treasure pass away.
Her tutor, also, was close by his side,
With all the calmness of a stoic's pride—
For she'd determined it should not be seen
That she had terror near Evangeline ;
She had a love that was too strong to weep,
For she'd averr'd that death was only sleep.
Evangeline beheld, with pitying eye,
Her there all callous, and she heav'd a sigh,
Then breathed, " Dear tutor, I shall soon be gone,
And you and father will be left alone ;
And I have thought of you so much of late,
With what you wished me to believe in fate.
Oh ! I am glad I did not heed you then,
For fate is but the deity of men.
I found a Rock on which I firmly stand—
A sure foundation-- not a sinking sand.
I'm on this Rock of Ages in the flood
Of Jordan's swelling, and the Rock is good ;
My mind is calm—Yes ; I have settled peace,
Although my time is short, my joys increase ;
While passing through the waters I can sing,
And to this Rock of Ages I will cling ;
While here I'm safe,—I on its strength rely :
It gave me life—and on it I shall die."

Her tutor rose and took her by the hand;
Then breath'd, " Oh! hush, my child.   I understand;
I'll think of what Evangeline has said,
When she is gather'd to the silent dead.
I love her much, and will hereafter prove
I have not slighted her unchanging love."
" Bless you," she whispered—"that has done me good;
It seems to cheer me in the Jordan flood;"
And then she rais'd her eye to him who there
Held her frail casket in his heart despair,
And whispered, " Oh! dear father, my heart warms;
Your Evangeline's so happy in your arms.
In them I wish to die; but here I trow
There are more loving arms around me now—
The arms of One who beckons me above—
My Heavenly Father's arms—the God of love.
I have no fear, although my end is nigh:
No fear in life, and shall not have to die—
For this one thought to me doth comfort give,
Though I must die, I shall but die to live.
And mother waits me on the peaceful shore,
Where I shall meet her—yes, to part no more.
And now, dear father, when I leave you here,
You must not shed for me one bitter tear,
For I shall be where all the weary rest,
With rapture leaning on my Saviour's breast.
And now I want to tell you all my mind
Before I leave you in the world behind:
I should like you to meet my mother dear,
Where there's no death and no distracting fear;
And I should be with both to join the song
That warbles from the ransom'd myriad throng;
But then, dear father, there must be a change
Before the plains celestial you can range,—
A change in heart and life before you dare

Look up with any hope for entrance there.
I found that change one day while I did look
Within the pages of this precious Book ;
And I have kept it like a treasure hid
Beneath the folds of my white coverlid ;
And here I read it when I am alone—
It seems to bring me nearer heaven's throne :
It gives me comfort more than I can state—
Far more than e'er can come from blinded fate :
It doth assure me, while it gives me rest.
That there are waiting mansions for the blest—
For all who live according to this Word :
Yes ; mansions in the kingdom of their Lord ;
And I should like you, father, to be there,
For they are bright, all beautiful, and fair, —
More beautiful than our loved Avondale
Those mansions are, and they will never fail.
No winter's winds will smite them at their will—
They're all secure on heaven's eternal hill ;
They cannot crumble 'neath old time's decay—
No, these will never, never pass away.
And father, dear, I want you ere I leave
To promise me that you will never grieve ;
And promise, also, you will sometimes look
Within the pages of this precious Book.
I leave it you as mother left it me :
Oh! try to read it on your bended knee—
To find the pearl—all priceless—that's within,
'Twill keep you from the luring paths of sin.
Now, father, tell Evangeline you will,
For my heart's failing : it will soon be still.
Now let me have this blest assurance given,
That you will meet us both at home in heaven.
I want you to be with us, free from care,
In the sweet home that's waiting over there."

Her voice grew fainter every word she spake,
And her fond father's frame began to shake.
Yet still he held her, and he gently press'd
His angel flower yet closer to his breast.
Then whispered, "Oh! Evangeline, my child,
Forgive thy father for a will so wild.
I now submit me to the will Divine :
Thy mother's God from henceforth shall be mine ;
I'll try to walk the path which thou hast trod,
And kiss the hand that smites me with the rod.
I see His wisdom here to take my child—
It is that I may become reconciled
To Him that loves me with a Father's love,
Though I from Him persistently did rove.
Forgive me, my Evangeline, the past,
Thy erring father is brought home at last.
A wayward prodigal I long have been,
But through my child my error I have seen.
I am repentant, though repenting late,
And here renounce the faith I had in fate ;
To modern thought no more I'll rear a shrine,
But cling to this good Book and things divine."
"Oh! bless you for those words," she faintly cried,
Then kissed him with her angel lips, and died.

CONCLUSION.

Just when the autumn leaves began to fall
From silver birches and the poplars tall,
Loud rustling onward, drifting with the gale,
Around the charming manse at Avondale,
Within its silent chamber might be seen
A lifeless treasure—'twas Evangeline.
She lay all placid in her coffin dress,

While near her stood her father in distress ;
And then her tutor came in very grief,
As though she wanted much some heart relief ;
Then he, the father of that angel flower,
Exclaimed, " We soon shall have her here no more ;
Yet we to heaven, through her, are reconciled :
We have learnt wisdom from a very child.
Oh ! let us henceforth walk in Wisdom's ways ;
All grateful spend the remnant of our days.
Improve the past, while in this world of strife,
By living in a sphere of nobler life.
Let it be ours to glory—not in word—
But in the Cross of Jesus Christ the Lord."
She breath'd, " It will be done by me, I vow—
I'll live for Him who is my Treasure now,
That I may reach at last the home above,
And greet the angel flower we both do love."
Then both bent o'er her, for they could not speak,
Implanting farewell kisses on her cheek.
The coffin-lid was closed ; a hearse was nigh,
And then was borne, 'mid many a tearful eye,
Beneath the cyprus shade, in Arno's Vale,
The angel flower of queenly Avondale.

PATIENCE.

THERE is a virtue, we often have read—
    One we should seek and retain ;
It has been cherished by martyrs who bled,
    Smiling on torturing pain.

These have possess'd it even to death,
    'Mid the world's rancour and strife ;
We should secure it— it is so useful
    In the strange battle of life.

A TRUE POET.

TRUE poet, wise men say,
   Ploddeth at his duty;
Diligent through his life's way,
   Penning thoughts of beauty.
He e'er sees, 'mid new delights
   On his treasured pages,
'Tis not for a day he writes,
   But the coming ages.

A true poet soars and sings
   On the wings of morning;
While to sleep the sluggard clings,
   He's the sluggard scorning.
He has joy upon his bed,
   Though his sleep's in snatches,
For new thoughts dance through his head
   In the midnight watches.

A true poet wise men heed—
   He has ills prevented;
Though some knowing ones, for greed,
   Have deemed him demented.
He's not one of their own choice,
   And these feel above him;
But he has this counterpoise—
   Little children love him.

A true poet looks above
   For his consolation,
While he pens new odes of love
   To exalt the nation.
Strains he writes with a true ring,
   And the world will know it;
Seeing God in everything—
   Such is a true poet.

VIRGIN SPRING, 1883.

VIRGIN Spring! Now I'll sing
 Thee a new refrain ;
 While thou'rt here in thy sphere,
Smiling once again.
Verdant hills, crystal rills,
 Their oblations bring ;
Nature's glad to be clad—
 Welcome, Virgin Spring !

Virgin Spring ! 'Neath thy wing
 Come the welcome flowers ;
Snowdrops white, crocus' bright,
 Near the woodland bowers.
Budding trees, humming bees,
 Thrush and linnet sing
In thy ear, sweet and clear—
 Welcome, Virgin Spring !

Virgin Spring! Valleys ring—
 For, in thy bright hours,
Flora comes to our homes
 With her precious dowers.
Violets sweet, primrose neat,
 And pure lilies bring
In her hand—oh, how grand !—
 Welcome, Virgin Spring !

Virgin Spring ! While I sing
 Thee thy birthday song,
Strains will flow, heavenward go,
 From my heart and tongue,
That my life, free from strife—
 (While thou 'rt on the wing)
May useful shine as doth thine—
 Welcome, Virgin Spring !

HOW I LOVE THE AUTUMN SEASON.

OH, I love the autumn season,
  When the golden corn appears—
  When the fields are white for harvest,
With their precious freighted ears ;
Then I've joy beyond description,
  And I linger o'er it long,
While I listen to the chorus
  Of the merry reapers' song.

Yes, I love the autumn season,
  It has such a charm for me,
As I gaze in thrilling rapture
  On the sylvan woods of Leigh ;
For they are so full of beauty,
  With their many tinted leaves,
When they 're belted by the corn fields
  Full of ready, ripened sheaves.

Oh, I love the autumn season,
  In the valley Nightingale,
For to me it is so pleasant,
  Just to ramble through the vale—
When the nuts are hung in clusters,
  While the rocky woodlands ring,
Where the crystal stream meanders,
  And the thrush and linnet sing.

Yes, I love the autumn season,
  And I feel the love is right,
For it fills my soul with music
  And a rapturous delight.
I shall always sing it welcome,
  While I have my dwelling here,
For to me it is the dearest,
  Sweetest season of the year !

"HOME, SWEET HOME."

Graciously accepted by H.R.H. the Duke of Albany.

John Howard Payne, the author of "Home, sweet Home," died at Tunis, April 1st, 1852, and was buried there in the Protestant Cemetery. His remains were exhumed January 8th, 1883, at the request of the United States Government, in the presence of the British authorities, and shipped to America.—*Bristol Mercury and Post.*

UNDER a choice, magnificent dome,
Bury the writer of " Home, sweet Home,"
Now he has gone o'er the raging sea,
Home to the land of the brave and free.

He has been to it a stranger long,
More than the strains of his own loved song ;
These have been heard in mansion and cot,
While he who wrote them was almost forgot.

Author of " Home, sweet Home," it is told
Thou once wert homeless, " out in the cold,"
Hearing thine own pure stanzas sung
From a grand hall by a lady's tongue.

Oh ! what a treat in a poet's life,
Writing to starve 'mid worry and strife ;
Writing, alas ! to help him to live ;
Writing for other hearts, comfort to give.

Why is it so in a land of light,
Where there is gold for the men who fight ?
Why should a poet, with brains in his head,
Wait for his guerdon until he is dead ?

Should not a poet have joy in this world?
Why should his hopes be constantly hurled
Down 'mid distraction, sorrow, and care,
Until he reaches the grave in despair?

Why not a poet have here some reward?
Why does the cold world use him so hard—
Make him as cheerless as the cold stones,
Value his life-blood less than his bones?

If he is worthy of honour at all,
Help to support him—don't let him fall;
Help him to live as long as he can,
Show you believe that the poet's a man.

DOING GOOD.

THERE is a work by Heaven blest,
    When it is understood:
    It is the true heart's luxury
Of only doing good.

When this is exercised, we know
There springs from it a joy—
That selfish man while here below
Nor demons can destroy.

ONLY PERSEVERE.

LIFE is one great mystery
    We must all explore ;
    And while searching we shall find
  Much we must deplore.
Yet its ending may be bright,
  If we do and dare ;
And for what is true and right
  Only persevere.

Many things in time doth vex,
  Many things doth please—
And some things our minds perplex
  When we 're on our knees ;
But if guidance then we seek
  We've no need to fear,
For the inward voice will speak,
  Only persevere.

Many a youth, while heeding this,
  Lasting fame hath won—
Found a ripe old age of bliss,
  Many a glad " Well done ! "
Bards have written thrilling lays
  'Mid the scoff and jeer,
For they learnt in wisdom's ways—
  Only persevere.

Let us, then, in our life's work
  Bear this truth in mind—
We must not our duty shirk
  When we duties find.
Then when this short life is past,
  In a brighter sphere
We shall reach sweet home at last,
  If we persevere.

THERE IS RESTING O'ER THE HILL.

LIFE is uphill work to-day,
  Some are saying, full of fears ;
And a very thorny way,
  Some are showing by their tears.
Yet it may be well to know,
  If we work with heart and will,
Living to do good below—
  There is resting o'er the hill.

Life is uphill work, we know,
  But we all were made to climb ;
'Tis not wise to grope below—
  'Twill not make our lives sublime.
We must rise, nor dare to stop—
  Have a strong, determined will,
Till we reach the mountain top—
  There is resting o'er the hill.

Life is uphill work, indeed,
  Yes, to many we have seen—
For so many things they need
  Here to comfort them, I ween.
'Tis to gladden these I write,
  Though they cannot have their will ;
If they live and do the right,
  There is resting o'er the hill.

Life is uphill work at best ;
  But beyond time's setting sun,
Through death's valley, there is rest—
  Yes, when all the toiling 's done.
Let us, then, be brave each day—
  Every duty well fulfil ;
Sing, as seasons glide away,
  There is resting o'er the hill.

WHAT THE WORLD IS WANTING.

H ! this is a grand old world,
   And it would be grander,
   If we did to truth and right —
Not to evil pander.
Were we but straight up and down,
   And had less of canting,
This would bring us true renown—
   What the world is wanting.

Yes, this is a grand old world,
   And it would be brighter,
If we did, for all we could,
   Make life's burdens lighter :
Seeking out the heart distress'd—
   Those for comfort panting ;
This would make the mourners blest—
   What the world is wanting.

Oh ! this is a grand old world,
   And would soon be giving
More true joy to one and all,
   Were there better living.
We have preaching that is good,
   And a deal of ranting ;
But 'tis more of Christian life
   That the world is wanting.

Yes, this a grand old world,
   And it would be better,
If we did all strive to be
   True in deed and letter.
Let us nobly do our part—
   Seeds of good implanting
Show true love to God and man
   This the world is wanting.

DOLLARS AND DIMES.

EARLY one morning, awake on my bed,
  I lay a thinking as I had before;
  Restless, yet hopefully tossing my head,
 While the dense darkness was shrouding me o'er.
There long I sigh'd for my own treasured muse,
  Wishing she'd bring me a theme for my rhymes;
When the pure angel soon came with the news,
  Whispering, "Thy subject is Dollars and Dimes."

Dollars and Dimes? I cried in my haste,
  Can I inordinate love of these stem?
If I succeed, there 's no time to waste,
  For this mad world is all mad after them.
Oh, what a cry from the babbling throng,
  "We must make money, and 'Go with the times;'"
This is the first and last of their song,—
  Oh, what a scramble for Dollars and Dimes.

Dollars and Dimes, soon echoed again;
  Dollars and Dimes, I cried in the strife,
Dollars and Dimes are sometimes a bane:
  These must not be the objects of life.
Craving for these is often a curse,
  Leading some poor erring mortal to crimes;
Usefully spent, when found in the purse—
  This should be done with Dollars and Dimes.

Dollars and Dimes are useful below,
  But we from these shall be taken away,
Or they from us will be taken, we know:
  Dollars and Dimes with us cannot stay.
Then it is better far, while we have breath,
  Giving the world good lessons in rhymes;
These will give pleasure through life and in death,
  More than will grasping at Dollars and Dimes.

THE NATION'S BALLAD.

Our Sailor Prince and lovely Russian Bride.

*Graciously accepted by their Royal Highnesses the Prince and Princess of Wales,
Duke of Edinburgh, &c.*

Air :—"*Auld Lang Syne.*"

WE welcome to this sea-girt isle,
　　Sweet home ! Old England dear !
　　Our sailor Prince and happy bride,
　With heart and voice sincere.
A nation's joy we thus present,
　Loud let the welkin ring ;
While throngs in each embellish'd home
　And peasant's cot shall sing :—

CHORUS.
God bless our gallant sailor Prince,
　And his fair Russian bride ;
May they through life, by love, evince
　They are our country's pride.

Loved daughter from a distant clime,
　Of noble birth and blood ;
With him who boasts a Princely sire—
　Our Albert, wise and good.
By ties endearing now made one,
　E'er may their union be
A glory to old Albion's shore,
　This land of liberty.

May pure affection's tender plant
　With blending fibres grow ;
Yielding sweet flowers of lovely hue,
　To wreathe them where they go.
And may fair Peace on angel wing,
　With fragrant incense, come,
And take up her abode for aye
　In their own palace home.

Long may those richer earthly gifts,—
    Blest health and unity,—
More precious far than Ophir's wealth,—
    Their lasting portion be.
May Charity's pure crystal stream
    Each tender heart o'erflow,
And her twin sisters, Faith and Hope,
    Inspiring bliss bestow.

Loud greet we, then, our sailor Prince,
    His fame hath spread afar ;
Like some attractive planet, he
    Has found the Northern Star.
Bright constellation in our land,
    Oh, may their lustre tell,
And prove a source of joy to her
    Whose name we love so well.

Long live our nation's noble Duke,
    Long live his Moscow bride ;
Loud swell the strain 'mid Scotland's hills,
    O'er Erin's ocean tide.
And brave Old England's sons shall rise,
    Her daughters' hearts shall glow,
And chorus this *best wish* to Him
    From whom all blessings flow !

In Memoriam.

———·—

REV. DAVID LIVINGSTONE,

LL.D., D.C.L.

Born at East Kilbride, Scotland, 1817; died at Lobisa, Eastern Africa,
August 15th, 1873. Aged 56 years.

D ied, ah! yes; the martyr's fallen, to his friends and country lost;

A ll his patient suffering ended, life's exploring desert crossed.

V ain we strive to tell the daring, tabulate his ventures bold

I n the trackless waste long written, yet the half can ne'er be told.

D eeds heroic are emblazoned, where no white man's feet had trod,

L ike the crystal fount of mercy, rising to the throne of God—

I n the forest, on the mountain, 'neath the scorching mid-day sun;

V enturing through the swamps and rivers, onward till his course
was run,

I n the land he loved and laboured, Africa, whose sons he blessed;

N obly for her slaves long toiling, there he passed away to rest.

G one where glides a stream more fertile than the winding Nile e'er
gave,

S weet and pure, for ever flowing, where the ransom'd spirits lave;

T here he finds his long lost Mary, where no fever's hand of pain

O n the banks of deep Zambesi e'er shall separate again.

N oble champion, Christian patriot! Livingstone has won

E ndless life, his Master's guerdon, and the glad " Well done!"

In Memoriam.

(SONNET AND ACROSTIC.)

ARCHBISHOP TAIT,

Born December 22nd, 1811 ; died December 3rd, 1882.   Aged 70 years.

A   nother loved one's gathered to his tomb,
R   ipe for the garner in heaven's harvest home ;
C   alled by the reaper Death, Tait bowed his head ;
H   e rests now in " God's acre " with the dead ;
B   ut in yon angel land his spirit sings,
I   n robe of beauty, with the King of kings.
S   trong Christian faith was his while here in time,
H   is death was peaceful, and his life sublime ;
O   n all mankind he looked with hopeful eye -
P   reached to them how to live and how to die.

T   hough he's now gone from his loved labour charge,
A   work there waiteth for the world at large—
I   t is, that all may nobly emulate
T   he Christian graces of Archbishop Tait.

HAST THOU HAD A FRIEND?

HAST thou ever been befriended
    When thy soul, alack !
    Was engulphed in deepest trouble,
And upon the rack ?

Then, as thou found timely succour,
    Unto others send ;
Unto others in their sorrow
    Be a friend.

BRISTOL'S GREETING SONG.

Respectfully dedicated to their Royal Highnesses the DUKE and DUCHESS
of EDINBURGH, on their visit to the Musical Festival, held in Colston Hall,
October 19th, 1882.

Air :—"*The Hardy Norseman.*"

WE welcome with a gladsome tongue
    Two royal guests to-day,
    To this our festival of song,
  In tributary lay.
Old Bristol's sons and daughters sing
  For these harmonious strains,
And make the very welkin ring
  With heart and soul refrains.

CHORUS.

All welcome, then, ye royal pair,
  We sing with hearty glee :
Ye come as guests, in royal sphere,
  To aid blest charity !

We sing them welcome from " sweet home "
  To City of the West ;
Old Bristol's glad to see them come
  To aid a work so blest.
Within this hall, with blooming hope,
  And faith Bristolia shares,
They come to honour his life-works
  Whose honour'd name it bears.

All hail we, then, our royal guests,
  May life with them be long—
It's future all be bright and blest
  With cheerfulness and song.
And when in time no more they meet,
  May both—with all they love—
Then join for aye, in anthem sweet,
  The festal song above !

IMPROMPTU.

The following Impromptu was sent to the Chairman of the Bristol Musical
Festival, for his lack of courtesy in not acknowledging the receipt of the
author's Greeting Song to their Royal Highnesses the Duke and Duchess
of Edinburgh—inasmuch as he had the honour of composing the Nation's
Ballad, sung in concerts at their marriage.

GOD-SENT genius came one day
    Knocking at a rich man's door,
    And he sent the maid away
Just because her dress was poor ;
Had she worn a college wreath,
    She would have most welcome been ;
But she came from Nazareth,
    And no good in her was seen.

MORAL—

Don't despise a jewel great,
    Though its casket may be rough ;
Surely Chatterton's sad fate
    Shows of this there's been enough.

IN THE STORMY WEATHER.

ONCE upon a time there sat
  In a stony cave,
    On St. Vincent's craggy rock,
  With a spirit brave,
A known poet at his work,
  Busy as could be,
When a friend drew near and said
  " I have news for thee."

" News, what news," the poet cried,
  " Dost thou bring for me ?
Surely there is nothing wrong
  In the woods of Leigh ? "
" No," he said, " it is not there,
  'Tis another way ;
'Tis a something of thy rhymes
  Knowing people say."

" What ! my rhymes," the poet said,
  Looking o'er Leigh Wood
(For his thoughts were thither led),
  " Is it any good ?
If it is, then let it come,
  If it's free from sin ;
If it is not, send it home,
  Or just keep it in."

" Well it won't give joy to thee,
  If the news be true ;
Yet, if it is right," said he,
  " Satan had his due.
It is right that thou shouldst hear
  Something of thy crimes—
What the knowing folk have said
  Of thy written rhymes."

" Knowing folk," the poet sighed,
    " Legion is their name ;
Yet some knowing folk have lied,
    Panting after fame.
But, pray let me have the news
    Thou hast brought to-day :
For my ready fertile muse
    Waiteth by the way."

" Well, these say thy written lays
    Are not polished much ;
And of course they cannot praise
    Such, and such, and such.
Thou hast ne'er seen college life,
    Nor a prize hath won ;
And these folk, amid their strife,
    Vow thy course is run."

" My course run," the poet said,
    "It has just begun ;
'Twill run on when they are dead,
    Till my work is done.
Tell them this, for all their pains,
    And their bitter lies ;
That a heaven-born poet's strains
    Never, never dies !

Tell them I am doing work
    That will live for aye—
Sowing seed to germinate
    When they're passed away.
If they wont believe their eyes
    Till my harvest's grown ;
They will judge me, if they're wise,
    By the seed I've sown.

DO THY DUTY, THAT IS BEST.

MOTTO for 1883.

SHELTERED in an old stone grotto,
   Where my muse did oft appear,
   I was waiting for a motto
For the virgin bright new year.
Soon my angel came, and whispered,
   Glad to set my mind at rest—
" Here's a motto, full of beauty,
   Do thy duty, that is best."

" Do thy duty," loudly echoed
   In the chamber of my brain,
And the echoe came attended
   By this thrilling true refrain—
" Better is a poet's pittance
   Than a rich man's tarnished crest ;
In the work thou hast assigned thee
   Do thy duty, that is best.

Life is given thee for something
   Better than for storing pelf,—
'Tis to love thy wise Creator,
   And thy neighbour as thyself ;
Write, that this world may be better,
   That all wrongs may be redressed,
And that men may serve each other—
   Do thy duty, that is best."

Then I blest my own pure angel
   For a motto so divine ;
And I promised her with gladness
   That this motto should be mine.
Then she bade me plainly write it.
   That mankind might be impress'd
With its teaching, and adopt it—
   Do thy duty, that is best !

MEMORIAM CENTENARY WREATH.

FOR

ROBERT SOUTHEY, Esq., LL.D., Poet Laureate, &c., born at No. 9, Wine
Street, Bristol, 1774.

CHEERFUL we come, with our bannerols waving,
  Pealing his name through the Queen of the West ;
  Bringing a wreath for this noble departed,
 Coming with guerdons enduring and blest.

Garlands we bring to the shrine of our SOUTHEY,
 Frankly the tribute of love to repay,
Placing bright chaplets of laurel and roses
 Where the sweet flowrets can never decay.

Son of Bristolia, boast of our city,
 Hero of thought ! through the press and the pen ;
Nations with loud acclamations have crowned thee,
 Written thee one of the princes of men.

Peace to thy manes, nature's essayist,
 Faithful biographer, honour to thee !
Kingly behests have enhanced thy immortelles,
 Laureate of England, the land of the free.

Days of thy boyhood, we pleasantly scan them,
 See thee in buoyant and vigorous youth ;
Culling rich gems from the stores of a Beaumont
 Fletcher, or Chaucer's memento of truth.

Hailing with joy the outbeamings of Spenser,
  " Prince of all Poesy," attractive and kind ;
Thrilling thy soul with his " Faerie Queen " sketches,
  Winning thy heart with the blending of mind.

Oft we have trod with enraptured emotion,
  Ere the soft summertide glided away ;
Carpet of green on the banks of the Avon,
  Thou gladly sought at the closing of day.

Fancied we heard thee with Coleridge thy brother,
  'Mid the famed Leigh Woods' musical trees,
Chanting your evensong, love's inspiration,
  Borne on the balmy and zephyr-like breeze.

Hallowed thy walks 'neath the foliage sylvan,
  Wooing thy muse with an ardour sublime ;
Sipping the sweets of her lavish bestowing,
  Prizing the choice golden talent of time.

Richly endowed with rare " Ossian " treasures,
  Anxious to grasp what a " Gebir " possest ;
Toiling with hope near the murmuring waters,
  Striving to glide to Elysian rest.

" Onward " thy motto ; with mountains before thee,
  Glaciers to scale far away from the light,
Bravely now setting thy feet in the pathway,
  Urging thy course to Parnassian height.

Catching the flame of undying devotion
  From a loved heroine's chivalrous spark,
Shouting Excelsior ! near thy first trophy,
  Orleans' fair maiden, brave Joan of Arc.

Then the nymph Graces came bounding to meet thee,
  Led thee on smiling to Helicon's bowers;
Hailed the aurora's pure silvery twilight,
  Blending with brighter meridian hours.

Tuning their lyres with Eolian sweetness,
  Filling the welkin with strains of delight;
Sang thy approach to the shade of the muses,
  Woodlands of Pilma resplendently bright.

Pure shone the glories of dreamland, converging,
  Stirring thy soul with immortal desire;
Giving thy pen a rich mystic outflowing,
  Flaming thy heart with eradiate fire.

Then, like reflection from crystaline fountain,
  " Madoc's " fair form its beauty displays;
Followed by " Thalaba," brilliant effusion;
  As " Curse of Kehama," pearl of thy days.

" Nathless with love and duty's " entwining,
  When far away from the land of thy birth;
Breathing sweet strains for thy own " Ancient City,"
  Nearest and dearest to thee upon earth.

Fond recollections around thee would gather,
  Vividly pointing to seasons of yore ;
When with "the spirit of Chatterton near thee,"
  In the dome-haunts of St Mary's once more.

Hail to thy memory bard of our city !
  SOUTHEY the Good, old Bristolia's pride !
Love for thy sweet home of childhood was cherished.
  Distance those tendrils could never divide.

Lisbon's rich palace, 'mid picturesque beauty,
  Cintra's rock mountains, and Tago's green sea;
Brought reminiscences from thy loved Severn,
  Near grand St Vincent's endearing to thee.

Sweet thoughts of home, like the harp notes of angels,
  Gladdened thy spirit while passing along;
Came, softly cadent, to cheer and sustain thee,
  Like the clear nightingale's eventide song:

Long ago heard in the valley sequestrate,
  Where thy feet ramble no more through the day;
Now through the valley of death thou hast glided,
  Passed to the fatherland meekly away.

Calmly now sleeping 'neath tablet of marble,
  Crosthwait ennobled is holding thy dust;
Finding the urn for thy slumbering ashes,
  Until the rising day dawn for the just.

Greta's clear lakes from thy vision hath faded;
  Skiddaw's high craggy top scaling no more;
Gone where the sapphirine sea of glass shineth
  In the fair city with beautiful shore.

Wordsworth, the friend of thy bosom, has written
  For the white polished slab over thy tomb,
Thoughts of the past from affection's plant blooming,
  Yielding sweet odour as Sharon's perfume.

Sculptors have chisled thy monogram chastely,
  Clearly portraying its beautiful parts;
But in the Queen of the West, "thy dear birthplace,"
  Thou hast a tablet in long-loving hearts.

Gladly we bring thee a palm centifolian,
   Bright are its petals of redolent flowers,
Culled from the Eden of love's own valerian,
   Sent from empyrean amaranth bowers.

Genius e'er found the a " generous Southey,"
   Guarding the lamp which the muses had fired,
Soothing the heart of the pale " martyr student,"
   Blessing thy name ere he meekly expired.

Friend of humanity, shall we forget thee ?
   Living to bless while thy mission was done ?
Never, no never, while life hath pulsation,
   Take our hearts' token for victories won.

Fragrant with roses this Wreath Centenarian,
   Gratitude's tribute, the festoon of love ;
Fitly bestowed for the deeds of our SOUTHEY,
   Written in letters of mercy above.

SEEK OUT THE NEEDY.

SEEK out the needy—these must be cared for
   In the dark alleys and slums ;
While they are helpless, they must be sought for—
   Hunger the lone one benumbs.

Seek out the needy, helplessly lying,
   In the drear attic are they ;
Some of them friendless, some of them dying,
   Will you go help them to-day ?

THE WONDERFUL AGE WE LIVE IN.

E have much that is bringing good folk surprise,
  In this beautiful world of ours—
    That is finding employ for the mind and eyes,
And a wonderful stretch for the powers.
We are so progressing in culture and art,
  In business are up to the chin,
With keen competition in places of mart—
  What a wonderful age we live in !

'Tis thought we are living a little too fast,
  And working the same, I declare ;
And some people wonder how long it will last—
  It seems to be passing compare.
It used to be slowly and surely, 'tis said,
  But now it is bluster and grin ;
'Tis hurry and scurry with hands and with head,
  In the wonderful age we live in !

What use is it making the blankets and shoes,
  With all this commotion and cry ?
These things, though much needed, all seem of no use,
  Unless there is money to buy !
The money wants moving that's hoarded away—
  To lock it up seems such a sin ;
If it was kept moving 'twould bring a bright day
  To the wonderful age we live in !

There is not a home in this beautiful land
  But might be well furnished, I know ;
Not a child or a wife but what might command
  Good clothing and comfort below.
There is plenty to do it, if money would move,
  And I cannot but think it's a sin
That this does not circulate in its right grove,
  In the wonderful age we live in !

COOK'S FOLLY.

PART I.

St. Vincent's Rocks—A noted Mansion, with its lofty Tower—Beautiful Surroundings—Lady Cook in Contemplation—Strange Gipsy Encounter, and its Results.

NEAR grand St. Vincent's rocky height,
    Where loved Cliftonia's blending light
        Gives fairy land reflection,
There stands a noted mansion high,
With turret pointing to the sky,
        A symbol of affection !

It was not built, as some suppose,
A safety tower from inland foes,
    Or pirates from the ocean ;
It boasts a legendary fame,
Enshrine's a loving parent's name,
    And filial devotion.

This turret, clad in ivy green,
From hills and valleys may be seen,
    'Mid shady sylvan splendour ;
And though COOK's FOLLY it is named,
From men of wisdom it hath claimed
    A tribute true and tender.

For where this tower meets the eye
The village swains and maidens sigh,
    While grandsires tell its story :
Relate the cruel fate of one—
A noble heir and only son—
    His father's pride and glory.

They in amaze declare it true,
The plaintive legend long review—
    For young and old believe it ;
We've heard them state, with bated breath,
How brave young Walter met his death,
    While many mourn and grieve it.

That cruel fate could thus deprive
A lovely boy of blooming life,
    May savour strong of fiction ;
But we will now in simple verse
This tale mysterious rehearse,
    And challenge contradiction.

'Tis near three hundred years ago,
That one Sir MAURICE COOK, we know,
   With much inherent pleasure,
Brought to a mansion's calm repose,
Near where the placid Avon flows,
   His lady bride and treasure.

This mansion had surroundings rare,
With charming walks beyond compare,
   And beauty scenes inspiring ;
For there, in peaceful glen and dale,
Were themes for many a fairy tale,
   All worthy of admiring.

His lady love, 'tis said, one day,
Near eventide, in pleasant May,
   Was walking at her leisure
Within a calm sequester'd shade,
In this retreat by nature made,
   With contemplative pleasure.

She walked alone without annoy,
And found a pure instinctive joy,
   Some sweetly thrilling feeling ;
It came like balmy zephyr breeze,
From o'er the welcome saline seas,
   With magic power of healing,

Her mind thus chain'd by pleasing thought
Of bliss to come, true rapture brought
   Amid those beauties vernal ;
For she in that retired alcove
Was musing of another love,
   The pure and good maternal.

This lady had inherent joy,
All free from faithless vow alloy,
 And jealousy's reflection ;
For she was soon a pledge to give
To him for whom she then did live,
 Of mutual affection.

She wandered through this woodland vale,
And thought the rich and charming dale
 Was free from all intrusion :
When, lo ! before her she did scan
A stranger from the gipsy clan,
 In this renowned seclusion.

How he, this outcast, dar'd to rove
Within the precincts of that grove,
 Was past her comprehension ;
She could not fully understand—
Was it a friend or foe at hand,
 Or, what was his intention ?

She started with a strange surprise,
For his now fascinating eyes—
 With sloey blackness shining—
Were fixed on her with some intent,
As though he were on mischief bent,
 Some daring deed designing.

But fears from this were soon allay'd,
For he in pleading accents prayed
 That she would yield to pity,
And furnish him with some relief :
He came with heavy pressing grief
 From old Bristowa's city.

She listened to his plaintive strain,
And thought perchance 'twas hunger pain
    Which tempted this intrusion ;
So in his hand without delay
She placed a coin that noted day,
    To quell her own confusion.

He took the proferr'd boon, 'tis true,
As though it were his rightful due,
    Then said in tone commanding,—
" 'Tis not enough. I must have more
From your well-furnished wealthy store—
    Now yield to my demanding !"

This bold demeanour of the man
All rules of etiquette outran,
    And needed a reminder ;
To check his seeming disrespect,
So that he might on it reflect,
    He had this trite rejoinder :

"What," said the lady, "art thou bent
To choose thy terms ?—pray be content,
    And cease this molestation :
One coin will buy thee needful food,
Be thankful for a present good,
    In this thy vagrant station."

" Alas ! " the stranger then replied,
While he approached the lady's side
    In suppliant condition :
" It is not food I ask to save
This wretched body from the grave,—
    Mine is another mission.

The fruits and herbs from nature's field —
These food for me abundant yield,
    I take them at my leisure !
And, like the thirsty dove and rook,
Drink from the crystal water brook,
    Fearless of man's displeasure.

But I will not your patience tire,
I crave for alms with strong desire ;
    And, though a foe may fear me,
You need not doubt me, lady fair ;
For I can tell you secrets rare,
    And true, if you will hear me.

Pray do not scorn my searchings deep.—
These sunken eyes long vigil keep.
    When man is rapt in slumber ;
And hear it, lady, in surprise,
I can most clearly read the skies,
    While stars I truly number.

The fates of men I trace them well,
Their planets rule and orbits tell,
    Pourtray such wondrous musing ;
The horn book to each scholar rare
May with my skill alone compare
    By its familiar using."

" What art thou," said the lady, " then ?
Astrologer to maids and men—
    Is this thy true vocation ?
To wander through earth's changing dell,
A secret future to foretell,
    To high and low in station ? "

" I can do this," he fearless cried ;
" And it is now my boast and pride,
　　If you will hear my story.
When Egypt's pyramids stood high,
That was my land of liberty,
　　Our heritage and glory.

But Israel's band—defiant, strong—
Vowed that our soothsayers ere long
　　Should perish in confusion ;
Their boasting thus was all in vain,
For they are scattered now in pain
　　By Judah's blind delusion.

They bend and cringe to other laws,
All helpless for their country's cause,
　　With branded malediction ;
We cringe to none, but stand alone,
Stern in a steadfastness our own,
　　The right of long conviction."

" Suppose I grant you your request
In this appeal, so urgent prest,—
　　I ask because I choose it ;
Pray tell me, ere I further go,
Of your intent I wish to know
　　How you intend to use it."

" The question, lady, you propose
I'll answer, but you may suppose
　　I deem it a transgression ;
And quite uncourteous thus to press
A son of Egypt in distress
　　To make to you confession.

Q

The cunning craftsman in his trade,
Would he have labour be repaid
   And shun all vex'd enthralling,
Cannot dispense with reason's rules,
Or toil with worthless broken tools,
   To grace his honest calling.

My tools are broken, lady fair,
It is for these I seek repair,
   For they have long been needing :
Please aid me now to pay the price,
Bestow a crown—this will suffice :
   Do heed my earnest pleading."

She listened to his plaintive tale,
All powerful in that woodland vale :
   And this unique communing
Brought yielding to his strange demand—
She placed the coin within his hand,
   To crown his importuning.

" I now have granted your request,"
She said ; and then this question press'd
   Upon his forced attention,—
"I here would ask from you a boon :
Give me a specimen, and soon,
   Of your renowned pretension."

" Pray to what purpose," said the man,
" My lady, would you have me scan
   Futurity's dread meaning?
Sure destiny runs sweeping on,
Long after our short life hath gone,
   Without an intervening.

This rushing and resistless tide
Mocks all the schemes of human pride,
    With knowledge all prevailing ;
Man cannot stem it by his will,
It onward flows for good and ill,
    'Mid joy and much bewailing."

" You will not profit by your trade,"
The lady then abruptly said,
    " If with such conversation
You treat those customers who come
To seek advice from you at home,
    'Tis such crude revelation "

" It is not for the sake of gold
I labour nightly in the cold,
    In my choice occupation.
I am alone upon the earth,
With none to love, and from my birth
    An outcast from our nation.

I've mixed not with the world of late,
Lest I should the deceiver hate,
    For its deluding madness ;
The present it is naught to me,
I commune with the spirits free
    That soar in land of gladness.

The glowing stars are now my home,
Historians of time to come,
    These bring me inward pleasure :
I gaze on them with raptured mind,
And in those orbs wise lessons find,
    More dear than wordly treasure.

The foolish sometimes come to me,
Demanding long some proof to see
 Of my star ruling powers ;
And then sometimes I gratify
Their childish curiosity,
 To wile away the hours."

" Well," said the lady, " I will lie
Under such imputation ; try—
 And give me, free from fiction,
The true and certain fate of one,
My unborn babe, perchance a son—
 I challenge thy prediction."

" You have obliged me," said the man,
" And I its horoscope will scan—
 But this I wish to mention,
Whene'er the babe doth see the light,
The moment note, by day or night,
 And you shall have attention.

I'll come again some early morn,
Or night, whene'er the child is born,
 And give its fate in writing ;
I cannot stay, for see, the stars,
Bright Jupiter and smiling Mars,
 My studies are inviting,"

Then with a bound, in hurried pace
And lightened heart, he left the place,
 With glowing exultation ;
While she returned, for night was come,
Regaining soon her stately home,
 In thoughtful meditation.

PART II.

Merry pealing Bells—Birth of a Noble Heir—Disclosures to Sir Maurice Cook : Astonishment, Consultation, and unexpected Surprise—A strange Visitor : Directions and Promises.

THE clamorous sound of merry bells,
Within a week—the legend tells—
   Was heard in sweet expansion :
Announcing to the vassals there
Sir Maurice Cook had now a heir
   To grace his noble mansion.

This known event that morning-tide
Was hailed with eager joy and pride ;
   The lady's hour of sadness
Had fled like transient mist away,
For wealthy friends came, blithe and gay,
   To fill the hall with gladness.

'Twas then she felt she must reveal
The secret of her woe or weal,
   In what was so surprising ;
And faithfully the scene describe
With him from out the gipsy tribe,
   And have her love's advising.

He listened, and in much surprise,
With wonderment in heart and eyes,
   At this strange revelation ;
And knew not who the man could be,
To hold such a strange colloquy
   With one above his station.

Then both some time, with good intent,
In a reflective converse spent,
    Which led to wise resolving—
How they might find a certain clue
To this mysterious interview,
    And give the problem solving.

And while they thought this matter o'er,
A pealing knocking at the door
    Was heard in loud decision :
While to their room, with some presage,
Their ruddy, ready waiting page,
    Came asking for admission.

He said, "Sir Maurice, please to know
You're wanted in the hall below—
    A gipsy man is waiting ;
This urgent message sends by me,
He wishes you at once to see,
    And give you some relating."

The page's voice and quick retreat
Soon brought Sir Maurice to his feet,
    He rightly understanding :
Then hurried o'er the chamber floor,
Pass'd by its richly pannell'd door,
    And reached his study landing.

'Twas there he found, against his will,
A stranger garbed *en-deshabille,*
    Devoid of fear enhances :
His hair and eyes were raven black,
And he displayed a clever knack
    Of braving circumstances.

" I'm here, Sir Maurice," said the man,
" Your infant's horoscope to scan,—
    I promised this your lady ;
I met her, as you now must know,
Within the vale some days ago,
    Beneath the cedars shady.

And when this morn I heard the bells
Send silver notes through woodland dells,
    I knew by merry pealing
Your lady's sorrow must have passed,
That you had found true joy at last—
    A parent's gladsome feeling.

And now I wish you to relate
The hour and momentary date,
    If you have no objection ;
The birthtime of your new-born heir,
All this please truthfully declare
    For my mature inspection.

You need not have undue alarm,
I claim no power the boy to harm,
    Or fill your breast with sorrow ;
But will perform the vow I made,
Your infant's destiny to read,
    And you shall know to-morrow."

Sir Maurice then, without ado,
Soon furnished what he wished to know,
    Gave dates for his divining :
And this bold gipsy went that night
From thence, while stars were twinkling bright,
    And lunar moonbeams shining.

PART III.

Shrine of St. Vincent—The Magician at Midnight—Mysterious Scroll, and
its contents—Strange forebodings—Filial devotion—Death of Lady Cook—Dark
Clouds again—A Tower rising—Cook's Folly.

HE morrow's sun's last golden ray
Was kissing fair departing day,
  In rapturous exciting ;
While o'er the downs with rapid stride
A traveller, in latent pride,
  Was seen with scroll of writing.

He passed in haste St. Vincent's shrine,
Regardless of the great divine,
  Intent on duty's calling ;
For he had yet some way to go,
And cross the ravine far below,
  With night shades quickly falling

He reached the hall, though jaded then,
Just as the convent bell struck ten,
  With destiny's indictment ;
When, lo ! Sir Maurice Cook did wait
All anxious, near the entrance gate,
  In feverish excitement.

" I come at last," said Egypt's son,
" But cannot stay,—my work is done—
  Here, read *this* at your leisure ;
It will your new born's future tell,
Go, ponder now its secrets well,
  It may bring *grief* or pleasure."

Thus saying, he with rapid flight
Departed 'mid the shades of night,
    To give no more intrusion ;
And then Sir Maurice closed the door,
Intent to scan the writing o'er
    In privileged seclusion.

He trimm'd the lamp and waning fire,
For he could not to rest retire
    With doubtful intervening ;
And thus alone within the hall
He opened wide the written scroll,
    To know its hidden meaning.

" Full twentie tymes shall Avon's pryde
(He read) in chains of ice be tyed,
    All glystening with brightness ;
And twentie tymes the wudes of Leigh
Shall wave their braunches merrylie ;
    With true sylvan politeness.

In sprynge they shall burst forth in graie,
And dance in summer's scorchynge ray,
    With rare fantastic gladness ;
And twentie tymes shall autumn's frowne
Wythere their grene to sombre broune,
    And bring them all to sadness.

'Till then the childe of yesterdaie,
Shall laugh the happie hours awaie,
    Nor wish for their returning :
That peryod past, another sunne
Shall not his annual journie runne,
    Ere thou hast pungent mourning.

For then a secrete sylente foe
Shall strike thy boy a deadlie blow,
 In that sad year of dangers ;
A cruel death his fate shall be,
Seek not to change his destinie,
 For fate permits no changes."

The Knight read this with eager eye,
Yet could not see the reason *why*
 This evil was impending ;
Resolving never to unfold
To Lady Cook, for love or gold,
 A secret so heartrending.

He tried to think the man he'd seen
Had long a rank impostor been,
 Through forest woodland straying :
For pelf alone to lead astray
The simple found upon his way,
 By this profess'd soothsaying.

For when his lady wished to know,
And prayed Sir Maurice to bestow
 Some favoured information
Which he had recently obtained,
Tell what the gipsy scroll contained
 Of her babe's future station,—

He told her with a forcèd smile,
Although his saddened heart the while
 Endorsed not *this* assertion ;
The man a vile impostor was,
A cheat from the low vagrant class,
 Who wrote for his diversion.

But yet, alas ! he had some fears,
Which haunted him in coming years,
   This scroll was not a fiction ;
For in the age in which he lived
Astrology was much believed,
   With fervent heart conviction.

And he determined soon to find
Its meaning out with earnest mind,
   Whene'er his will inclined it ;
So placed the scroll, as hidden lore,
Within a secret escritoire,
   Where none but he could find it.

The baby boy of this loved pair
Grew up in health and beauty fair,
   His parents' hearts delighting ;
And though with other pleasures blest,
This treasure was their brightest, best—
   With promise all inviting.

For oft Sir Maurice did declare
His large estates were rich and rare,
   And crowning his endeavour ;
Posterity would find his name
Now handed down in worthy fame,
   Through his own heirs, for ever.

He doted on this darling boy,
The sum and substance of his joy,
   Each daily bliss enhancing ;
Anticipating every need,
From cares his youthful mind was freed,
   In life's pathway advancing.

And yet, though strange it may appear,
The knight soon had inherent fear,
    His anxious bosom thrilling ;
That in some future day or night
The writing of the gipsy might
    Result in true fulfilling.

This feeling, with its pungent smart,
But served to bind him to his heart
    With ties of strong affection ;
He scarce could bear him from his sight,
The boy was now his chief delight,
    His own true love's reflection.

While time revolved, to his bright home
He had two welcome daughters come,
    To grace his hall and table ;
But these, though loved, could not beguile—
All blandishment and ready smile
    Were vain from Rose or Mabel.

Whate'er a father's purse could buy,
Or ingenuity supply,
    Was furnished *for his using ;*
A graceful boat with glowing pride
Was moor'd along the Avon side,
    That he might have amusing.

And through his boyhood's sunny days
Some hired minstrels sang his praise
    At every festal meeting ;
Whene'er they met for gladsome song
Young Walter's name was toasted long,
    With jubilantic greeting.

In chase, Sir Maurice, full of pride,
Would have him mounted by his side,
    The very woodlands ringing
With sound of merry huntsman's horn,
And tally ho ! at early morn,
    Good news of Reynard bringing.

Then when at night the sport was o'er,
And huntsmen coming from the moor,
    They thrilled with glowing pleasure
To see brave Walter onward push,
In triumph bearing Reynard's brush,
    His own acquired treasure.

And when he hied with dog and gun,
When shooting season had begun,
    His company, uniting,
Would stand aside to give him fame,
And let him bag the choicest game,
    To his intense delighting.

But there are clouds in every sky,
And sorrows for the low and high,
    To rich and poor repelling :
And these Sir Maurice did descry,
With his fond daughters and his boy,
    Now hanging o'er their dwelling.

For she who loved them ardently
Was fast approaching, they could see,
    The end of all the living ;
And from her bed of waiting death
They heard her faltering, failing breath,
    Love's valediction giving.

This sad bereave Sir Maurice bore,
Though long his loss he did deplore,
  And yet it had a tending
To make him feel with anxious mind
For that lov'd son she'd left behind,
  A double care depending.

'Twas then he purpos'd in his mind
His future life should action find
  To save his son from danger ;
For eighteen years had passed away
Since he, on that eventful day,
  Had seen the gipsy stranger.

And he had plans devised of late,
Which if matured on his estate
  He thought might bring confusion ;
Would aid to foil and stultify
The proud Egyptian's prophecy,
  And prove it a delusion.

This settled, he his steward sent,
Gave building plans of his intent,
  Investing him with power :
To have erected near his home
A spherical rotunda dome,
  With castellated tower.

The style of this peculiar place
Brought wonderment in every face,
  While many wish'd instruction ;
They yearned to know the true wherefore
Of its strong walls and single door,
  So strange in their construction.

The builder could no answer find
To satisfy the craving mind
    Of every passing stranger;
Some thought it was for time of need,
(For all was mystery indeed,)
    A hiding place from danger.

The knowing class who went that way
Had often very much to say,
    When they were very jolly;
And one who saw himself allwise,
But was not so in wisdom's eyes,
    Then named it old Cook's Folly.

PART IV.

The Tower finished—Strange building—Sir Maurice and his Son—Explanation—Reasoning and acquiescence—Walter's Soliloquy—Sisterly affection.

TWO fleeting years had nearly gone
    Before the finishing top stone
      Was placed on this high tower;
But now it had completed form,
And bade defiance to the storm,
    In winter's darkest hour.

'Twas then Sir Maurice wisely thought
He as a filial duty ought,
    Without delay, to mention
To his loved son the reason why
This turret pointed to the sky;
    And tell him his intention.

He sent for him in pleasant May,
The morn of *his last* natal day,
  To wish him joy and plenty ;
And let him see the scroll of fate,
Its hidden mystery relate,—
  For Walter's age was twenty.

And in his study's calm retreat
Sir Maurice sat his heir to greet,
  While from its secret hiding
He took the written gipsy scroll,
Whose contents pain'd his very soul,
  The whole to him confiding.

Young Walter listened to his sire,
Until Sir Maurice, by desire,
  Removed the strange inditing ;
He said he thought it was a ruse,
And worthy only of abuse,
  Such worthless, gipsy writing.

He had no doubt Sir Maurice meant
Him well in this his good intent,
  But he might have reliance ;
He could not bring his mind to try
And live so near the cloudy sky,
  In giving death defiance.

What would his boon companions say,
To find him absent every day
  From their convivial meeting ;
The thoughts of this he could not bear,
They could not find him hid up there,
  To give him welcome greeting.

His merry friends could join the chase,
Or leap the fence with gallant grace,
    All dauntless and unfearing ;
But he must then contented be
These daring feats alone to see,
    A prison tower sharing.

The trilling lark at opening day
Could rise and sing sweet roundelay,
    On freedom's soaring pinion ;
And why should he deprivèd be
Of that sweet boon called liberty,
    Because of man's opinion ?

The sea gull passing swiftly o'er,
To reach the waiting ocean shore,
    Near to the Avon's flowing ;
Could fly all fetterless and free,
And pluck from out the briny sea
    The silver fish a-glowing.

But he, forsooth, in blooming health,
The heir to rich estate and wealth,
    Must live in lone seclusion ;
Because a son of Egypt had
Once tried to make his father sad,
    By writing such delusion.

Sir Maurice heard his son's address,
Delivered with a firm express,
    And ardent telling power ;
Then tried to satisfy his mind
That he would no discomfort find
    In that constructed tower.

R

It was for his dear Walter's good
This monument of safety stood,
　　Although amazement giving ;
To save from fate his threatened life,
He built it 'mid much din and strife,
　　Just to prolong his living.

It was a maxim in his day
That sons their parents should obey,
　　Let this have his reflection ;
And if he wished his father's peace
Through life's declining to increase,
　　Remove this raised objection.

Young Walter listened to his sire,
And ere to rest he did retire,
　　Right cheerfully consented ;
Determined he would nobly try,
No more his parent's will defy,
　　But make himself contented.

Next morning's sun right joyfully
Was gilding all the eastern sky,
　　With matchless, glowing beauty :
Apprising Walter Cook that day
He must his promised tribute pay,
　　Prepare himself for duty.

For time with him was not prolix,
And while the convent clock struck six—
　　The legend states the hour ;
He, with his sire's wish in view,
To outside friendships bade adieu,
　　And occupied the tower.

'Twas then there came foreboding pain,
While gazing on the wild domain,
    In solitude expressing ;
That he, though free from all molest,
Would miss the merry welcome jest,
    And this was so depressing.

He saw the gallant ships in pride
Come dancing with the swelling tide,
    Upon the Avon riding ;
Their pennants fluttering in the breeze,
With captains sitting at their ease,
    In pilots' skill confiding.

But he was there, and all alone,
Surrounded by a wall of stone,
    Defying time's resistance ;
While craggy rocks of sombre hue,
Uprearing to his searching view,
    Were looming in the distance.

These thoughts, accompanied by sighs,
Brought tears of anguish to his eyes,
    With much o'erwhelming sorrow—
That he would hear loud thunder shocks,
And fierce storms ringing through the rocks,
    In winter's stern to-morrow.

But kind Sir Maurice all the while
Made preparations to beguile
    His hours of gloomy sadness ;
He had the hired minstrel's song,
The grotesque morris dancers long,
    To give his Walter gladness.

His loving sisters, too, would come
From out their beautiful, bright home,
　　To give him joyful cheering ;
They sent him up their choicest flowers
To wile away the lagging hours,
　　And banish all his fearing.

Then while the seasons passed away,
They brought him dainties every day,
　　His basket well supplying ;
And he the treasures upward drew,
Well pleasing to his ready view,
　　For he had no denying.

Sir Maurice greeted him with joy,
And bade him not his hopes destroy,
　　The time was fast expiring ;
When he would come to them with glee,
In all the bliss of liberty,
　　Ennobling and inspiring.

PART V.

Secure and not secure—The Morning Song promised—Increasing Joys—
Last Request for the Night : One more Faggot—A Father's Fears—Walter's
Confidence—Bright Star—Good-night—Early Morn—Boding Sorrows—Love's
Appeal—No answer—Alarm—The Tower entered—Thrilling Discovery—
Walter dead—The deadly Viper seen—Overwhelming grief of Sir Maurice, and
the Prediction fulfilled.

ECURE beneath his parent's eye.
　　The days and months soon glided by,
　　　　With Walter's joy unceasing ;
But while the son was growing glad,
Sir Maurice Cook, the father, had
　　Anxieties increasing.

He knew the morn was drawing near
Which was to give him back his heir,
    Restore his household gladness ;
Or that prediction be fulfilled
The gipsy gave, which often filled
    His mind and heart with sadness.

On the preceding afternoon
Young Walter hailed the coming boon,
    In spirits high appearing ;
And from the lofty tower tried
To cheer his sire, with glowing pride
    He bade him have no fearing.

As night drew on his sisters came,
He loudly welcomed them by name,
    While they returned the greeting ;
They promised him with ready tongue
That they would wake him with a song
    At their next morning meeting.

And ere they left him for the night,
They asked him in the waning light
    If he was aught requiring ;
Could they send up the lofty tower
More comfort for the midnight hour—
    Had he both food and firing ?

He thank'd them for such kind regard
To him in his high prison ward,
    A sister's sphere adorning ;
Then told them with a brother's pride,
He thought his wants were well supplied
    With needful good till morning.

" But yet," said he, " I'm scarcely right,
The air feels chilly here to-night,
    I will the basket lower:
Please send me from the rocky cleft,
For I have little fuel left,
    One faggot up the tower."

They with *his last request* complied,
As they before, with vieing pride,
    All sisterly did cater ;
He thanked them for past favour grants,
And said he'd dip no more for wants,
    Like old maids did for water.

For such employment had no charm,
The work had wearied long his arm,
    But now it all was over ;
No longer he would fret or pout,
To-morrow's sun would find him out—
    A free and easy rover.

His sisters left him for the night,
With hopeful, blooming, true delight,
    To greet him in the morning ;
But yet Sir Maurice lingered near
The spot, as though portending fear
    Was on his spirit dawning.

He held long converse with his son,
Until the convent clock struck one,
    When Walter, long desiring,
Said to Sir Maurice's appeal,
" I will retire : I drowsy feel,
    Although the moon's inspiring,"

Then while he closed the window, said,
" Cheer up, dear father, raise your head,
  The stars are bright appearing ;
My fate star Mars, with much delight,
Looks smilingly on me to-night,
  With its fair silver cheering."

Sir Maurice lookèd up to see
The star of Walter's destiny
  In its resplendent shining ;
When, lo ! a dark spot came to mar
The beauty of the planet star,
  And give it woe divining.

He shuddered at this omen cloud
Appearing like a deadly shroud,
  To thwart his vigil keeping ;
Forbidding him to leave the spot,
It was a dire forget-me-not,
  To rob him of his sleeping.

For there he stay'd throughout the night,
Long waiting for the morning light,
  His breast with anguish burning;
He paced the court with rapid tread,
As though his reason long had fled
  To have no more returning.

Old Bristow's loud cathedral bell
Struck two, and like a funeral knell
  Its hollow tone came sounding ;
But yet Sir Maurice watched the tower,
Nor wearied in the lonely hour
  With gloominess surrounding.

At length the morning light's appear
Brought Walter's sisters running there,
    With merry song to cheer him ;
They called his name, he answered not,
One thought he had contrived this plot,
    But yet they could not hear him.

The youngest sister of the two
Cried, " Walter, come, this will not do,
    Our fears you are but courting ; "
And she Sir Maurice then addressed,
By saying " This is but a jest,
    I know he's only sporting."

'Twas then the father stood aghast,
Some thrilling tremor held him fast
    In its all potent power ;
And soon a servant, being taught,
A ladder from the coppice brought
    To scale the lofty tower,

He then ascended, and in haste,
For there was now no time to waste,
    The aged sire was weeping ;
And when he reached the window's height,
He shouted loudly in delight,
    " Sir Maurice, he is sleeping."

He heard his trusted servant's voice,
Yet that did not his heart rejoice,
    It made his spirit languish ;
For he desponding bow'd his head,
Then slowly murmur'd, " Walter's dead,
    And I a prey to anguish."

The servant quickly broke the glass,
And forced the casement from its place,
    While Walter's room he entered ;
And then Sir Maurice rushed to see
His boy, in frantic agony,
    On whom his hopes were centred.

They drew the curtains from his bed,
And found young Walter lying dead,
    As though he were but sleeping ;
His nightdress was all stain'd with blood,
While near him his loved father stood,
    In loud distressing weeping.

    For there a living viper clung
Around that boy, whom it had stung
    To death, and not retreated ;
From that last faggot it had crept,
And, while young Walter sweetly slept,
    The work of death completed.

Sir Maurice spent his days in grief,
Loved friends could give him no relief,
    His son and heir was killed ;
That gipsy's scroll which marred his bliss
Was burnt, for he had found that his
    PREDICTION WAS FULFILLED !

MORAL.

Parental Anxiety, Parental Affection, and Parental Duty.

AND now to this renown'd legend
    A moral *finale* we append,
        To benefit each nation ;
It is that parents high in sphere,
Or lowly birth, with offspring dear,
    May have consideration,—

That when they fain would build a tower,
To save their sons from danger's power,
    By polished education;
They all may show, by thoughtful care,
No deadly viper lurketh there
    To bring them degradation.

The age in which we live demands
This much at every parent's hands :
    All sons now need protection
From what is worse than fate's decree,
A sure and deadly enemy,
    And full of sore deception.

The foe is one to mind and soul,
It lurketh in the flowing bowl,
    Loved homes it maketh sadder ;
The book of Proverbs names it right,
'Tis ruby wine that sparkles bright,
    This stingeth like an adder.

Will thoughtful parents then declaim
Against this foe, our country's shame,
    It brings dire melancholy ;
If not, some day their homes may be,
For keen heartrending misery,
    Far worse than poor COOK's FOLLY.

SECRETS OF A YEAR.

THE POET AND WHISPERING ASPEN ON ST. VINCENT'S ROCKS : WHAT
THEY SAW, WHAT THEY THOUGHT, AND WHAT THEY SAID.

IT was piercing, cold November,
 And the leaves were falling fast ;
 Wintry winds, I well remember,
Blew with an appalling blast.

Standing in my path of duty,
 Near the noted woods of Leigh,
Gazing on their sylvan beauty,
 All enrapturing to see,

I was roused—my rapt attention
 Startled by some blasting shocks,
Near the Bridge of grand Suspension,
 Planted on St. Vincent's Rocks.

Pealing sounds from their vibration
 Woke me from my reverie,
Just in close approximation
 To a waving aspen tree.

There my eyes found strange inspection—
 For beneath its partial shade
Stood a poet in reflection,
 One by God and nature made.

His outflowing thoughts were winging
  To the tree above his head ;
While its falling leaves seemed bringing
  Answers to the words he said.

Seeing this, I drew quite near him,
  Sheltered by the rocky height,
Where I could distinctly hear him
  Speak, to my intense delight.

Some who saw him in this station
  On that cold November day
Might have thought from observation,
  He had better been away.

And they who knew not his mission
  Would have doubtless said, " How sad ; "
Pitied him in such condition—
  Thought him, by such conduct, mad.

He, to all this crude conclusion
  From the passing sneering foe,
Would have vowed 'twas their delusion—
  They were mad for thinking so.

He was there this bleak November,
  Life reviewing in the blast ;
Taking stock, I well remember,
  Calmly looking o'er the past.

For that tree while winds were blowing,
  Whispered in the poet's ear—
" What hast thou been doing, doing
  In the fleeting passing year ?

Tell me, for my long befriending :
    I have sheltered thee with pride,
With my green-clad branches bending,
    Through the lovely summertide.

Let me have a true narration,
    For what purpose thou dost live—
Some account of life's probation,
    Like a faithful steward, give."

HEARING this, the poet answered,
    In his own accustom'd way—
    " Graceful Aspen, hear my story ;
I have much I wish to say.

I was thinking in my quiet,
    When I saw thy sere leaves meet,
Disarranged, in seeming riot,
    On the greensward at my feet,—

Such is life : the bright leaf springeth
    In the blooming days of youth :
And through fairest summer bringeth
    Sylvan hopes to man, forsooth !

But when autumn winds are blowing,
    And the winter's drawing nigh,
Life's last season quickly going,
    And without a parting sigh,—

Then 'tis wise to have inquiring,
    While the feet are nearing home,
If the heart hath hope inspiring
    For a better life to come.

Had the field of my employment,
   In which I had toilèd hard,
Brought me true and pure enjoyment,
   That which hath the best reward.

And I pondered, in my musing,
   O'er the work I had begun—
Found, by clearer light infusing,
   Much could better have been done.

Yet a cheering voice within me
   Spake as with a trumpet blast—
' Persevere ; and if I win thee,
   I'll forgive thee for the past.

I am from Parnassus' mountain ;
   See ! I bring thee water pure !—
Drink it from the living fountain,
   And thy musings shall endure.

I have flowers for thee to furnish
   Garlands for our rising youth ;
Gems for riper years to burnish,
   From the precious mine of truth.

Rise to duty ! hear me crying !
   Now my pealing accents ring ;
Father Time is swiftly flying—
   And he has no leaden wing.'

Hearing this, my spirit, soaring,
   Cheerfully looked up to thee ;
Then I heard thy voice imploring,
   My beloved Aspen tree.

Wilt thou grant me patient hearing,
 If my story should be long?
Nay, I crave for some forbearing,
 Lest perchance I mar the song."

I WILL listen, never fear me,
 As a true unchanging friend;
And for thy regard to hear me,
 I will hear thee to the end.

I have watched, with heart elation,
 Thee throughout the passing year;
And I make asseveration,
 Thou hast naught from me to fear.

How I thank thee, lovely Aspen—
 Thee my heart shall ne'er forsake;
May the rocks thy roots are clasping
 Witness to the vow I make.

Long may they, while thou art shaking,
 Know, when feeling thy entwine,
I was observations making,
 While thou hast been making thine.

For when thy fair leaves were budding
 In the welcome opening spring,
And thy branches were bestudding
 Where the feathered songsters sing—

Then I came with expectation,
 'Neath thy shade with poem stand,
Fashioned, after meditation,
 With my own long-toiling hand.

And I deck'd it with effusions
    From my brain and trusty pen—
Placing there no vain delusions,
    Nothing that would injure men.

Leaves as bright as thine were showing
    Truths that might be understood,
In their varied colours glowing,
    Valued by the wise and good.

Yet the stranger did not know it,
    And would often turn aside ;
Some would not a thought bestow it,
    Showing a contemptuous pride.

Thou, I know, this winter morning,
    Did such rude behaviour see :
Was it right, this heartless scorning ?
    Tell me, truthful Aspen tree.

AS thou pleadest for an answer,
    I will give it thee, my son ;
    I beheld the necromancer
        Sporting at what thou hadst done.

But why trouble at this sneering ?
    It such minds may well befit ;
Thou from these need have no fearing ;
    They have not examined it.

All who sneer without inspection
    Have what reason ever dreads—
This I state from long reflection—
    Shallow minds and empty heads.

HUSH thee, Aspen ; how excited
    Thou hast suddenly become ;
    Thy strange tone has me affrighted—
    Softly speak, or else be dumb.

I can understand thy feeling—
    How thou o'er such conduct grieves,
When to reason's son appealing,
    In thy trembling, falling leaves.

But the world has not discovered,
    Yet, that trees and faithful pen
Evils can denounce, untroubled,
    Without evil thoughts to men.

Let us try to treat them kindly,
    Silver lining give the sky ;
Some may yet be sneering blindly—
    They'll be wiser by-and-by.

HOW I thank thee, thoughtful poet,
    And will treasure what I've heard ;
    I was foolish not to know it,
    As my branches have averred.

But I never can dissemble :
    When I view the wilful blind
Every leaf begins to tremble,
    Then I always speak my mind.

And I ever need excusing,
    For I'm but an aspen tree ;
This was not of my own choosing—
    Therefore, please to pardon me.

S

And when I, in conversation,
  Err—oh, pray do set me right;
Then I shall adorn my station,
  On St. Vincent's rocky height.

For I saw with sincere pity,
  When thou first for shelter came
From the outskirts of the city,
  Bringing lays of worthy fame,—

When the fair and bonnie lasses
  From their varied training schools,
Passing by here, and in masses,
  Subjected to certain rules,—

While they glanced at these productions,
  Looked askance at what you'd done,
Then I heard some loud instructions—
  "Ladies, ladies, please move on."

I once nearly said—"You snarlings,
  By my early opening bud,
There is naught to harm the darlings;
  Let them read—these themes are good."

Long I trembled, I remember,
  For one made so great a stir;
If it had but been September,
  I'd have thrown some leaves at her!

WAVING Aspen, how pugnacious
    You have recently become;
  Don't, I pray, be so ungracious
    To the ladies, when from home.

You must aim at giving pleasure,
   And enhance it day and night ;
This surpasses golden treasure :
   Learn and practise what is right.

For the cultured lady teacher
   Has a mission to fulfil ;
And, I pray, do not provoke her,
   Or attempt to thwart her will.

She, when with her pupils airing
   Near the noted woods of Leigh,
Has great need of long forbearing
   With a youthful progeny.

For their parents have commended
   Loving offspring to her care,
Wishing to have them defended
   From each hidden, hurtful snare.

And in this our age, abounding
   With productions from the press,
There is need of earnest caring,
   All the evil to suppress.

Now you see, my watchful Aspen,
   There's a change come o'er them all
And they bring their eager pupils
   Round this pure production stall.

They don't find one vulgar slander
   Lurking in the flowing rhymes—
Nothing that will ever pander
   To the lewdness of the times.

But they certainly discover
  Truths that may of service be
Unto these, while time is over,
  And throughout eternity.

Did you not, in summer season,
  When arrayed in your green dress,
See some ladies, blest with reason,
  Underneath your shadow press?

Near the poet's stall they listened
  To a teacher, well equipp'd—
Reading, while their young eyes glistened,
  From a written manuscript.

YES, that scene I well remember—
  It was in the month of May;
Brighter than this cold November—
  And I noted down the day.

For I thought the sky was clearing
  When I hailed the early dawn,
And beheld this group appearing
  On that welcome summer morn.

Long I listened to the lady;
  And my branches, full of glee,
Formed a canopy quite shady
  For the youthful band and thee.

She was reading what was written
  Of a Christian hero gone—
Brought from Africa, death smitten—
  Our immortal Livingstone!

Of the dying words he breathed
  Ere he entered life to come ;
Praying much at Muilala ;
  Saying, " I am going home."

How those young hearts were excited,
  I shall never more forget ;
His last words their minds delighted,
  And are in my memory yet.

I rejoiced with ardour glowing ;
  Long I blest that lady fair ;
And with my soft zephyrs blowing,
  Fanned those youthful listeners there.

Then I breathed a benediction
  On the happy group I knew ;
While my leaves, for love inscription,
  Sprinkled them with early dew.

BLESS thee, Aspen —how I love thee,
  Swaying on thy rocky bed ;
May thy branches, green above me,
  Flourish after I am dead.

And whene'er the passing stranger,
  From his distant home away—
Be he fearless ocean ranger,
  Or the comer for a day—

Passes underneath thy branches,
  And with joy looks up to thee,
Whisper welcome assurances—
  Say, " I am the the poet's tree.

He has gone, but I am growing,
  With my graceful boughs and stem ;
And I chant, when winds are blowing,
  My beloved's requiem."

HUSH ! I cannot bear this longer—
    We must not for seasons part ;
  Thou, perhaps, may be the stronger,
    For I am decayed in heart.

Old Boreas is so chiding,
  It has broken me some limbs ;
Two were snapt, at thee deriding,
  Once when thou wert writing hymns.

It was cruel—and thou lookèd
  Up to see its crashing strides ;
I suppose it felt rebuked,
  So blew off thy Christmastides.

Some have said the North Wind's frantic—
  Does this work by evil power ;
And I thought to see its antic—
  It was true that stormy hour.

For it scattered thy productions
  Far and wide upon the grass ;
While thou questioned its instructions,
  And its right to break thy glass.

Long I thought the fiend possessed it—
  Bade it sweep thy stand away ;
For thou dost not interest him
  In thy work, the people say.

I can understand it's trying
   Every means to thee molest ;
But why it is me defying.
   'Tis perplexing, at the best.

When I grow a little wiser
   I may know the reason why
That old roaring, loud surpriser,
   Comes in such mad revelry.

AY, beloved Aspen, truly
   That will long remembered be—
   When the rushing gale, unruly,
   Made sad work for thee and me.

Yet, although it came annoying,
   It has not been always so ;
When the zephyr notes were blowing,
   Then we did not say them " No."

For we here had joy together,
   Heard the thrush and linnet sing ;
When the May-bloom, like a feather,
   Flew and kissed departing spring.

While the chirping sparrows, standing
   On the many sheltered boughs,
Heard thee, with love's voice, commanding
   Them to pay their morning vows.

How we listened to their chanting,
   Heard them chirp their early lays—
With their little fledged ones, panting,
   Joining in the song of praise.

Then were men of commerce going
  To and fro beneath thy shade—
Telling of some joy or sorrow
  In the mysteries of trade.

And some hopeful pairs, united
  By a sanction from above,
Told that tale, so often plighted,
  In the mystery of love.

Then, my Aspen, we had pleasure :
  Let us long the thought retain ;
And if we but wait, my treasure,
  We may see fair spring again.

We can both rehearse, with gladness,
  Some good work that we have seen—
Yes, and done, to banish sadness,
  When the Downs were clad in green.

WELCOME, poet, I will hear thee
    Speak of this in cheering strain ;
  I rejoice thou art so near me,
    Giving me new life again.

Now give me some explanation,
  Ere I take my winter's rest,
Who that was in conversation
  With thee once, and by request ?

He appeared of noble station,
  I could see with ready ken :
From his bearing and behaviour,
  One of nature's gentlemen.

THOU art right, my Aspen treasure,
  I can never him forget;
There was something more than pleasure
  From this English baronet.

For he came that lovely morning,
  Glancing at my poem stand;
His true face betrayed no scorning,
  When he held some in his hand.

He then read, with thoughtful vision,
  And complacently he smiled
Over one called " Love's Decision,"
  Written by a poet's child.

It portrayed her first production,
  Penn'd as pure affection's proof;
Answer to a parent's question—
  If she did her father love.

When he had the sequel learned,
  This true English gentleman
Said the writer meed had earned
  For her touching, tender strain.

Then he read her father's rhyming—
  Came to see him day by day,
And to give him farewell greeting
  Just before he went away.

Bade him persevere in writing,—
  He had bright example set:
What he wrote was pure inditing,
  And his path would open yet.

Favoured Aspen, dost thou hear me ?
This I state with latent pride :
It is true as thou art near me
On this rocky mountain side.

But his name I will not mention,
It is one beyond dispute ;
And deserving our attention
As an Author's of repute.

GLAD I am to hear thee, poet :
Such rehearsal gives me joy ;
Take my blessing, long enjoy it,
And thy talents well employ.

Rest assured I will repay thee
For thus heeding my appeal ;
Yet there's something more, I pray thee,
For my pleasure now reveal.

It is this : while I was shady,
In the early summertide,
Thou wer't listening to a lady,
Long in converse at thy side.

What had she so good to tell thee ?
For I saw, while she did speak,
Something from within impel thee,
Yielding pleasure for the week.

I AM glad, my wise inspector,
Thou wert watching us so keen ;
That good lady—Heaven protect her !—
Gave me bliss and joy serene.

She was speaking at her leisure ;
  And that gladsome day she told
Me what gave my heart true pleasure,
  More than richest mine of gold.

It was something from a poem
  Written when a mind was mild,
Of a darling Eva's triumph,
  Fair Cliftonia's dying child :

How she was the means of bringing
  Her loved parents to her side,
Pleading by her pure love clinging,
  Until both were reconciled.

And while she her home was leaving,
  Blessèd both that parting day,
When like breath of summer evening
  This fair angel passed away.

Long within a home of beauty,
  As one means to gain right ends,
This true lady did her duty,
  Reading it to many friends.

Said they heard it with attention —
  Treasuring the pleasing lore—
Wishing then the hand that penn'd it
  Soon would write a many more.

And when she at length discovered
  He who brought it forth was there,
All false etiquette she spurned,
  Thanking him with heart sincere

Then he told her with emotion
    That love's victory unfurl'd,
Had in numbers cross'd the ocean,
    Given blessing to the world.

It had moved the heart of mothers,
    While from sin restraining men ;
But the glory was another's—
    Man was but His Maker's pen.

Now, my guardian, I have told thee
    Why that lady came to me ;
May she live, to long behold thee
    In thy graceful symmetry.

I ASSURE thee, welcome poet,
    I have heard this with delight ;
And that many more may know it—
    Our long conversation write.

For I have so much to ask thee—
    Many questions great and small ;
And although no wish to task thee,
    I could not remember all.

GLADLY will I do thy bidding—
    I was never deem'd a lout ;
And I would the world be ridding
    Of what it can do without.

Yet, my Aspen, thou well knoweth
    What a world we're living in,
And what way the wind oft bloweth
    When we strive the right to win.

What strange eyes we have beholding,
   And what varied states of mind ;
While we try, by truth unfolding,
   To instruct the seeming blind.

How our motives are impugned,
   We with egotism charged ;
By some critics roughly pruned,
   Vowing we are too enlarged.

WHAT hast thou to do with critics?
     Poet, listen unto me :
   I know crusty paralytics
     Cannot crush or frighten thee.

Hear me, I am now appealing :
   Though I'm not in beauty drest :
Write regardless of such feeling,
   Do thy duty—that is best.

If thy Master kept on braving
   Cynic's sneer and make believes,
Long endured the rabble raving
   In a noted den of thieves,—

Why should thou of lower station
   Dread the piercing satire pen—
Polish'd shafts of self-inflation,
   Shot by worldly wisdom men ?

Lay aside this squeamish fearing,
   And to please thy Master try ;
If the carpers are appearing,
   They will vanish by-and-bye.

THANK thee, Aspen, thou art growing
　　Into a true wisdom tree ;
If we live, there is no knowing
　　What may come from thee and me.

And as thou art not yet tired
　　Of my varied flowing strain,
I will do as thou desired,
　　Hasten to my theme again.

Only it is not quite pleasant,
　　After years of toiling pen,
To endure such inconsistent
　　Treatment from unthinking men.

They had better, my inciter,
　　For a time their judgment stay ;
And the motives of the writer
　　Leave until the reckoning day.

He and his good Elder Brother
　　Then will free their mind from fears ;
They have understood each other
　　Well for very many years.

His frail vessel holds the treasure
　　But in trust, till life is gone ;
And though both now work together,
　　All the glory's due to One.

Every work of man's existence,
　　He knows well, is incomplete ;
And, that his may find acceptance,
　　Lays it at the Master's feet.

Tell them this, I do implore thee —
  It may give them peace at home,
Save them trying much to bore thee
  And thy son for years to come.

NOW I'm glad at this recital :
    I have wondered why thy mind,
  Once appearing so triumphal,
    Seem'd uncertain as the wind.

It was this that thee distressed—
  But thou never need to quake ;
Thou hast read that they are blessed,
  Suffering for thy Master's sake.

Take thee heart, I will not tease thee,
  But through life to thee be true ;
If I cannot always please thee,
  I will always try to do.

Now then, while the sky is clearing,
  May I here inquire from thee,
Who thou wert so gladly hearing
  Once beneath thy Aspen tree ?

He I mean, that graceful stranger—
  Dark, yet in his manners bland—
Seemingly had pass'd through danger,
  Coming from a foreign land.

He was rapt in meditation,
  Like a man enduring loss;
Yet in peaceful contemplation,
  As a herald of the cross.

Long he gazed on thy productions,
  Read them to himself awhile;
And when thou convey'd instructions,
  Gave a pleasant, welcome smile.

OH, I well remember seeing
    Him on that auspicious day;
  He was from a mission station
    On the Coast of Africa.

He was toiling for the Master,
  Though he'd studied for the law;
But was now a Christian pastor,
  Since the clearer light he saw.

He related through what trials
  He had passed—what sorrows had,
From the world's vindictive phials,
  Pour'd out to make him sad.

Yet amid this proud resistance,
  Which to check him ever strove,
He had sweet and blest assurance
  Sent to soothe him from above,

Then he tried to give me cheering
  In the work of my employ—
Told me what I then was sowing
  Would bring harvest home of joy.

Bade me use the pen in writing
  Themes like these and persevere;
They would give true heart delighting
  In this world of grief and care.

Then he made a choice selection,
　　Giving me his friendly hand ;
And with a " God speed you, brother."
　　Started for a foreign land.

Words like these sent fervour glowing
　　Through my throbbing, beating heart ;
It was full to overflowing,
　　While I grieved with him to part.

And I came to this conclusion—
　　Just imparted from above—
Sneering men may bring confusion ;
　　But give me the men of love.

THOU art right ; I'm glad to hear thee
　　　Thus conclude this pleasing lay :
　　　It is true, for I was near thee
　　　　On that lovely summer's day.

And I saw another visit
　　Thou had'st from some gentlemen :
Two there were ; to be explicit,
　　Photograph these with thy pen.

One seemed very shrewd and knowing —
　　Taking thee at once to task—
As though he was then bestowing
　　Favour—anything to ask

From a man of thy calibre,
　　Yet he wished an answer then—
Quite forgetting, as a neighbour,
　　Infant poets are not men.

T

I was trembling with emotion,
　And my tears came falling down:
For there was so much commotion,
　From this man of some renown.

What was his demand that morning?
　From thy heart an answer give;
For he seemed to ask in scorning
　Something strange, I could perceive.

OH, I well remember, Aspen,
　　This, and answer for thy sake—
　If I'm not thy patience taxing—
　　Why that stranger made me quake.

Stranger? Nay, he's not a stranger,
　Soon I plainly understood;
But his name I would not mention
　To thy spring-time's early bud.

Yet he made report so thrilling—
　Like a cannon, to be sure;
And, though it was far from killing,
　I had something to endure.

For the friend who stood beside him
　Thought he could a liner poke;
And, in his known skill confiding,
　Heard him thus the rhymer joke—

" Who," said he " made you a poet?
　Pray relate before I go:
Can you answer? Give, then—do it
　Now; for I do wish to know."

"As you've askèd me the question,"
  Said the bard, " I'll answer give :
Take it with you for digestion,
  It may serve you while you live.

The Almighty thus endowed me,
  And in this I do not err.
Now, please, will you deign to tell me
  Who made you a Canon, sir ? "

Hadst thou seen him, lovely Aspen,
  Very soon recoiling back,
When he had not aimèd surely,
  For he did precision lack.

Quickly turning from the warfare,
  Stayed no more to sneer and scoff ;
And though he did not explode there,
  He immediately went off.

Showing by his quick retreating
  What the wise may truly see—
Men sometimes have had defeati ng
  With infallibility.

Now I've given thee relation
  Of that scene in summertide,
With its varied derivation
  On St. Vincent's mountain side.

There are storms to mar our sunshine
  In the changing path of life ;
And mankind still hold a carbine—
  Some for peace, and some for strife.

HAT is true, and needs attention
    In this busy world of ours ;
For this age of much pretension
    Grows its weeds as well as flowers.

Yet, if we, by earnest toiling,
    Can the lovely flowers retain,
Live and work for evil spoiling,
    We shall not have lived in vain.

HANK thee, Aspen, for this lesson ;
    I will bear it in my mind :
Now I ask thy parting blessing,
    For I feel the piercing wind.

TAY a little longer, poet,
    On my rocky mountain steep ;
And I will with joy bestow it,
    Ere I take my winter's sleep.

This frail life is so uncertain -
    We may never meet again ;
And more scenes I wish describing,
    That I may more knowledge gain.

I should like to hear the story
    Of a scene I viewed with pride,
When a gentleman and lady
    Halted here in Whitsuntide.

Looking o'er the poem-writing,
    Asking questions loud and long—
Some that gave thee much delighting,
    Answering with ready tongue.

Thou must well these two remember,
   For they bought thy varied rhymes,
And they read the joint memoriams
   Of two eminent Divines.

YES; I do remember having
   Converse with that loving pair ;
But I cannot truly tell thee
   Whence they came, or who they were.

For I wanted much to know them—
   Yet they kept the news from me ;
And what I would fain now show them
   I will tell my Aspen tree.

I discovered, by appealing,
   They were worthy of true fame—
Having Christian life revealing,
   More than having Christian name.

For at parting one declared
   He, like me, had toiled long ;
And while we our notes compared,
   I found him a son of song.

Then he told me, with much pleasure,
   How one Sabbath he was blest,
When he came for quiet leisure
   Near the city of the west.

Entering one hallowed temple—
   Not for fashion's sake, or whims—
He had heard the people singing
   One of his own written hymns.

Then he wished me Heaven's blessing,
   Bidding me with joy toil on ;
Said the Master would reward me
   When the Master's work was done.

Then he said—" I print and publish
   Many works from day to day ;
Providence with means hath blessed me,
   And I give my themes away.

Never mind my name or station ;
   Let us both with earnest love
Labour for man's elevation
   Until we shall meet above.

Now then, Aspen, I have given
   One more true relation here ;
And to please thee I have striven,
   But shall weary thee, I fear.

NAY, nay, poet—never fear thee,
   Thou may yet thy themes prolong ;
   I am well content to hear thee,
   And will listen to thy song.

For I see so many coming
   Now to view thy rhyming stand,
I conclude it is receiving
   Some attention in the land.

One especially came near thee,
   When bright nature's tints were seen,
Pencilling the woods of Leigh
   With their amber, gold, and green.

And he stayed awhile entranced,
　Marking what thy hand had done—
Reading there, with joy enhanced,
　In the brightness of the sun.

Who was he ?—pray tell me, poet ;
　I have seen him day by day
Give thee greeting—thou must know it—
　When he passes by this way.

He had very thoughtful bearing ;
　And I saw, upon the whole,
When he for thy health was caring,
　That he had a noble soul.

And I blest him for this labour
　More than any tongue can tell,
For I saw he loved his neighbour—
　This I do remember well.

I should like to hear thee give me
　Some account of this kind man ;
Do proceed while I am with thee,
　Ere my yearly course is ran.

For yon silver bells are ringing
　The decadence of the year,
And the waits will soon be singing—
　" Merry Christmastide is here."

YES ; I hear thee, yet unfearing,
　　And with threefold pleasure, now
　Will impart some news worth hearing
　　Of this gentleman, I vow.

I had heard, before I saw him,
 He was in his duty sphere,
For a time, at least, located
 In Cliftonia the fair.

And I wished I could but meet him,
 For his princely brother's sake—
Have the joy to see and greet him,
 And his counselling partake.

Yet to have this longed-for pleasure
 Seemed so difficult—alas !—
To a mind of my expressure ;
 But at length it came to pass.

For he came one day, all glowing,
 Looking o'er my varied rhymes ;
And I saw he was bestowing
 Thoughtful care on them betimes.

Then he had one full of humour—
 " Uncle Peter " it was named—
Written by a strange transgressor,
 Who of it was not ashamed.

Some few words at this known visit
 Were exchanged ; and I could trace
Lineament of our own Laureate
 In the welcome stranger's face.

Soon we both had recognition,
 Breathing forth our minds' parole,
Flowing sweet in heart-agnition
 From the chambers of the soul.

He then told me of his travels
　　In the land where poets go—
Where they gaze on skies of beauty,
　　And the muses' fountains flow.

Then we talked of something better,
　　Written in a good Old Book—
A kind Father's loving letter
　　Unto all who in it look.

And we came to this conclusion—
　　While we then our views express'd—
That this Book was no delusion,
　　But the purest and the best.

For in it were priceless treasures,
　　Many precious hidden gems—
Yielding all-enduring pleasures,
　　More than wearing diadems.

And that all who from this fountain
　　Sip their inspiration pure,
Had it from the love-cleft mountain,
　　And their musings would endure.

Then we convers'd of his brother—
　　He the princely son of song—
Long unbosomed to each other,
　　While we whispered nothing wrong.

And we were of kindred feeling
　　On the laureate's volume,
For I had been just revealing
　　I was reading it at home.

And I told him with much pleasure
　　How enraptured I had been,
On its front to find a treasure
　　Written for our gracious Queen.

Then another gave me thrilling—
　　Truth and warning were combined ;
It commenced with this instilling—
　　" Vex not thou the poet's mind."

And I'd read his " Enoch Arden "—
　　Touching, tender, on the whole ;
With his offspring's " Model Warden,"
　　Philip Ray with noble soul.

And I very well remember
　　Reading one for loving folk,
Penn'd, perchance, in bright September :
　　It was named " The Talking Oak."

Then I thought, my graceful Aspen,
　　If the laureate could see
Wisdom in an ancient oak tree,
　　I might find some sense in thee.

If that oak, with cups and acorns,
　　Could so many secrets tell,
Why not thou, when old St. Vincent
　　Gives thee nectar from his well?

Alfred's oak of summer chases
　　Wisely spake without restraint ;
Yet it had not half thy graces,
　　Nor had it a patron saint.

This I told the poet's brother,
  And he gave a pleasant smile ;
Saying men lived for each other,
  And were debtors all the while.

Then he, in solicitation,
  Sought to find if I was blest
With a true discrimination
  Of the fairest and the best

Of his kinsman's vast productions—
  Could I find his richest gem ?
And I said, without instructions,
  It was " In Memoriam."

There I found a boundless ocean,
  Where I had enraptured swam—
Ay, and plunged with deep emotion
  Down this " In Memoriam."

I had gone beneath its billows,
  In hope's diving bell to scan—
Hidden from the roaring breakers—
  Love depths for a brother man.

But my strength was soon exhausted,
  And I rose in mute despair,
For an under-current whispered,
  " Love for Arthur's flowing here."

Now I've told thee, my fair Aspen,
  What I feel has brought delight :
When this treasured friend comes near thee,
  Welcome him by day or night.

And if he should pass beneath thee
    In the coming opening spring,
Let the songsters perching on thee
    Loud their sweetest carol sing.

Let it be a pure refreshing
    To the winter's interlude,
Falling as a song of blessing
    With a poet's gratitude

I WILL heed thy loud invoking,
    And I wish thou could but stay ;
Yet I know it is provoking
    On this dreary winter's day.

But a little longer hear me—
    Do relate me something more ;
I will treasure it, assure thee,
    In my now capacious store.

Who was he that came at springtide,
    And thy varied writings conned ?—
Thinking thou, perchance, hadst stumbled
    In the slough of deep despond.

And, with kindly voice uplifted,
    Tried to cheer thee in the mud,
Where he once had surely drifted,
    When he was not understood.

Who was he ?— nay, tell me, poet,
    For I know he's not a dunce ;
No excuse—or I'll compel thee
    Here to witness, and at once.

A S thou wilt not have denial,
 I must yield to thy request—
Although he may be decrial,
 Wishing it to be suppressed.

Yet he need not know it, Aspen—
 Secret this for thee and me ;
For he's been a friend ungrasping,
 One of untold worth to me.

When he saw me first a stranger,
 Some attention I did win ;
And when he could see no danger,
 Then he kindly took me in

To a home for the wayfaring,
 One where envy cannot part
Those who are true friendship sharing,
 In the region of the heart.

He has furnished for my reading
 Many books of hidden lore—
Some that I was greatly needing,
 Never having seen before.

For my life has been so varied,
 Interlaced with doubt and fears :
Fitly it has been declared—
 " Sowing hope and reaping tears."

Yet take heart, my Aspen treasure—
 Though man is to trouble born ;
True life roses, yielding pleasure,
 Do not grow without the thorn.

And when this friend comes beneath thee,
　Let thy branches chant his name ;
Say—" Our blessing we bequeath thee ;
　Thou art worthy of more fame."

I WILL note thy wise instruction,
　　If we live till opening spring ;
He shall have true joy affluxion
　　While the feathered songsters sing.

Then some more dost thou not wish us
　To give hearty serenades —
When they may be passing near us
　In the summer even shades ?

YES, my Aspen, I entreat thee
　　Love's pure anthem sweetly sing,
For two friends who here may greet thee
　　When the bee is on the wing.

One has been to me a brother
　In life's fitful chequered way ;
And his spouse a second mother—
　For my own is far away.

In the storm as well as sunshine,
　They were my unchanging friends ;
And when they approach this incline,
　Waft them blessings without end.

When their children pass in springtide,
　Give them benediction free—
Tell them their loved sire and mother
　Are two treasured friends to me.

For when storms once raged with blindness,
   And my frail barque sinking fast,
Then their soothing loving-kindness
   Brought me to the port at last.

Let thy benizon attend them,
   Lovely Aspen, where they rove,
And the shield of Heaven defend them
   At their home in Clifton Grove.

IT shall be as thou requirest,
   And will give me joy, I vow :
Tell me what thou more desirest—
   For the old year's waning now.

I WILL do it, patient Aspen—
   Only one more song to trill ;
Then pray take thy winter's slumber
   On this famed St Vincent's hill.

Yet I know thou wilt forgive me,
   Asking just this one refrain ;
And, though last, not least, I beg thee,
   Whisper not the subject's name.

Thou art smiling—I can see thee—
   And art guessing who I mean :
If thy guessing's right, believe me,
   Thou hast penetration keen.

I CAN guess, this dull December,
   Though I am benumbed with cold ;
And I guess—a city member,
   One whose worth can ne'er be told.

THOU are right—I thought thou knew him;
    He has lookèd up to thee,
Where thou could'st distinctly view him,
    My observant Aspen tree.

YES, I saw him in a moment;
    And to save me from disgrace,
Without any further comment,
    Welcom'd him with smiling face.

When he stayed to view thy musing,
    My fair leaves were his convoy;
And they had a day's carousing,
    Sipping in the dew with joy.

We could see thy anxious features
    When he halted near the stand,
And took up an " Uncle Peter,"
    In his work of mercy's hand,—

Reading it with pleasant humour,
    And some others, I could see;
Glancing with his eyes benignant,
    Until they were fixed on thee.

I should like if thou wilt tell me
    What he said on that glad day;
Some kind words I know he told thee
    Long before he went away.

AS thou asketh this one favour,
    And the last in this old year,
I will be of good behaviour,
    And comply without a fear.

For I had no cause for sorrow,
  While this senator did stay;
Seeing it brought bright to-morrow,
  And the clouds were swept away.

He expressed his heartfelt pleasure
  I had written such a theme
As this youth's friend, " Uncle Peter : "
  For he held it in esteem.

Giving patronage assuring,
  Purchasing with good intent—
Which, with other themes enduring,
  I to London city sent.

Then I told him I was writing
  Sonnets sweet for ladies fair,
With some marriage odes delighting,—
  And acrostics could prepare.

But I always had determined,
  In my flowing, simple verse,
Writing to make this world better,
  And to never make it worse.

Then he saw the " In Memoriams "
  Of two eminent divines—
And their treasured photos., showing
  Life-like features with the lines

Two whom he with joy regarded
  With esteem till life did last ;
Now he has the both to look at,
  As reminders of the past.

U

Well, my Aspen, I have told thee
    All I need of this good man—
One whose philanthropic bounty
    Has through our old city ran.

And a many more can witness
    Of his ready helping hand ;
Orphan homes and other claimants
    Yet proclaim it through the land.

Sing him, Aspen, when he cometh
    Underneath thy shade again,
A pure anthem, as becometh
    Thee, to a true gentleman.

Let it echo through the valley,
    Then across the Avon flood—
Sending high, with flowing sweetness
    Chorus through the famed Leigh Wood.

And if passing strangers ask thee
    Why the air is filled with song,
Tell them it is for a noble
    Senator, who hates the wrong :

Or e who lives to aid his country,
    That she may be truly blest—
Representing our loved city,
    Grand old City of the West.

I WILL surely do thy bidding ;
    And my branches, leaves, and stem
Shall join in this worth ovation,
    When in spring I welcome them.

Much I thank thee, toiling poet,
  For the news I've had from thee ;
And though both are loth to show it,
  We must part awhile, I see.

For the cold north wind is roaring,
  Coming o'er the distant deep ;
And my branches are imploring
  Me to take a little sleep.

I am weary ; thou art weary ;
  Here thy toiling has been long ;
Let my benediction cheer thee
  For thy very lengthy song.

THANK thee, Aspen, for thy blessing ;
  Yet the half has not been told
Of my work beneath thy branches,
  Since last winter's piercing cold.

I have written many ballads—
  Some have gone across the sea,
Cheering hearts that once were lonely,
  Waiting words of sympathy.

Many stanzas for the living,
  Budding ere I left my bed ;
Many mourners comfort giving—
  Weeping o'er their lov'd ones dead.

This alone has given cheering
  'Mid the sorrow and the pain :
He who toils for good, unfearing,
  Never can have lived in vain.

THOU art right; I love such theming;
　　And when I to sleep am gone,
　　May I dream, as thou art dreaming;
　　Let us both for good dream on.

And if some loud brawler cometh
　　'Neath my branches with a scream,
Vowing tree and poet 're tainted
　　At the core with self-esteem.

If he rouses me from slumber,
　　I will give him this response—
" Crimin ls won't do for judges:
　　' *Honi soit qui mal y pense.*' " *

　　* Evil be to him who evil thinks.

AS IT SHOULD BE.

WHAT a different world it would be,
　　If mankind would do their best—
　　Bearing one another's burdens,
　　When the weary needed rest.
We should have, instead of sorrow,
　　And a load of pressing care,
Many a gladsome, bright to-morrow—
　　Where we now have dark despair.

What a different world it would be,
　　If each acted well their part;
This, we know, is as it should be
　　To bring joy to every heart.
Let us, then, to all our neighbours
　　Try to give this precious boon;
Heaven will bless our loving labours,
　　And the world be better soon.

ISABEL AND I.

An Old Man's Christmas Story.

THE old Church bells of Clifton sweet
   Rang out one joyful Christmas-tide
   Their silvery tones, while well-known feet
  Were hastening on with glowing pride
To spend a Christmas eve, 'tis said,
  Within a very charming dale,
And to a well-known table, spread
  With Christmas cheer, in Clifton Vale.

In this sweet home the holly green,
  And mistletoe with berries white,
With joy sprays festoon'd might be seen
  To give the visitors delight.
While here and there, in tasty frame,
  A practis'd eye could surely ken
Nice mottoes of immortal fame,
  For peace on earth, goodwill to men.

Sweet peace and plenty reignèd there,
  And welcome guests that plenty shar'd ;
For many dainties of the year
  On dishes smoking hot appeared.
Then when the first repast was o'er,
  The room was filled with new delight;
For there were richer joys in store
  For them, this merry Christmas night.

The guests then gather'd round the fire,
   To watch the kindled yule log blaze;
Its welcome flame kept rising higher,
   Reminding them of bygone days.
When one known friend a wish expressed
   That some one would a story give,
Or something that would interest
   To pass away the Christmas eve.

This met with favour, and at once;
   But who the one should be to tell
His story first found no reponse,
   Until a lady from Hotwell
Suggested that their oldest friend
   Should give the first—he was a sage,
For wisdom they might all depend,
   And they must pay respect to age.

" Hear, hear," was heard from all the throng,
   And eyes were fix'd with great delight
On he who had been absent long,
   And whom they met with joy that night.
Yet ere he tried, at their request,
   There from his breast escap'd a sigh;
And then he said, " I'll do my best,
   The story 's ' Isabel and I.'

" I must go back for sixty years,
   For I am seventy-five to-day,"
He said, while a few silent tears
   Down on his cheek had found their way;
" I then had seen but sweet fifteen,
   My hopes and heart were beating high;
A sprightly youth from Leigh Woods green,
   The home of Isabel and I.

" Now Isabel was just as old
 As I—at least within a day ;
And if the truth must now be told,
 We met, and often by the way
That leads from Abbot's Leigh to Pill ;
 Where smugglers did the laws defy,
And often robb'd her father's mill—
 A dread to Isabel and I.

" For Isabel and I were young,
 Yet we had found a treasure trove ;
Not like the daring smugglers' strong,
 But in the treasur'd store of love.
And though we had not yet confess'd,
 We by some pleasant arts would try
To draw the secret from each breast,
 That dwelt in Isabel and I.

" Until one day in pleasant dream
 We saunter'd through a woodland dell,
Where flow'd her father's wide mill-stream,
 A spot I have remember'd well.
For Isabel there look'd at me,
 When from my heart had come a sigh ;
A sigh that brought felicity
 That day to Isabel and I.

" For just beside the gliding brook
 A water lily droop'd its head ;
'Twas blooming in a little nook,
 A distance from the mill stream-bed.
I took it from the water course,
 While Isabel was standing nigh,
And held it her from true love's source,
 Well known to Isabel and I.

" She took the lily from my hand,
   And then my lily droop'd her head ;
Yet soon she made me understand,
   When I four welcome words had said,
Her heart was mine, and had been long,
   And I might on her love rely ;
And though some prudes might think it wrong,
   'Twas right for Isabel and I.

" We rambled by the winding stream,
   In pleasant chat with cheerful will ;
Until in true love's pleasant dream
   We near'd her cottage by the mill —
When, lo ! her father's form appeared,
   And when he saw us drawing nigh,
His smiling face our spirits cheer'd,
   This pleased both Isabel and I.

" For we had wander'd by the way,
   And had confess'd it with our tongue,
If he we met, what he would say,
   As we were both so very young.
But then her father understood
   That love's pure fount would never dry ;
And took me kindly by the hand,
   Delighting Isabel and I.

" He said, ' I saw you coming on,
   As though your two young hearts agreed,
And sweetly blending into one ;
   I will not thwart you ; no, indeed.
Be true, be brave, and love sincere,
   You'll both be older by-and-by ;
Adorn through time your duty sphere.'
   ' We will,' said Isabel and I.

" Her father loved my Isabel,
　　For she was then his only child ;
And he would very often tell,
　　His joy was when his daughter smiled.
For he had lost her mother dear—
　　She'd reached that home above the sky ;
And yet he often thought her near,
　　And so did Isabel and I.

My widow'd mother loved her boy,
　　And tried to plan his path through life ;
While in our cottage full of joy,
　　Away from all the din of strife,
Oft she would wish that at the mill
　　I would a miller's calling try ;
And she was glad it was her will,
　　And so was Isabel and I.

" Now Isabel's loved father heard
　　My mother's wish in this respect ;
For some sweet early singing bird
　　Had bade him not her suit reject.
Nor did he, for he gave consent
　　That I a miller's trade should try ;
And his consenting brought content
　　To more than Isabel and I.

" I went at once to try my skill,
　　For I was old enough to toil,
And would within the water mill,
　　Although I could not till the soil.
I could apply my mind to this,
　　And honest labour I would try ;
Then onward look to coming bliss,
　　For lovely Isabel and I.

" And so I went to grinding wheat,
   One well remembered joyful day ;
The birds were singing carols sweet,
   For it was in the month of May.
And while the water wheel went round,
   It seem'd to say, ' You may rely
Each closing day will joy abound.'
   It meant for Isabel and I.

" This joy increased from year to year,
   For when my daily toil was done,
Did Isabel and I repair
   To watch the setting of the sun.
Or we would climb St. Vincent's height,
   Beneath the vaulted starlit sky ;
And found intensive soul delight,
   That cheer'd both Isabel and I.

" Or if a storm began to stir,
   We back to home would gladly steal ;
And I would sit and read to her,
   While busy at her spinning wheel.
And she would sing a welcome song
   I loved to hear, ' Sweet by-and-by,'
That doth to those who love belong,
   And did to Isabel and I.

" Thus time sped on, and mother dear
   Began to sink from time's decay ;
But death to her did bring no fear,
   And soon she sweetly pass'd away.
But while she yielded up her breath
   Both I and Isabel were nigh ;
She kiss'd us in the vale of death,
   And blest both Isabel and I.

" Then Isabel's fond father, he
   Began to fail from sickness soon ;
And in the mill would say to me,
   While resting in the hour of noon,
Since he had lost his own true wife,
   He ne'er forget her parting sigh ;
And he would soon depart this life,
   And leave both Isabel and I.

" But he had form'd his plans, that we
   Should, ere he had resigned his breath,
Be joined for life, that he might see
   Us one, then sweetly sleep in death.
And he had told his Isabel,
   And mine, he then in peace could die ;
His Father had done ' all things well,'
   And would for Isabel and I.

" We heard him in the eventide
   Breathe forth for us a fervent prayer ;
And while we knelt at his bedside,
   We found true consolation there.
For he had lasting peace within,
   That took away the fear to die ;
A freedom from the power of sin,
   That cheered both Isabel and I.

" And just a week before he died,
   At his request we were made one ;
He took my hand with glowing pride
   And blest me as his only son.
Then Isabel he kiss'd with joy,
   And bade us live as we would die ;
In wisdom's ways e'er find employ,
   'Twas best for Isabel and I.

" Then soon we saw him glide away
    To where the city needs no sun,
The land of everlasting day,
    Where he has heard the glad ' well done.'
And we were left to mourn alone,
    Alone to breathe the sorrow sigh ;
For he had gone to find a throne,
    And left poor Isabel and I.

" We placed his form beneath the sod,
    Near loved ones laid in Arno's Vale,
Whose spirits had return'd to God,
    Safe anchor'd now within the vail.
And then we had to sigh and moan,
    And face a world with darken'd sky ;
Till we sought light from One alone,
    Who gave it Isabel and I.

" And long in our sweet home at night
    We told Him all our varied care ;
And while we did we had delight,
    His presence then was ever near.
We found Him to His promise true,
    When we did on His word rely,
While thanking Him for mercies new
    Bestow'd on Isabel and I.

" And now the world we had to meet
    In somewhat new and varied form ;
Yet we had hallowed moments sweet,
    That well prepared us for the storm.
We lived without a jarring strife,
    To pull one way we both did try ;
And mutual joy in married life
    Was seen in Isabel and I.

" When life's path was not very smooth,
    As we went through the vale of time,
We tried each other's minds to soothe,—
    This brought us both a joy sublime.
If trade was bad she did not swoon,
    Nor did she choose to fret and sigh ;
But sang, ' A good time is coming soon,'
    This cheer'd both Isabel and I.

" Then to our home there came new joy—
    We had a little daughter born ;
Some said it should have been a boy,
    But Isabel and I that morn
The little welcome darling blest ;
    And would you know the reason why ?
We thought our Father knew the best
    To send for Isabel and I.

" Our little treasure grew apace,
    And all who saw it wish'd it well ;
'Twas like its mother in the face,
    And we had named it Isabel.
This name had such a pleasant sound,
    It many names did far outvie,
No other nicer could be found,
    So thought dear Isabel and I.

" Oh, those were very happy days,
    And blithesome went the mill wheel round :
While with the sun's departing rays
    We in our own sweet home were found.
And I would baby take with glee,
    Then lift it towards the ceiling high ;
While one I loved prepared the tea,
    For joyful Isabel and I.

" And oft when in the room we sat
 Would baby perch upon a chair,
Put on her father's miller's hat,
 And whiter make her glossy hair.
Or after this, while looking pale,
 She would with little fingers try
To pull poor pussy by the tail,
 To please loved Isabel and I.

" Or when her little welcome feet
 Could just begin to trot about,
And Isabel for baby's treat
 Would let her for a time go out,
She'd toddle to the old mill door,
 To kiss me in her passing by ;
And having her we were not poor,
 But rich, both Isabel and I.

" But, ah ! there came a trial day—
 To me it seemeth but a dream ;
Our little loved one lost her way,
 And fell down in the deep mill-stream.
We miss'd her when the clock struck one,
 And sought her with a tearful eye ;
Yet whither was our darling gone
 Was strange, to Isabel and I.

But poor old Rover, he had seen
 Her fall from off the grassy bank,
And with an instinct doubly keen
 Swam to the place where she had sank.
It was too late—the current strong
 Did all his failing strength defy ;
And carried her with speed along,
 Away from Isabel and I.

" Just as the sun was going down
    We found her near the little nook
Where Isabel's love flower had grown,
    Her lily from the water brook.
And now our little lily there
    Had drooped its head to fade and die—
The first dark day in married sphere
    That came to Isabel and I.

" Poor Isabel ! she felt the blow
    As only loving mothers do ;
Yet while we laid our darling low,
    We lean'd upon a promise true,—
That God is love, and doeth right,
    And while we did on this rely,
The darkness soon was lost in light
    To weeping Isabel and I.

" I cheer'd her in the noontide hour,
    And sooth'd her in the silent night :
Then tax'd my every thinking power
    To give her solace and delight.
And though she never did complain,
    I often heard her plaintive cry,
' I soon shall meet my child again,'
    The flower of Isabel and I.

" These words brought pain to me, I know,
    For I had watched her sunken cheek,
With its consumptive, hectic glow—
    Yes, day by day, and week by week.
And I heard something on life's way
    Keep telling me, when I did sigh,
That there would come a parting day,
    And soon, to Isabel and I.

" Alas ! I did not think so soon
   This woe for me would come to pass,
For she had seen but time's bright noon,
   Yet sands were falling from her glass ;
And quickly, for we had alarms
   One autumn eve that she would die,
And cruel death with outstretched arms
   Soon parted Isabel and I.

" I kiss'd her placid, treasur'd cheek,
   And placed my hand upon her brow,
Then felt as though my heart would break,
   My earthly all had left me now.
And soon her coffin'd form was laid
   In God's own acre rising high,
Beneath a weeping willow's shade,
   In grave, for Isabel and I.

" And then I felt myself alone—
   The house, the mill, a vacant place ;
I did not care the cot to own,
   I long'd to see a well-known face.
But it was vain, my love was gone,
   And I was left to grieve and sigh
In home that, when the day was gone,
   Had pleas'd both Isabel and I.

" Then times grew bad, for trade was dull,
   And slow and dreary pass'd the day ;
For bags that once with grain were full
   Upon the floor now empty lay.
Then I resolv'd to cross the sea,
   And on a distant shore to try
If peaceful hours would come to me,
   As came to Isabel and I.

" I sold my stock, and then set sail
   To settle on Columbia's shore ;
And thought when I had left the dale
   I ne'er should see Old England more.
I bade adieu my native land,
   Breath'd out to it a parting sigh ;
For once I knew 'twas doubly grand
   To lovely Isabel and I.

" I reached the land of plenty soon,
   And took two mills beside a stream ;
This water power it was a boon,
   And cheaper far than using steam.
Then trade was brisk, for flour I made,
   I sent it here in barrels dry,
To cheapen food for those in trade,
   In land of Isabel and I.

" And there for more than forty years
   My mills were running day and night ;
For loss of trade I had no fears,
   Trade came that gave me true delight.
And now I have abundant store,
   I have no need to sell or buy ;
And I have come again once more
   To land of Isabel and I.

" I've been to see the dear old mill
   That was a treasur'd spot on earth ;
But now the water wheel is still,
   And there is now no infant mirth.
The mill-stream flows as heretofore,
   With its own waters swelling high ;
But no one opes the cottage door,
   As did loved Isabel and I.

W

" I wander'd by the mill-stream side,
   And noted many precious spots,
Where Isabel and I with pride
   Had gather'd sweet forget-me nots.
And in this Christmas season mild
   I gathered some with tearful eye ;
Reminded of a long lost child
   Of my loved Isabel and I.

" And I have been to-day to see
   The grave where both are lowly lain,
For it is hallow'd unto me,
   I long'd to gaze on it again.
And there I left the priceless flowers
   I took from out the mill-stream nigh ;
Spent near the grave some precious hours,
   And thought of Isabel and I.

" I've seemed to breathe a purer air
   Since I have Clifton seen again,
And did to Arno's Vale repair,
   Where my two Isabels are lain.
I mean to spend my latter days
   Near Clifton Grove, you may rely ;
And while my outer man decays
   I'll think of Isabel and I.

" I'm glad to meet you here to-night
   To spend the welcome Christmas eve —
This is a season of delight,
   Though time brings seasons of bereave.
For here I recognise but few
   That knew me in the years gone by,
While many faces here are new,
   Not known to Isabel and I,

"I'm glad to see your Christmas cheer
Is better than it used to be ;
This festive board displays no beer
Or wines to mar our harmony.
We can enjoyment have, I'm sure,
By only drinking when we're dry,
And quenching thirst from fountains pure,
As did loved Isabel and I.

"Where I have been for forty years
I have beheld what gave me pain—
I've seen the drunkard's wife in tears,
But not within the State of Maine.
The law has done what it should do,
And could, if it would only try ;
Prevent this woe the wide world through,
That grieved loved Isabel and I.

"And now my friends, I wish you all,"
He said, "a merry Christmas-tide ;
I have obey'd your pressing call,
And told my story at your side.
Allów me then to wish you here,
Before we part, without a sigh,
A bright and welcome sweet new year—
As once had Isabel and I."

The old man's story now was told,
And those who heard it there confess'd—
The blithesome young and thoughtful old—
It gave them thrilling interest.
Though many themes produced delight,
This story did the rest outvie ;
The loved recital of the night
Was that of "Isabel and I."

TRUE LOVE SHALL NEVER DIE.

I'LL sing to thee with joy, true love,
    A sweet and cheering song ;
    Thou art a spirit from above,
  Invincible and strong.
A dear, long-tried, unchanging friend,
  On whom I can rely ;
My solace to life's journey's end,
  And thou shalt never die.

CHORUS.

I'll pledge thee, then, from morn till night,
  Loved angel from the sky ;
Through time I'll sing with heart delight,
  True love shall never die.

In bygone days I sang thy praise,
  For thou art ever true ;
And this new song to thee I'll raise,
  For thou art ever new.
Without thee this cold world of ours
  Would be a cheat and lie ;
But thou dost bring the sunny hours,
  And thou shalt never die.

           I'll pledge thee, then, &c.

UNDERNEATH THE TREES.

A Lyric composed in twelve minutes, June, 1880.

WELCOME ! bright and sunny June—
  Beautiful and gay ;
  Nature seems in sweeter tune
Than in merry May.
Now the woodland valleys sing
  In the zephyr breeze ;
Fanning like an angel's wing,
  Underneath the trees.

Welcome ! blithe and gladsome June,
  Thou art dear to me ;
I will to the coppice soon
  Haste with cheerful glee.
By the winding brooklet long
  Hear the humming bees
Sing their honey-seeking song,
  Underneath the trees.

Welcome ! pleasant month of June,
  Now the woodlands ring ;
From the early morn till noon
  Thrush and linnet sing.
There till eventide I'll dwell,
  Full of thoughts that please ;
'Till I hear the nightingale,
  Underneath the trees,

Welcome ! hallow'd month of June,
  Thou art rich indeed ;
Bringing me a priceless boon,
  Solace in my need.
And I hasten to my home
  With my heart at ease ;
Thankful for a peace that's come,
  Underneath the trees.

"I SHOULD LIKE TO DIE IN MY FATHER'S ARMS."

HESE words were breath'd 'mid the twilight grey,
One eventide in the welcome May;
While a loved one sigh'd for a waiting rest,
With her head reclined on her father's breast.
Her plaintive voice did the strains repeat,
As she only could, with an accent sweet:
"There is rest in heaven, and unending charms;
I should like to die in my father's arms"

Her fragile form it was sinking fast,
For consumption's hand with a deadly blast
Had touch'd the stem of this treasur'd flower,
And it bent 'neath the stroke of the wasting power.
But yet from her heart, with a joyful breath,
She could say to the ghastly monster, Death,—
"I can smile on thee and thy fierce alarms,
If I may but die in my father's arms.

I have pleasing hopes of a home above,
Through a dear Redeemer's dying love;
He is calling me to the climes of day,
Where the painful tears will be wiped away.
I shall soon be far from a world of care,
With the loved ones landed over there;
This pleasing thought my spirit calms,
Oh! let me die in my father's arms."

It was noontide in the month of June,
When nature's voice was in sweetest tune,
This treasured child, as the summer's day,
On her resting couch ready waiting lay.
And there she said, with her failing breath,
"Yea, though I walk through the vale of death,
I will fear no evil—no alarms."
And the loved one died in her father's arms!

SERVED HIM RIGHT.

A GENTLEMAN, the other day,
    Came down St. Vincent's height—
At least in dress he one appeared,
  Though not in manners right ;
For, halting near the Poet's stand,
  With haughty voice he said,
" Why don't you get a business
  To earn your daily bread ? "
" A business," the Poet cried,
  " Now, pray, sir, who are you ?
Where have you lived, not to have known
  That I have long had two ? "
" Two businesses," he sternly cried.
  " What businesses are they ? "
Now this the Poet's patience tried,
  And quickly he did say,
" One business, sir, I long have had
  Since I a man have grown—
Is this, by having common-sense,
  To try and mind my own.
The other I will give to you
  'Till you have wiser grown—
It is to let the business
  Of other men alone."

A NEW YEAR'S CAROL.

THE FADED LEAF AND ITS LESSONS.

A True Incident.

ECEMBER'S gloom, with its sombre sky
  And a blighting frost, had come,
  While roaring winds were raging high
O'er manse and the cotter's home ;
When an old man came, with silv'ry hair
  And faltering steps, to see
The playful mood of a faded leaf
  That clung to the poet's tree.

This leaf alone, on a slender bough,
  Had many a storm defied :
Just like a weird, defiant thing,
  With an aspen's latent pride.
It seemed to say to the tempest fierce,
  And the hoary frost, in glee—
" Ye may smite and bite ; 'till the opening year
  I'll cling to the poet's tree."

The old man gazed at this faded leaf
  While it waved in the passing wind,
And then he smiled, for a something pass'd
  Through the chambers of his mind ;
And his long thin arm was soon stretched out
  As high as an arm could be,
For he sought to take this faded leaf
  That clung to the poet's tree.

His zeal this cold and wintry day
  Was great and beyond compare,
For the rough blast sway'd this faded leaf
  And drifted his silvery hair ;
Yet he could but touch with his finger's end
  The leaf he rejoiced to see,
Though he tried, and tried, and tried again
  For it on the poet's tree.

At length he look'd from the faded leaf
  To the ground on which he stood,
And there he saw many better leaves
  Than the one he thought so good.
And he took them up in his horny hand,
  While his heart was filled with glee,
And stored them well in his open vest—
  These leaves from the poet's tree.

Then on he went up the craggy height,
  With a joy-lit mind and eyes,
His faltering feet fresh vigour found,
  As though he had gained a prize.
He had won this joy by looking down,
  Found leaves all good—and free,
More choice than that poor shrivell'd thing
  That clung to the poet's tree.

That old man's deed was beheld by one
  Who was standing near that day,
And it touched the chords of his waiting harp
  For a new year's virgin lay ;
And he sang, " Old man, thou hast brought me joy,
  Heart-strains I will chant to thee,
For a lesson good from a faded leaf
  On the whispering poet's tree.

" I saw thy zeal for a faded thing,
  As though it would give thee cheer ;
Perchance thou hadst read of its parent stem,
  In the ' Secrets of a Year.'
And yet that is only a faded leaf
  That sports near the woods of Leigh,
Like a sere and wasted wreck of grief
  That clings to the poet's tree.

" Thou thought that leaf had a mystic charm—
    'Twas seen in thy anxious look ;
This truth was read in thy outstretch'd arm,
    As though it were Nature's book.
Come into my heart of love, old man,
    Thou art more than a friend to me ;
And thou shalt live, after I am gone,
    As a leaf on the poet's tree.

" Thou hast been like some who live to-day,
    And seek for their soul's delight,
Who long for the world's short, fading joys,
    As a boon to their waiting sight.
These reach, and reach, and reach again,
    To take them, with inward glee—
Just as thou didst the faded leaf
    That clings to the poet's tree.

" But while they hope that the next long reach
    Will bring them the tempting prize,
There's a wind-storm comes with fearful blast,
    And tear-drops blind their eyes.
They cannot take with an outstretch'd arm
    What they wished as a good to be ;
The taunting cheat is beyond their reach,
    As the leaf on the poet's tree.

" Oh, were they wise, these would all look down,
    And find, with a joy complete,
Those richer, fairer, purer joys
    They had trampled beneath their feet.
Then take them up with willing hands,
    And a grateful heart, as he—
The poor old man with his silvery locks—
    Did leaves from the poet's tree."

NEW SONG.

I'LL DO THE BEST I CAN.

THEY sing that life's a thorny way,
    And has no pleasant bowers ;
A wilderness, where many stray
    For weeds instead of flowers.
But I a sweeter song will sing,
    For weal of every man ;
To make the best of everything,
    I'll do the best I can.

There 're ups and downs we know in life,
    In every mortal's cup ;
But looking down won't quell the strife,
    We'd best be looking up.
I thought this over long ago,
    When I was looking wan ;
Then said, " Good-bye to moping woe,
    I'll do the best I can."

There are some folks—well-known, forsooth,
    A lot of wretched elves ;
Who value neither right nor truth,
    Nor try to help themselves.
But I have found it best, I know,
    To labour like a man ;
And through life's vale I singing go,
    I'll do the best I can.

This glowing theme I sing at night,
    As well as every morn ;
The welcome strains bring true delight,
    Whene'er I feel forlorn.
They cheer me with a joy sublime,
    And check fell sorrow's ban ;
I'll sing them to the end of time,
    And do the best I can.

MAGGIE GRAY.

I N the summer twilight fair,
On a landscape green,
'Mid the sweet and balmy air,
Maggie Gray was seen
Looking on the ocean foam,
Very far away,
For a gallant ship to come,
Dear to Maggie Gray.

In the pleasant eventide
You would find her there,
Pacing with a lover's pride
O'er the heather rare.
There each morn she'd lightly skip ;
Pleasant as the May.
Watching for a coming ship,
Known to Maggie Gray.

There she went till autumn came,
Then her heart would quail,
While she breath'd a well-known name,
Echo'd by the gale—
'Till, like speck of something dark
On the ocean way,
She beheld the welcome barque,
Dear to Maggie Gray.

Then a brave young seaman's arms
Clasp'd a loving prize ;
Maggie now had no alarms
In her joy-lit eyes.
"Safe at last !" she softly cried ;
" Safe," he breathed, "for aye ; "
And they homeward walked in pride,
He and Maggie Gray.

KEEP YOUR HONOUR BRIGHT.

’LL sing in joyful strain to-day,
   To banish what is wrong,
   A new and interesting lay
And tributary song.
I trill it for a world’s esteem,
   That all may have delight ;
The subject of my glowing theme
   Is—Keep your honour bright.

Whate’er would lead away from this
   Brings much distressing woe ;
True honour points the way to bliss,
   Wherever we may go.
The path of life will brighter shine
   If we, with heart and might,
In every life act would combine
   To keep our honour bright.

Our path sometimes may not be clear,
   And difficult our lot ;
Dark days may bring the rising fear
   In manse and peasant’s cot.
Yet then it will be always best
   To aim at doing right,
For this alone will make us blest,
   And keep our honour bright.

Then let us on the world’s wide stage
   Well guard each danger door ;
That we may greet the golden age
   Our bards have sung of yore,—
The age when man in man shall find
   A friend to cheer his sight;
And bear the golden rule in mind,
   To keep our honour bright.

NEW SONG.

"I'LL KNOW HE WILL COME TO-NIGHT.

LOV'D Lillie was singing a sweet new song,
    One summer-tide's cheering day ;
And her dulcet stains went trilling along
    To where a lov'd listener lay.
On a mossy bank he had stretched a time,
    To catch, with a heart delight,
The welcome notes of a true love's chime—
    "I know he will come to-night."

A rippling brook that was flowing near
    Was singing the same sweet tune ;
And it cheer'd a mind that was waiting there
    In the gladdening month of June.
But Lillie knew not he was resting nigh
    On the greensward from her sight ;
Yet he heard her sing, and without a sigh,
    "I know he will come to-night."

She rose and sped to the window pane
    That opened upon the green ;
Then look'd around for her love again,
    Yet her darling could not be seen.
So she went to practise her song once more,
    And sang with a pure delight —
"He was always true to his word before,
    I know he will come to-night."

Her room, whose door had been left unlatched,
    He entered with smiling face ;
Two lovers, then, who had been well matched,
    Were locked in fond embrace.
Then he urg'd his Lillie with joyful tongue
    To trill him a lay at sight ;
And she sang to him for a greeting song,
    "I knew he would come to-night."

BE UPRIGHT EVERY DAY.

Y harp is tuned, and I must sing
    A new and treasur'd song ;
I feel it has the proper ring,
    Though it may not be long.
Yet it may be to you and me
    An interesting lay ;
The subject 's this—" Where'er you be,
    Be upright every day."

This world we know 's a crooked thing,
    With many ins and outs ;
But we should find more time to sing,
    And have less time for pouts,—
If we will try, while passing through,
    To walk in wisdom's way ;
And this is best to always do,
    Be upright every day.

'Tis said there are some people now
    Who love dishonest gain ;
But this in after life they'll know
    Will bring remorse and pain.
'Tis best to do the thing that's right,
    For this will always pay ;
To give the heart a pure delight,
    Be upright every day.

Uprightness will give constant joy,
    And make time's duties light ;
Then give our eyes without annoy
    Refreshing sleep at night.
Beneath its shadow we have bliss,
    While conscience guards the way ;
Then let us well remember this,
    Be upright every day.

NEW SONG.

"DO YOU THINK THERE'S A LETTER FOR ME?"

THE golden sun with his rays of cheer
  Was smiling from out the east,
On a lady fair with a soul sincere,
  Who was seeking a true love's feast.
For she could not wait for a well-known tread,
  But tripping along in her glee,
On the open street to the postman said—
  " Do you think there's a letter for me ? "

He smiled, because he had heard those words,—
  Yes, many a time before ;
Then he looked at once with a good intent
  Through the piles of his varied store,—
'Till he found one bearing her own sweet name,
  It had come from over the sea ;
And her heart replied, "Oh, I am so glad
  That there is a sweet letter for me."

'Twas sent from one who was dear to her,
  And one to be loved for aye ;
In a sweet new home that was waiting now,
  Because she had named the day.
And she read her letter with joy-lit eyes,
  Near the " Whispering Aspen Tree ; "
Then cried aloud with a glad surprise,
  " This indeed's a sweet letter for me."

Then home she sped to her anxious friends,
  Who waited for her and long ;
These wish'd to hear from her welcome voice
  A pleasant glad morning song.
And she sang them one with a new refrain,
  It was this, and as sweet could be,—
" My true love is coming to Nellie again,
  There has been a sweet letter for me."

NEW SONG.

LILIAN AND I.

T was in the spring-tide sweet,
    Lilian and I
      Sat beside a trellis neat,
  Looking in the sky,—
Watching clouds of beauty pass,
  Ravishing the eye ;
While we sat upon the grass,
  Lilian and I.

Oh, how strange we felt that day,
  Lilian and I ;
Wishing we could something say
  On sweet "by-and-by."
Yet right words were us refused,
  And we had to sigh
What we meant, and this confused
  Lilian and I.

Yet we soon did understand,
  Lilian and I ;
When I gently pressed her hand,
  They were coming nigh.
And I whispered, " Be my dove ; "
  Then she said, " Oh, fie ! "
Thus we tried at making love,
  Lilian and I.

Soon she breath'd what truly pleased
  Lilian and I ;
And my anxious mind was eas'd
  By her joy-lit eye.
" I will be your own true wife,"
  This was her reply ;
And we lived and loved through life,
  Lilian and I.

MERRY, MERRY CHRISTMAS BELLS.

A New Carol for the Times.

RING on, ring on, ye Christmas bells,
On mountain side, in woodland dells ;
Ring on, 'mid town and city's street,
Your cadent sounds of music sweet.
Ye seem to say with silvery tongues,
As sweet as any angel songs—
" Good news, good news we bring again :
For peace on earth, goodwill to men."

Ring on, entrancing Christmas bells,
Your sweet intoning sorrow quells ;
Ye strike the ear in busy mart,
And comfort bring the lonely heart.
Attuned ye fill your customed sphere
With welcome chiming once a year ;
We love to hear your sweet refrain
Of peace on earth, goodwill to men.

Ring out your music, Christmas bells,
Let notes as pure as crystal wells
Now fill each home with cheerful glee,
And deeds of heaven-born charity.
Let all around the festal board,
To home, sweet home, and friends restored,
With gladsome voice and heart, again
Sing peace on earth, goodwill to men.

Ring on, harmonious Christmas bells,
To me your pleasant chiming tells
Of Him who came that wrong might cease,
The advent of a Prince of Peace.
With consentaneous sounds ye bring
Glad tidings of the new-born King ;
As though some better days ye ken
Of peace on earth, goodwill to men.

Ring on, ye thrilling Christmas bells,
And ring for aye the funeral knells
Of shaming discord, strife and hate,
And then, oh, ring with strains elate—
That men have now determin'd mind
To seek the good of human kind ;
That hand and heart will join again
For peace on earth, goodwill to men.

Ring on, endearing Christmas bells,
Through sadden'd homes and cloister'd cells,
And soothe lone hearts made sad by war,
Then scatter those who love it far ;
That men may learn, a nation's laws,
And sacred honour's righteous cause,
Receive their best promotion, when
There's peace on earth, goodwill to men.

Ring on, ye faithful Christmas bells,
And let your merry pealing swells
Rise higher than the clash of arms,
And higher than dire foe alarms.
'Till nations lasting quiet find,
And man to man is true and kind ;
Oh, sweet will be your music then,
With peace on earth, goodwill to men.

Ring on, ring on, clear Christmas bells,
'Till fields of blood—those fiendish hells—
And they who use them for delight .
Shall perish in unending night :
And when from ashes of their fire
Shall rise an army we desire,
That only use the press and pen—
For peace on earth, goodwill to men.

Ring on, and loud, ye Christmas bells,
And make it known through distant dells
That men, to settle their disputes,
Must act like men, and not brutes.
That this must now be understood,
To shed an unknown brother's blood
Is not the way our rights to gain,
Nor peace on earth, goodwill to men.

Ring on, sweet-throated Christmas bells,
Until your harmony dispels
The murky clouds that yet appear,
And fill with gloom our hemisphere.
Ring on, and sweep them all away,
And bring a brighter, better day ;
As when the angels' joyful strain
Was peace on earth, goodwill to men.

Ring on, ye merry Christmas bells,
Despite the war dogs' awful yells ;
And sound this truth from shore to shore,
That nations shall learn war no more.
Ring down the Saviour from above,
To fill men's hearts with peace and love ;
Then ring the war fiend to his den,
With peace on earth, goodwill to men.

Ring out, ye true-tongued Christmas bells,
To those on whom your chiming swells,
And say that men love's mission mar,
Who preach the fame of horrid war.
Ring out, ring out, and do not cease
Until they preach the Christ of Peace,
And tell that He can only reign
With peace on earth, goodwill to men.

Ring louder yet, brave Christmas bells,
Until your earnest clangour tells
To all who plead that we must wait,
Instead of slaying, warlike hate.
Oh, tell those priests, so slow to learn,
The new-born King would have them spurn
This bygone teaching's doleful strain,
For peace on earth, goodwill to men.

Ring on, inspiring Christmas bells,
And sound, 'mid continental dells,
To rulers dwelling o'er the sea
That they must live in unity.
Ring out through this terrestrial ball,
The one good Father made us all ;
As links in love's all golden chain,
For peace on earth, goodwill to men.

Ring on, euphonic Christmas bells,
Until your warning sound compels
Each nation, with its false alarms,
To close the forge for making arms.
And let their sons, with horny hand,
Have nobler work, to till the land ;
Be peasants in each rural glen,
For peace on earth, goodwill to men.

Ring out, O gladsome Christmas bells,
Till your glad tidings evil quells;
That every heart both far and wide
May have a joyful Christmas-tide.
Ring out pure strains from shore to shore,
And let the days of wrong be o'er ;
Then hail the good time's coming train,
With peace on earth, goodwill to men.

Ring on, O joyful Christmas bells,
Ring on, ye mercy's evangels;
Ring out from every steeple dome
Some music sweet for every home.
Ring on, and bid the virgin year
In peaceful robes to soon appear ;
And let three angels sing again
Of peace on earth, goodwill to men.

Ring on for aye, lov'd Christmas bells,
Your cheering notes are magic spells ;
Ring out the old year's hate and strife,
And then ring in a better life,—
When man shall be to man a friend,
And loving-kindness have no end ;
That earth may be like heaven again,
With peace on earth, goodwill to men.

SHE BLOOMS IN EDEN NOW.

THE virgin rose is faded,
　　Our blooming flower has fled ;
　　And sorrow's voice would whisper—
"Your lovely plant is dead."
But there 're two welcome angels,
　　With lustre on their brow ;
Bright Faith and Hope are singing—
　　"She blooms in Eden now."

We bore her to God's acre,
　　In peaceful Arno's Vale ;
And mourned our coffin'd treasure
　　With pungent, sad bewail.
Yet while the tears were falling
　　O'er Mary, then laid low,
The angels still were singing—
　　"She blooms in Eden now."

One chair at home is vacant,
　　And her lov'd childhood bed :
For now the elm and cypress
　　Are waving o'er her head.
Yet while, with heart submissive,
　　To Heaven's will we bow,
We hear the angels singing—
　　"She blooms in Eden now."

THE DAYS OF MY CHILDHOOD AND YOUTH.

HOW sweet to my memory still
　　The days of my childhood and youth ;
　Their past reminiscences fill
　My mind with irradiate truth.
I mourn, and with tears o't bedew
　My couch—it avails not, forsooth,—
And sigh for the quiet I knew
　In the days of my childhood and youth.

I walk through the fam'd Kilton Wood
　I rambled in school-days of yore,
And see the old yew as it stood
　With evergreen covering in store.
From the bank near its trunk I could rid
　Wild flowers with manners uncouth ;
They smell not so sweet as they did
　In the days of my childhood and youth.

I stroll by the Ryton's clear stream,
　Where its gurgling waters flow ;
And feel as awak'd from a dream,
　While watching the spray fall below.
I hear in the distance a sound
　Of the mill, and to leave it am loath,
For its wheel went merrily round
　In the days of my childhood and youth.

I haste to the Abbey churchyard,
　And gaze on the graves of the dead ;
How vast are the numbers interr'd
　Since the days of my childhood are fled.
My friends I perceive are lain there,
　And then did I learn the sad truth :
'Twas their loss that brought me despair,
　Since the days of my childhood and youth.

But why should my spirit repine,
  Since my Father 's appointed my way?
To Him I would cheerful resign,
  And to Him I for guidance will pray.
For sure His kind wisdom displays
  A fountain of joy and of truth ;
And will give to me happier days
  Than the days of my childhood and youth.

GATHERING WAR CLOUDS.

May, 1866.

WHEN will the clarion notes of horrid war,
    When will the booming sound of cannon cease ?
    When will these dogs of hell be banish'd far ?
  When will the dawning come of endless peace ?

Why do the nations strive with potent might ?
  Why do the kingdoms arm in fierce array ?
Why do the crown'd ones marshal to the fight ?
  Why do the princes hasten to the fray ?

What is the cause that rampant armies fly ?
  What is the cause now man to man is stood ?
What is the cause that thousands doom to die ?
  What is the cause that sheds our brother's blood ?

Where is the need for desolation's hand ?
  Where is the need for sorrow'd widow's groan ?
Where is the need for fell ambition's brand ?
  Where is the need for helpless orphans' moan ?

Would that the world were wise in this our day ;
  Would that the peoples join'd with heart and hand ;
Would that they hail'd with joy true wisdom's way ;
  Would that they chas'd fell despots from the land.

When will the great ones learn to covet not ?
When will the cause of right be own'd by men ?
When will the name of might and tyrants rot ?
When will our weapons be the press and pen ?

Wait for the good time, wait ; it draweth near ;
Wait, for the bright star hope illumes the sky ;
Wait for the bursting cloud of sombre fear ;
Wait for the minstrel angel liberty.

Watch for the dawning of the joyful day ;
Watch for the Master's footsteps at the door ;
Watch, for the time 's at hand, yes ! watch and pray ;
Watch, for the nations shall learn war no more.

Work, that the promis'd day may swiftly come ;
Work, that the sound of war may ever cease;
Work, that this world may be one brother's home ;
Work, that this world may kiss the Prince of Peace !

ON THE DEATH OF A BLIND CHILD.

By Request.

DIEU ! dear child, a fond farewell !
Lov'd parents mourn around thy bed ;
Sad, pungent grief, their bosoms swell,
To find thee number'd with the dead.

Lent only for a few short years,
Child of affliction thou hast been ;
Thy pathway has been wet with tears,
Thy sorrows have been felt, not seen.

A cancer's keen relentless pain
Depriv'd thee of the light of day ;
Nor could physician's skill again
Bring back the sight to cheer thy way.

Cold death has now thine eyelids press'd,
　Released thee from affliction's rod ;
With holy angels thou art blest,
　And seeing now thy Father God.

—————

M Y   S T A R .

*A reply to a Poem of the same title from I. L. O., in the " Bristol
Gazette," 1880.*

HINE eyes grown dark !　And so have mine,
　　While gazing on the stars ;
　　Yes ! drearily as e'er have thine
From sorrow stricken scars.

I've watched each strange unquiet star
　With mind as ill at rest ;
Yet while I watched those gems afar
　My heart and soul were blest.

For while I dream'd like thee at night,
　With sorrowing to cope,
My dreams have brought me true delight
　And brightest stars of hope.

E'en when I scann'd the milky way
　From where I often stood,
The twinkling beauties seem'd to say—
　Have faith, for God is good.

Their voice came in irradiate form,
　Harmonious from above,
Like messengers to quell life's storm,
　And whisper'd—God is love.

I heard this then, my loss was gain,
　For I have lost like thee ;
Yet I found solace for my pain,
　By waiting patiently.

And now I know the reason why
 The world was made so fair :
It was that man might glorify
 His wise Creator here.

I learnt that in the silent night,
 While gazing on a gem—
Earth's brightest star and heaven's own light,
 The Star of Bethlehem.

CARNARVON CASTLE.

AIL ! Cymra's pride, Carnarvon's gem !
 On this glad festal day,
 We'll sing in our Eisteddfodd
 For thee a pleasant lay.
All beautiful 's thy castle dome,
 Thy woodland, hill, and dales,
Where royal Edward's son became
 The first-born Prince of Wales.

Six centuries have nearly fled
 Since on our rich ore lands
Thy time-worn turret reared its head,
 By toiling peasants' hands.
In one short year thy structure rose,
 A chieftain's tribute true,
To show Prince Edward's sire a work
 Old Cymra's sons could do.

This Edward came with fearless host,
 And scaled our mountain heights,
With slaughter sword along our coast
 Engaged in hottest fights ;
But thy rare stones, Carnarvon's gem,
 Now in their grandeur set,
Proclaim in deeds of noble art,—
 Wales is not conquer'd yet !

CLIFTON OBSERVATORY.

THIS ivied, castellated tower,
  All pleasing to the sight,
  Stands forth in majesty and power
  On famed St. Vincent's height.
Where from its summit's calm repose—
  Rich, beautiful, and grand—
The camera obscura shows
  A thrilling fairy land.
Beneath it, through a tunnell'd way
  That rugged nature gave,
Is Ghyston—or, as thousands say,
  The noted giant's cave—
Where Roman chiefs from Roman camp
  Close by, with hearts aglow,
Performed the duties of their church—
  Four centuries ago !

MY MOTHER.

On an unexpected visit in her 78th year, July, 1877.

WHAT ! come at last, my mother dear,
   With pure maternal joy,
And near two hundred miles, to see
   Thy first-born darling boy ?

I long had wondered day and night,
   'Mid pleasure and some pain,
If ever I should see thy face,
   Or kiss thy cheek again.

When, lo ! I find thee in my home,
   Calm seated near my side ;
And thy lov'd form has charms for me
   Which nothing has beside.

For in my life's unshapen track,
   When all seemed dark to thee,
Thou wert in loving-kindness true
   A mother unto me.

Thy brow is wrinkled more, I find,
   With thy advancing years,
Than when I climbed thy waiting knee
   With all my childhood fears.

But yet I readily confess,
   With willing heart and pen,
I know I love thee better now
   Then I could love thee then.

And this one thought doth give me joy,
  Whate'er my failings be,
I have not brought one bitter pang
  Though life's long day to thee.

Though thou wert absent from my sight
  Whene'er I bowed the knee,
My orisons thy name have borne—
  I have remembered thee.

My mother—nay, I cannot tell,
  'Tis only known above,
How my fond heart yet clings to thee
  With unabating love.

I feel as though some mystic stream,
  Outgushing with my tears,
Comes flowing from a fount of love
  For thy declining years.

May Heaven's blessing crown thy life
  With mercies yet to come,
And grateful songs thy lips employ
  In my loved childhood's home.

And when thy latest hour arrives,
  While life's pulsations cease,
I pray thy latter end may be
  Serene with heavenly peace.

THINKING OF THEE.

THINKING of thee in my home to-day,
  Thinking of thee in the twilight grey ;
  Thinking of thee in the silent night,
Thinking of thee with a pure delight !
Thinking of thee in the early morn,
Thinking of thee when weary and worn :
And, whenever I bow the knee,
Then, my love, I'm thinking of thee !

Thinking of thee with a heart's desire,
Thinking of thee when I strike the lyre ;
Thinking of thee while I touch the strings,
Thinking of thee sweet music brings !
Thinking of thee I trill my strains,
Thinking of thee removes my pains :
And, when my song is sung with glee,
Then, my love, I'm thinking of thee !

Thinking of thee with thy joyful look,
Thinking of thee as a treasured book ;
Thinking of thee while I use my pen,
Thinking of thee in the woodland glen !
Thinking of thee, my precious dove,
Thinking of thee, my own true love :
And, though absent awhile thou be,
Yet, my love, I'm thinking of thee !

Thinking of thee this summer-tide,
Thinking of thee with a glowing pride ;
Thinking of thee while I write my song,
Thinking of thee, who will not be long !
Thinking of thee I send thee this,
Pure as a true affection's kiss :
It is for one who is dear to me,
And 'tis from one who is thinking of thee !

In Memoriam.

MY MOTHER.

Died December 13th, 1884, aged 84 years.

N queenly Clifton's rocky height
    I take my seat in saddened plight,
Thy death memoriam to write—
           My mother.

Yes ; near the spot where years ago
    I penn'd my father's, thou didst know,
For I had often told thee so —
           My mother.

And now, as by some mystery,
    While leafless are the woods of Leigh,
I have to do the same for thee—
           My mother.

For here, one cold December day,
    I had a telegram to say
That thou from time had pass'd away—
           My mother.

This news, alas ! was sad to read ;
    And off I went with railway speed
Where thou wast oft a friend in need—
           My mother.

I found thee in my childhood's home,
    From whence we years ago would roam,
And then again there smiling come—
           My mother.

But thou wast in it free from pain,
    Whom I had hoped to hear again,
Yes ; in an oaken coffin lain—
           My mother.

Thy peaceful spirit had gone where
   There are no days of dark despair,
To the sweet home that's over there—
                  My mother.

I gazed upon thy cheeks all cold,
   And kiss'd them with a grief untold,
For thou wert more to me than gold—
                  My mother.

And now I write 'mid blinding tears,
   That thy loved voice could quell my fears,
E'en till thou died all ripe with years—
                  My mother.

No mother's love to me like thine,
   And yet I must not dare repine,
But bow me to the Will Divine—
                  My mother.

For Him who gave me unto thee,
   And He who gave thee unto me,
He always doeth right, I see--
                  My mother.

And so I lay me in the dust,
   For He is now my hope and trust,
And recognise His sentence just—
                  My mother.

I feel that thou art on the shore
   Where all death throes and pain are o'er,
And loved ones meet to part no more—
                  My mother.

I think I see thee happy now,
   Where angels reverential bow,
With a love garland on thy brow—
                  My mother.

And greeting one by one of those
   Our loved ones who had found repose
Near where the living fountain flows—
               My mother.

Perchance my own dear father's voice
   Hath welcom'd thee, his fond heart's choice,
To where the ransom'd ones rejoice—
               My mother.

There three loved children pass'd away
   In boy and girlhood's hopeful day,
May now have clasp'd thy form for aye—
               My mother.

And three are left to mourn for thee,
   Their guardian from frail infancy,
To whom a better could not be—
               My mother.

What watchful care thou hadst for these,
   Not caring for thy own life ease,
If they could have what would them please—
               My mother.

To rear them was thy anxious care,
   And often did their burdens bear,
For thy strong love was past compare—
               My mother.

'Twas thy life study and thy pride
   That there should come no woe betide
To loved ones nurtur'd at thy side—
               My mother.

Yea, even unto thy last day,
   Thy love was such in this life's way ;
It ceased not 'till thou pass'd away—
               My mother.

What mothers can do thou didst do,
   For what thou set thy hand unto
Was always sure to be got through—
                My mother.

But when thy time was come to die,
   Thou whisper'd all a sweet " Good-bye,"
And found the Home beyond the sky—
                My mother.

Thou left a message for thy son,
   That thou a crown of life had won;
And soon would hear the glad " Well done "—
                My mother.

This message gave him joy complete
   To know thou had a blest retreat
Where all who love the Master meet—
                My mother.

And while he writes thy ode to-day,
   He feels as though he heard thee say,
That it is well with thee for aye—
                My mother.

For where thou art are no more sighs,
   But glad unspeakable surprise
Of beauties rare beyond the skies—
                My mother.

And there thou seem'st to beckon me,
   Where thy loved form I hope to see
In the fair land of purity—
                My mother.

How long or short the time will be,
   Is wisely hidden now from me;
But when it comes, I'll come to thee—
                My mother.

KILTON WOOD.

This charming sylvan retreat stands on the outskirts of Worksop, in the county of Nottingham, bounded by the Dukeries of Portland and Newcastle, and was once in the possession of His Grace the Duke of Norfolk. It was a favourite place of resort for the author in his youthful days ; and the following touching incident occurred during a visit there in the prime of manhood, just after passing through a severe domestic bereavement.

'WAS summer ! with its golden light
    And fragrant balmy air,
When nature, smiling with delight,
    Pourtray'd all bright and fair—
A lone one contemplative stood
To meditate in Kilton Wood.

The sky was clear, the sun shone bright
    His last refulgent ray,
And gave new beauty to the sight,
    To cheer departing day.
Sublimely pure, so grand and good,
'Twas heaven's own temple—Kilton Wood.

And yet, though beauteous was that scene
    To him who wander'd there,
Dark gloomy thoughts would intervene
    To check aspiring prayer :
For he had found such flowers might bud
And germinate in Kilton Wood.

The birds they join'd in evensong,
 And pour'd forth notes so clear;
While all around, in language strong,
 That sad one tried to cheer.
But, ah! 'twas vain—o'erwhelm'd he stood,
A prey to grief, in Kilton Wood.

" Ye birds," cried he, " have pleasure here,
 Your homes from pain are free ;
But mine, alas ! is desolate,
 No comfort there—ah, me !
Oh, had I wings, and if I could,
I'd join you here in Kilton Wood."

Just at that moment from a bush
 A pretty spink did fly,
And fluttering past with eager rush
 It raised that sad one's eye.
When lo ! a nest before him stood,
With five bright eggs, in Kilton Wood.

Without a thought, with eager hand,
 He seized that poor bird's nest ;
And on he went, then tried to stand,
 But, oh, he could not rest.
Two birds they cross'd his path for good
Before he left fair Kilton Wood.

They seem'd to say, " O stranger, dear,
 Can you thus cruel be,
To fill our trembling breasts with fear,
 Our home with misery?
'Tis all we have, pray be so good
As leave our nest in Kilton Wood.

How keen the pang that touch'd his heart,
    There's no one knows but He
Who with one glance the secret part
    Of man can fathom'd be ;
Suffice to say, it stamp'd for good
That visit paid to Kilton Wood.

For hastening back with rapid stride
    To that lone spot he press'd,
And then as best he could, with pride,
    Replac'd that poor bird's nest.
This done, pure joy came like a flood,
And fill'd his breast in Kilton Wood.

That sad one now had heart relief
    In summer's crepuscule ;
He found the balm for healing grief
    Lay in a golden rule.
Outspringing from a heaven-born mood
Of priceless worth in Kilton Wood.

For this pure act of justice done
    Was by the angels blest,
And though the wearied golden sun
    Was sinking into rest,
It gave a benizon for good
On that love deed in Kilton Wood.

Returning home again, he thought,
    " How happy men could be,
If they through life untiring sought
    To give true sympathy ;
Such work of love well understood
Might make this world a Kilton Wood."

LOVE'S TRIBUTE.

Written by Request.

THIRTY-TWO long months to-day,
    Dear Elein,
 Since I came from thee away,
    Dear Elein.
Many changes I have seen,
With their varied intervene ;
Many faces passing fine,
None to me so fair as thine,
    Dear Elein.

Thee I sigh to meet again,
    Dear Elein.
Though across the bright blue main,
    Dear Elein,
Ocean waves now roll between
Thee and me, my fairy queen :
Yet their surges cannot part
Thy loved image from my heart,
    Dear Elein.

New York city is thy home,
    Dear Elein ;
I in other cities roam,
    Dear Elein.
I am viewing beauties rare,
Charming and beyond compare :
Wert thou here I should be blest,
Near the city of the West,
    Dear Elein.

Fair Cliftonia is grand,
> Dear Elein,

With its matchless fairy land,
> Dear Elein.

On St. Vincent's rocky height
There is thrilling, pure delight,
Near loved Leigh Wood's sylvan ridge
And the famed Suspension Bridge,
> Dear Elein.

Here I range o'er lovely Downs,
> Dear Elein,

Far from turmoil din of towns,
> Dear Elein.

Could'st thou see each passing sight,
They would fill thee with delight—
In this quiet peaceful shade,
By the God of nature made,
> Dear Elein.

Yet I'll come to thee again,
> Dear Elein,

If the Higher Will ordain,
> Dear Elein.

Take thee heart, my treasured dove,
This is from thy own true love ;
I am coming o'er the sea,
Bringing joy and love for thee,
> Dear Elein.

ODE TO MY MARY.

THOUGHT that life's sweet cup of joy
  For ever from my lips was wrung:
Sad hours of grief without alloy—
  My harp upon the willows hung.
I could not sing—sad hours for me—
  My Mary, till I met with thee.

When morning's voice my slumbers broke
  And to life's duty called away,
My powers so drooping, scarce awoke,
  Were feeble as the falling spray :
I felt o'erwhelmed in life's rough sea,
  My Mary, 'till I mêt with thee.

But thou, like some kind angel come
  From peaceful shore, my woes did feel,
And left thy kindred friends and home
  My bleeding heart's deep wound to heal ;
For it was crushed—sad truth to me—
  My Mary, till I met with thee.

And thou wilt now, my own true wife,
  Those griefs assuage by tender love—
Help me to brave the storms of life,
  And reach the better home above !
I oft despaired that rest to see,
  My Mary, till I met with thee.

But now thy love will cheer my way,
  And soothe my fluttering, throbbing breast,
Allure me on to realms of day—
  The Christian's joy, and pilgrim's rest—
Until the better land we see,
  Where, Mary, I shall meet with thee.

GWENDOLINE.

A Leigh Wood's Story, in Five Parts.

B Y charming Clifton's beautiful Leigh Wood,
    An antiquated mansion long hath stood,
    Which an observant eye may clearly see,
While travelling on the way to Abbot's Leigh :
Where princely Charles the Tenth did safely hide,
Found place of shelter, and would fain abide.
For generations it hath stood the breeze
That swept upon it from the western seas ;
And it seems more enduring every hour
Than doth Cook's Folly with its ivied tower—
Where Egypt's son foretold a father's woe,
Fulfill'd, 'tis said, two centuries ago.
This mansion, be it known, stands on a ridge
Not far from the world-famed Suspension Bridge—
A bridge all ornamental in its place,
That spans the Avon with a queenly grace ;
Close by the valley Nightingale, where sing
Sweet songsters, till the merry woodlands ring
With music, as from heaven to cheer the spot—
True poets feel it their forget-me-not.
A century ago, in this loved home,
A fair young lady lived, who oft did roam
In spring and summer through the Leigh Wood bowers,
And gather'd from their moss beds choice wild flowers—
The primrose, violet, and woodbine sweet,
Which she would fashion into bouquets neat,

And carry them safe home as precious store,
To give new beauty to her neat *boudoir*.
This loved young lady's name was known, I ween,
While she dwelt there, as "graceful Gwendoline."
Now Gwendoline was daughter of a pair
Who had for many years been dwelling there ;
They'd had two sons as well, but now, ah ! me,
One died in battle, one upon the sea.
But Gwendoline was left to dry their tears,
And comfort them in their declining years ;
And this she did with a fond daughter's pride,
In fitting solace sitting by their side.   And
Well they her remembered that sad night,
When her young brother was engaged in fight ;
How she did try to cheer them with the thought
He would be safe in battles that he fought.
He'd find protection where he had his lot
From sword or bayonet and raking shot ;
And then return with joy to give them cheer
In the last month of the declining year.
Alas ! how human hopes are built in vain—
They never saw their youngest son again !
For he had met with an ill-timed defeat,
With Sir John Moore in his sad death retreat
In battle at Corunna : for he died
While fighting bravely at his leader's side.
And when the news came home that he was dead,
It seem'd as though their reason must have had fled ;
But Gwendoline sustained them in their grief,
And tried to give them both some heart relief,
By telling them of One who, if they'd go,
Would find a sovereign balm for all their woe ;
Who sympathised with them in their sad loss—
For He was slain for them upon the cross,
Yet lived again, that He might comfort give

To all His creatures while they here do live
Then, when their elder brother died at sea,
And news came home—all sad as sad could be—
That he was lost beneath the briny wave,
And in the ocean found a sailor's grave,
And they would never meet at home again—
This gave to all of them heartrending pain.
But Gwendoline was found to give them cheer
By telling them, though they would not meet here,
There was a good time coming, when the good
Would meet again beyond the Jordan flood ;
And meeting in the land of no more pain,
Would have true bliss and never part again,
This seem'd to comfort both their hearts awhile,
And soon they greeted her with a love smile,
And call'd her darling with a joy serene,
Their own belov'd, entrancing Gwendoline :
For in the wintertide's long hours she'd sit,
And by their side all cheerful she would knit
Warm stockings for them, as in days of yore
The rich folk knitted for the helpless poor ;
And she would tell them stories in her glee
That she had heard while in the woods of Leigh,
Of old St. Vincent, who his rocks once clave ;
Or the great giant who has left his cave,
As each observant traveller may see
Under fair Clifton's Observatory.
Then she would tell them of a strange report
She'd read in history of famed Leigh Court,
How this known structure that Sir Miles doth hold
Was never once intended to be sold ;
But how in old St. Mary's years ago
Its rightful owner, ere he was laid low,
Laid his own parchments on God's altar free,
And Leigh Court lands bequeathed to charity.

Then Gwendoline would tell them there with pride,
How she had watch'd the flowing Avon's tide,
And seen large ships from the Atlantic come,
Bringing the merry sailors to their home,—
While these would dance upon the decks with glee,
When they old Bristol's welcome port did see ;
Or how the foreign seamen would not dine
Until they pass'd by old St. Vincent's shrine,
Lest they should miss a treat that fiction shocks
And thrills the gazer on St. Vincent's Rocks.
Thus hour by hour she interested them,
And they regarded her as a true gem
Bestowed by heaven to cheer them all the days
That they were passing through life's varied ways.
Thus Gwendoline was busy day by day—
Life duties pressing hourly on her lay
Not only at her own sweet home with glee,
But in the cotters' homes surrounding Leigh ;
Where one was sick there quickly might be seen
The all entrancing form of Gwendoline.
Her kindly face and her all soothing voice
Had often made the widow's heart rejoice,
And many times she cheered with her love breath
Their loved ones passing through the vale of death ;
And when the time had come that they must die,
She then would point them to the joys on high,
Where death and grief and parting are no more,
Within the veil on the all peaceful shore.
Then ofttimes she'd wander by the hill,
Across the greensward on the way to Pill ;
In summer's beauty she would gladly roam
Until she ventured past the smuggler's home.
But she was safe wherever she was seen,
The smugglers whisper'd, " It is Gwendoline."
These daring men who braved the briny deep,

And reckless made a many strong hearts weep,
Would never harm sweet Gwendoline, they said,
Who lived to aid the living and the dead.
When in the darkness, or 'neath starlit sky,
If these did meet her they would pass her by ;
She'd done that night, they knew, had Gwendoline,
Some work of mercy on the village green.
And they knew well, though making many a moan,
'Twas wise to leave good Gwendoline alone ;
For she well knew these smugglers were a ban,
Though they were fashion'd in the form of man.
They had low sunken in the gulf of sin,
And while in the sad chasm they were in,
She would have rescued them with all her heart,
And to do this she bravely did her part :
For many an erring one her voice did win
From the alluring paths of secret sin.
Yes ; Gwendoline's sweet voice these men had heard,
And her loved name was like a household word.
One night when she was coming home from Pill,
And near Leigh Court, on an adjacent hill
The moon was shining with its silvery light
As though to cheer the traveller at night ;
While lustrous stars with beauty o'er her bent,
And dotted like rich gems the firmament.
Sweet Gwendoline, ere she had reached Leigh Wood,
Saw in the distance a fine charger stood ;
And while she hastened onward all alone,
She fancied she could hear a stifled groan.
Then to the spot at once she quickly fled,
And saw a man to all appearance dead ;
While by his side his faithful horse was found,
As though determined not to leave the ground.
Good Gwendoline advanced, and kneeling down,
She found it was a neighbour of renown ;

Young Brentoline, that lived by Ashton Court,
Who had been riding out for a day's sport.
And on that morn as he had cross'd the green
Had raised his hat as he passed Gwendoline ;
She knew him well for reasons she could give,
And hoped for years young Brentoline would live.
She then breath'd softly, " Can I give you aid ?
Are you much hurt ?   Oh, speak, be not afraid ;
I'll do my best to help you.   Will you come
And have a shelter at my own lov'd home ?
Oh, speak and tell me, I will do my best
To now relieve you, and to give you rest."
He rais'd his head a little from the ground
Where it in close proximity was found,
And breath'd, " Where am I ? "   " On the Leigh Wood's green."
" Is that your own sweet voice, Miss Gwendoline?
My horse hath stumbled.   He at something shied,
And I have fallen heavily on my side.
I know you'll help me ; see my bruises dress'd.
Oh, haste, Miss Gwendoline, and do your best "
Sweet Gwendoline then told him she would haste—
Indeed, she felt there was no time to waste,
For she could see 'neath the all brilliant moon
The loss of blood might make him quickly swoon ;
And she breath'd softly, " She would fetch relief
And do her best to mitigate his grief."
Then off she sped as only ladies can
Who wish to solace a young gentleman,
Whom dire misfortune brings near their estate—
They do this duty with a heart elate.

PART II.

WHEN Gwendoline reached home with some alarm,
  Her friends began to think she'd taken harm ;
  But soon she quell'd their fears, and made it known
What she had seen while coming home alone ;
Then bade the servants come with her to where
Young Brentoline was groaning in despair.
While giving orders e'er they onward fled,
There must be there for him prepared a bed ;
Then on they went all speedily, and found
The brave young horseman bleeding on the ground.
And placing him on a strong stretcher there,
They bore him onward to her homestead near ;
While one man-servant hastened in a trice
To Clifton Mall for surgical advice.
Soon help was there, and of a useful kind
For easing both the body and the mind ;
Good Doctor Frear had on a fleet horse come,
And left his carriage at his well-known home.
He could not wait for it on that dread night,
While one was suffering there in such a plight.
He carefully examined, and at once,
Young Brentolıne's disfigured, bleeding sconce ;
And found a scalp wound freely oozing there
That would require his utmost thoughtful care
To probe it, as it should be, for his good :
For it was saturated with his blood.
But he was skilful, and had won a fame
That would be as enduring as his name ;
And he discovered to their great delight
It was not dangerous, and would soon be right.
This news to listening Gwendoline was glad,
For she was waiting there with features sad ;

z

And every word from Doctor Frear to her
Was eagerly drank in, she did aver.
And lest he should in the lone night be worse,
She volunteered at once to be his nurse ;
With one maid near her to assuage his pain,
And trusted he would soon be well again.
This pleased the doctor and her parents too :
They knew good Gwendoline saw what to do ;
She'd had much practice in the Homes at Pill,
For inmates there were often taken ill :
And she would gladly with these—taken worse—
Be kind companion, doctor, or a nurse.
Good Doctor Frear knew this, and when he'd dress'd
Young Brentoline's sad wounds, and done his best,
He left for home– from Leigh Woods rode away,
With a true promise to be there next day.
Then Gwendoline, with thrilling heart delight,
Sat by her patient through the livelong night :
His wants were studied with a thoughtful care,
And she felt glad young Brentoline was there—
Yet sorry he was there in so much pain,
But trusted he would soon be right again :
For, strange though it may seem, she loved him well,
Far more than any human tongue could tell ;
Yet how to show it was to her a task—
She wish'd to learn, and yet she dared not ask—
Lest some false teachers with a ruthless start
Should crush the longing of a faithful heart.
And so she trusted with her common-sense
The guidance of an all-wise Providence,
Who in its own right way on Leigh Wood's Green
Made plain the path of treasur'd Gwendoline ;
And soon she found, to her intense delight,
That all who trust in Providence do right.
His parents came to see their only son

Next morn, before the rising of the sun :
All glad to find he was not injured worse,
And in the home of such a thoughtful nurse ;
Then soon they left him in her watchful care,
Well satisfied that Gwendoline was there.
Young Brentoline grew better day by day,
By well regarding what his nurse did say :
For somehow in a way he understood,
And felt that it would be for his own good ;
And what she'd done for him in every part
Had found its way to his all grateful heart.
For she was its loved object, he well knew,
He loved her now with an affection true ;
But how to tell it was to him just then
A subject he could best do with his pen ;
And he resolved, his faithful love to show,
He'd write sweet Gwendoline a *billet doux*.
Soon he began to gather strength with ease,
For Gwendoline would do her best to please
Her doting patient both by night and day,
To make the hours glide pleasantly away.
When he could leave his bed, she'd softly glide
And lead him like a treasure at her side,
To a nice cosy room fit for a king ;
Then take her harp and play, and sweetly sing
Of what young ladies wish when hearts beat high,
And true young gentlemen, " Sweet by-and-by "—
Those pure sweet trillings that will welcome find
From all who have an elevated mind,
And leave no longings, though they please awhile,
Or base incentives to the low and vile.
Good Doctor Frear came to him day by day,
And soon concluded he might go away ;
But this news was not good, it might be seen,
While looking in the face of Gwendoline

And her young patient : for he then did sigh,
Because he soon would have to say " Good-bye "
To one before him who look'd neat and trim,
And one far more than all the world to him.
But this one thought brought solace to his mind :
He would for her sake try to feel resigned ;
But he determined e'er he went that night
That he would to his heart's true treasure write,
And tell her all he could not with his tongue,
Although his letter might be very long.
He told sweet Gwendoline that afternoon
He wish'd to be left there some time alone :
For he had something for a friend to do,
It was important, for that friend was true.
This strange request of his was granted soon,
And when old time had pass'd the hour of noon,
He went to where he could all free indite,
And Gwendoline a true love letter write :
Which she might read at leisure on some day
When he from her sweet home had gone away.
This letter it was finish'd in a bower,
And sealed securely in the twilight hour ;
Then he soon went were Gwendoline did stand,
And placed the lengthy letter in her hand,
And said, " Miss Gwendoline, I humbly pray
You'll read this o'er when I am gone away ;
Its contents may surprise and trouble you,
Yet I will vouch that you will find them true.
If when you've read them will you please reply,
I shall on you, Miss Gwendoline, rely ;
I thank you much for all your service shown,
Since that sad night you found me all alone.
I cannot tell you all I wish to say,
But I shall feel your debtor every day ;
And I will tell you this with grateful pride—

Had it not been for you I must have died.
My life was saved by you within your doors,
And if you wish it, from henceforth 'tis yours ;
My carriage I see waiting on the lawn,
And I feel glad Miss Gwendoline was born.
Farewell at present, my devoted nurse,
I'll come to you if I again am worse ;
My love to all your friends I cannot see,
Give these my kind regards for care to me :
I trust to see you all and soon again,
And you, Miss Gwendoline, must write me when.
Good-by, loved Gwendoline. *Au revoir.*"
He clasp'd her hand, then sought his carriage door,
And she look'd after him with feelings strange,
For over him she knew had come a change ;
And over her, as well she then could prove,
A change embodied in that sweet word, Love :
Not low bred passion from a mind impure,
But love all faithful that will e'er endure.

PART III.

YOUNG Brentoline reach'd home with heart elate,
Lov'd parents met him at the hall yard gate ;
And gave him greeting that was past compare,
Like parents give their only son and heir,—
When they have reach'd again their home with glee
From varied perils on the land or sea.
His mother clasp'd him to her throbbing breast,
And felt her anxious mind once more at rest :
For when the news arrived that he had been
In sudden danger on the Leigh Wood's Green,
And that his horse had thrown him to the ground,
The startling news his mother did astound ;

And she had fear'd, as mothers do in pain,
She might not see her darling son again,
But now he stood before her and was well—
Oh, she had rapture more than heart could tell.
And then his father with a joyful mind
Told him how pleased he was again to find
Him home once more, his hope for future years,
And he was free from all foreboding fears.
Then at their table on that meeting night
Young Brentoline his parents did delight :
He told them why it was he went to roam
That autumn morning from his own lov'd home,
And how his horse on their return at night
Had thrown him over, owing to a fright
The noble creature had near old Leigh Wood,
That neither did the horse or rider good ;
But he was better now—and with good sense
He said he owed it all to Providence,
Who had provided him with such a friend
As found him when all hope seem'd at an end,
And nurs'd him as a sister would have done
A brother, and his parents' only son.
He said she seem'd to him a fairy queen,
He never could forget Miss Gwendoline ;
His life he felt had been preserv'd by her,
And this all fearlessly he did aver :
And while he valued her above all price,
His parents exchang'd glances in a trice,
And felt there was a spirit in their boy
From love's pure source that added to his joy,
And would to theirs if they had rightly seen
That love was fixed upon good Gwendoline ;
And when he'd done his story they were blest,
Then said good-night, and sweetly went to rest.
But Gwendoline was at her home alone,

For when the carriage of her love was gone
She hasten'd with the letter in her hand,
And laid it on the cover of her stand
Beneath the window of her chamber neat,
To read it over as a fond heart's treat
Soon as the setting sun had gone to rest—
For it was slowly sinking in the West,
And then 'twas scarcely light enough to read
Without—a light she certainly would need ;
In a short time she'd read it without fear
Beneath her waiting taper that was near.
But while the twilight moments pass'd away,
She sang a lyric to departing day,
And looking through her window in the shade,
She watch'd loved objects in the distance fade—
Old Dundry Tower, of which, 'tis often said,
Looks like a giant that has lost his head ;
And near it something it could not resist,
It seem'd envelop'd in a cloud of mist.
Then Ashton Court in that declining day
Seem'd like a spectre that was clad in grey,
While o'er the meadows and the crystal rills
There was a shadow of the Mendip Hills ;
And Gwendoline was dreaming, as she sat,
Of one she loved, who would in pleasant chat
Delight her ; but he now from her had gone,
And she was thinking of him there alone—
Yet while she mused she fancied she had seen
The shadow of a man upon the green,
And started with a fear no tongue can tell
Until she heard anon the hall door bell,
And to her room at someone's strange command,
A servant brought a letter in her hand,
Then placing it before her as her due,
She said, " Miss Gwendoline, this is for you."

She took it from the maid as in a fright,
And wish'd her kindly to bring in a light :
This she did swiftly to dispel the gloom—
Then Gwendoline was in her lighted room.
And when the maid was gone her head soon bent
To glance upon the letter that was sent :
Its envelope was scented she did find,
Yet this brought no true pleasure to her mind :
For she knew the handwriting was not his
That would have brought her an inherent bliss.
His writing was before her on the stand,
This was not like it she had in her hand
Where could it come from ? It was strange indeed—
It had no post-mark on it, she could read :
But she would open it at once—'twas best,
And that would set her troubled mind at rest.
She broke the seal amazed—for it was seal'd
As though it held what someone wished conceal'd
From any eye but hers : lest they should read
What only was for Gwendoline indeed.
The letter opened with, " Miss Gwendoline,
Will you excuse me ? I have lately seen
You very often—though I here must say
You don't know me, I'm living miles away :
Yet visit in this neighbourhood at times,
Close by Stoke Bishop, my old Uncle Chrimes ;
Who has some riches, and he's taking care
Of these, 'tis said, for me, his only heir.
He's growing feeble, and I often come
To see this uncle at his quiet home.
And he's worth looking after, I see this :
He holds the money to give mankind bliss,
And womankind as well, or I mistake—
Though it has given many the heart-ache.
But what I want in truth to you to say,

Is what I trust will give you joy to-day.
Will you bestow on me your heart and hand?—
Then I will ever be at your command.
I should rejoice if I could call you mine,
And this is sent to lead you to incline
Your ear to a true lover, you may tell,
And one who wishes you through this life well.
I've heard much of you from my uncle's friends,
And as my fortune on uncle depends
I wish to please them, and my uncle too—
And I should do it if I could have you.
I will confess I like a jovial life,
And shall do after I have won a wife :
I don't believe that when a couple's wed
They should grow mopish, as if they were dead.
I love to go to theatres at night,
And dance in ball-rooms till the morning light ;
And I enjoy the races year by year,
To do a little betting—quietly, my dear—
With some known flats, who often there are bold,
And ease them of a little of their gold.
To do it right I get them on the spree,
And then 'tis easy work, I know, for me :
I treat them well to brandy if it's cheap,
And then I fleece them as they do the sheep.
I think I've told you most of my delights,
Excepting that I'm fond of all prize fights :
I rather like to see two bruisers meet—
It is to me, I know, a welcome treat.
I brought this letter on myself to-night,
And ask you earnestly that you will write
And tell me after this, my first advance,
If you suppose I shall have any chance
To claim for life a lady I have seen,
The Leigh Wood's beauty—you, Miss Gwendoline.

Let not this letter fill your mind with wrath,
But write at once to my address at Bath:
'A Fortune Hunter, daily on the stump,
At number sixty, near the city pump.'"
This letter gave Miss Gwendoline some fear,
She could not think why he should then come there:
He might have sent the letter through the post,
'Twould not have hurt him for the price it cost—
Although the postage then was more, we know,
Than in this age, when for one stamp they go.
And he dare not for shame, the roving blade,
To send the letter, were it not prepaid:
But visiting his uncle he did roam,
And left the letter ere he started home;
While no doubt thinking in the Leigh Woods green
He might by chance have met good Gwendoline.

PART IV.

ISS Gwendoline at once this letter placed
Aside, and wished its contents were erased
Both from her mind, and his who sent it there:
Because she knew 'twould add to his despair
What he would gather from her quick reply—
There was no hope for him, he might rely.
Then taking from the table, all serene,
The other letter from young Brentoline,
She opened it with glee, intent to scan
What was for her from this young gentleman.
The letter read: " Miss Gwendoline, I write
This long epistle with intense delight:
That you may read it over day by day,
Now I from your sweet home have gone away.
I tell you here all that I could not tell

When I in Leigh Woods bade you fond farewell ;
I long admired you I can truly prove,
And soon my admiration changed to love—
The love, I mean, that changes cannot part,
Which issues only from the faithful heart ;
A love increasing, and that will endure,
Because the fountain whence it flows is pure.
Not ill-flamed passion that corrodes as rust,
And only emanates from warring lust.
No ! mine is love from an affection strong,
That will not lead its wise possessor wrong.
I offer it to you because 'tis just,
The free-will offering of a true heart's trust.
You saved my life, and with devotion true
That life with gladness is now offered you ;
You were my nurse when I in danger stood,
And I have named you Gwendoline the Good ;
You have been good to me in nature's strife,
Now crown that blessing, and become my wife.
My mode of life is somewhat known to you :
I love life pleasures if they are but true.
But what to some is pleasure I disdain,
Because it brings its mad possessor pain.
I never take the blighting drunkard's drink,
And to proclaim it I will never shrink ;
It is our country's curse I long have known,
Producing widows' and the orphans' moan.
Then I ne'er visit places I could name—
The midnight dancing with its doubtful fame ;
The theatre contains no charms for me,
Nor does the maddening haunts of revelry.
I love to go to places where I know
I shall have pleasure and shall wiser grow :
Where friends convivial meet, and try to find
Some elevating culture for the mind,—

That I may be to others living here
Of true life service in my duty sphere.
My fortune here I cannot tell to you,
Because I know not yet what is my due.
You know I am my parents' only child,
And with them I now here am domiciled;
But they would joy to know that you and me
Were one day joined, as all who love should be,
In bonds that Hymen forges with delight,
For those who wear them with a purpose right.
They have connubial bliss from day to day,
Because they live and love, and pull one way.
When I shall have my fortune 'tis not known,
Nor am I anxious, I am free to own.
I wish my parents to have long life here,
Because I them with filial love revere;
Their life to me is dearer far than wealth,
And I shall glory in their long good health:
Yet when they leave the world, they've made it known,
Their wealth will then descend to me alone;
And until that time comes they have confessed
To make me happy they will do their best.
Now if good Gwendoline the same will write,
That welcome message will my heart delight;
Think o'er what I have written on the green,
And send me quick reply, loved Gwendoline."
She held this letter like an angel meek,
Till crystal tear drops trickled down her cheek,
While these all pleasing thoughts passed through her mind:
Oh! what a loving letter, and how kind
To think of me who found him on the green—
A nurse that he has named good Gwendoline.
And now he loves me; well, I must love him—
My cup of joy is filling to the brim;
He's worthy of my love, I see this clear,

More than a fortune hunter, fond of beer.
He is so frank, and opens out his soul,
A true bred lady could his life control;
I'll see my parents and without delay,
And send my answer on an early day.
Both letters they shall see, and all be told—
For one is dross, the other sterling gold.
The clock struck ten just as good Gwendoline
Had read her letters with a soul serene,
And she sped to her chamber with delight,
When she had kissed her parents sweet good-night.
Next morning to the breakfast table came
Good Gwendoline, to win a daughter's fame
From her loved parents, who were waiting there,
To see her seated on her 'customed chair;
But ere she sat, she did not let them miss
Her sweet "Good morning" and the welcome kiss.
And then she showed them what she had in store—
Two letters she'd received the night before;
And sitting on her chair without ado,
She read both letters to her parents through.
One did surprise them very much indeed—
That from the fortune hunter in his need;
They thought he needed not to her apply,
She did not want a man that's always dry.
Not always seeking, as a venture bold,
To have his way with a young lady's gold:
And so they told good Gwendoline to send
By post: he need not on their child depend.
The other letter gave them true delight,
It was what they expected from that night
Their daughter found him, ere it was too late,
In his great danger near the abbot's gate.
The marked attention she had shown him then
Had brought this frank avowal from his pen;

And they were glad indeed, from what they'd seen,
For they respected much young Brentoline.
The contents of his letter to the brim
Had well established what they'd thought of him ;
His love for his dear parents seemed to them
More than a jewel to a diadem :
For jewels perish by the hand of time,
But love to parents was a joy sublime,
That yields its true possessors no sad sigh,
And no misgivings when they have to die.
They told good Gwendoline, when they did find
That they could read the longings of her mind,
That she might ask young Brentoline to tea,
And say he was a welcome guest at Leigh ;
And that their daughter, Gwendoline the Good —
Who his long letter fully understood—
Would be delighted, as their treasured gem,
To say he had a welcome, and from them.
And then she left the breakfast table glad—
Good Gwendoline had no cause to be sad ;
Her parents had endowed her with full powers
To welcome him she loved to Leigh Wood bowers :
This would give pleasure, she could plainy see,
To have dear Brentoline for company.
It seemed to her the dawning of a life
That augured for her the new sphere of wife —
For she knew well his letter was designed
To comfort two in heart, in soul and mind.
And so she hasten'd to her quiet room —
The morning sun had banished all its gloom,
And then was shining through the window bright,
As though to add to Gwendoline's delight ;
While famed old Dundry's tower stood out all clear,
As though it had to guard the Mendips near.
Then Gwendoline sat down and took her pen,

To write in haste to two young gentlemen.
Her first epistle she resolved should be
Addressed to him who boldly came to Leigh
The fortune hunter, seeking after game—
This she concluded from his noted name,
And his pursuits in varied walks of life :
For he was hunting for a wealthy wife.
Her letter it commenced, " Dear sir, I write
To answer yours that came on yesternight :
In which you state, in language all serene,
You wish to have for wife Miss Gwendoline.
My answer, sir, to you is simply this,
I cannot condescend to give you bliss,
By sacrificing mine to be your wife—
For this might bring to both unseemly strife.
When marriage is intended, I oft read
It must be shown the two are well agreed :
But you and I, sir, differ —and so much,
On subjects I have scarcely time to touch,
That we should be, I fear, were we to wed,
Regarded as two subjects off our head.
I'll give my reasons, then you must decide
If I have not true reason for my guide :
You are a fortune hunter—yes, 'tis true,
And you have relatives, 'tis said, like you,
Who hunt young ladies, in a manner bold,
To get possession of the lady's gold.
And when 'tis gained, if he can have control,
She must not then dare breathe she has a soul :
But on his fancies she must ere depend,
While he her gold in riot lives to spend—
Instead of husbanding it well through life
To benefit his family and wife.
Then, sir, you say the theatre you love,
But I do not, and you shall have the proof ;

I hold the theatre, in this our day,
Though more refined, still lures the young away
From paths of virtue by each lustful dress,
And through its glitter brings them soul distress.
If not, why is it on each crowded night
The painted harlots flock there with delight,—
And when the young play-lovers go away,
Are hovering round them like the birds of prey?
Are these not facts that heart conviction brings?—
And facts, you know 'tis said, are stubborn things:
I may be hiss'd at for these facts by you,
But I must give to every man his due.
What if you hiss, your hissing only makes
You like a cousin to the geese and snakes;
That is their language in this age of ours,
As I have heard it near the Leigh Wood bowers.
Then you have told me you're a racing man,
And I will tell you as I have began,
That betting men, with all their store of gold,
When buying others are as often sold;
And if they sometimes win as on they go,
Their winning is another's overthrow:
And wealth that's won by betting, I must tell,
For true enjoyment never weareth well.
Then you have told me one of your delights
Is found when you are visiting prize fights:
Oh, what refinement, what a cultured taste,
To see two men stripp'd naked to the waist,
And beating one another like two tools
To please some gaping empty-headed fools!
And you a gentleman.   Oh, what a blot!
If you are fond of bruising, I am not;
Were I your wife, I might at some day tell
That I came in for bruising blows as well:
Your proposition, sir, I must decline

For one more reason, you are fond of wine—
I mean the wine, that poisoner of the brain,
The love of which has fill'd the world with pain ;
Our country's curse, the blighter of its life,
That severs oft the husband and the wife,
And leaves their starving children prey to crime,
Like pity's beacons on the sands of time.
I now must close this letter," she did write,
" Its contents, sir, may not yield you delight :
Yet I shall joy, if in this dark world's strife
These lead you onward to a better life—
And now, conclude this note from Leigh Woods' Green
As a *finale* from Miss Gwendoline."

PART V.

AND now came Gwendoline's delightful part,
        To write to him whose love was in her heart ;
        And with a willing hand she dipp'd her pen,
Then wrote to one of nature's gentlemen
As a devoted and young lady can—
For with her heart and love she thus began :
" Dear Brentoline, I hasten with delight
To send reply to what I had last night
In that sweet letter near the woods of Leigh,
For its contents brought true heart joy to me.
I read it o'er and o'er, when you were gone,
In my own chamber, quiet and alone ;
Its every word was precious to my mind,
Although 'tis said by some that love is blind ;
It may be blind at times, but you'll agree
It was not blind when finding you and me.
Love might be shy once, on its new trod ground,
But it was joyous when it us two found ;

And now it 's found a way to both our hearts,
We will sustain it in its varied parts.
I read your letter to my parents dear
This morning while at breakfast, without fear :
For I have always found it best to ask
Their wise advice when I have had a task—
And I had one this morning, I confess :
For there had come last night to my address
Another letter from a would be friend—
And I have just another to him penn'd—
A fortune hunter from a city near :
But I have answered him all free from fear,
And such an answer as he will not prize
When it has come in contact with his eyes.
His letter you shall see some future day,
When you are coming by the Leigh Woods' way ;
My parents heard his letter with disdain,
And I know well he will not write again—
Though o'er its contents he may chance look grim,
I feel assured my answer settled him.
You will excuse me when I tell you this,
The subject of your letter gives me bliss ;
And what is now a priceless joy to me,
Is that in all our tastes we well agree.
You love true pleasure, as I always do,
Because true pleasure it is always true ;
It seeks to elevate the heart and mind,
And on its leaving leaves no sting behind.
Like me, I find, who live by Leigh Woods' bowers,
You have no longing for the midnight hours ;
But well believe, to have a life all blest,
Before the midnight you must go to rest.
And then with gratitude I joy to think
That you ne'er drank the blighting drunkard's drink :
In this one thing we cordially agree

In what is meant by true sobriety—
An abstinence from that which I disdain,
Strong drink—the harbinger of woe and pain.
And though so many plead its moderate use,
And only condemn men for its abuse,
They cannot see what you and I well know,
For strength and health it is no good below.
'Tis but a stimulant to leave folk worse,
Instead of blessing, 'tis a nation's curse ;
And blest are they who from this drink abstain,
That poisons both the healthful blood and brain.
But I must not this letter close to you,
Until I've told you what I feel is true.
It is that I have had much joy to find
That Christian principles possess your mind ;
Together we in this may well rejoice,
For I have made this, too, my early choice.
It doth sustain me in the way of life,
Amid the world's anxiety and strife ;
And with it we shall find true bliss below,
For with its guidance we shall wiser grow.
And now I close this letter, and invite
You to my own dear home on Friday night.
My parents will be glad to see you here,
And so will Gwendoline, you need not fear.
Write by return, and say if you can come,
For we shall sure expect you at our home ;
And till I hear from you at Leigh Woods' Green,
I will subscribe myself—your Gwendoline."
This letter reached young Brentoline that night,
And filled him with an exquisite delight :
For when he'd read it at his domicile,
He went to his fond parents with a smile,
And told them all, like an obedient son,
What he had said and Gwendoline had done.

This gave them joy that only parents know
Who wish their offspring happiness below.
Young Brentoline at once began to write,
To answer his loved Gwendoline that night;
And he arranged, as men of honour do,
With heart sincere, when they desire to woo.
He promised Gwendoline, with love inspired,
He would be there the evening she desired;
And on the promised night, near famed Leigh Wood,
This worthy lover made his promise good.
He was received with rapture on that night
By her loved parents, for they deemed it right
To thus receive him who had favour won
From their prized daughter, and to be their son.
Good Gwendoline was glad as glad could be,
To once more there her first true lover see;
And through the evening they had pleasure new,
In planning through life's future what to do.
Then they recalled the wonders of that night
When his own faithful horse received its fright,
And it was found by her, on Leigh Woods' Green,
Who was to be through life his Gwendoline.
And though to him it was a dangerous fall,
They thought they saw a Providence in all.
He had the bitter to his joy complete,
And what was bitter had now brought the sweet.
Thus gladly did the evening glide away,
And her fond lover could no longer stay;
But he'd improved the moments as they sped,
And so had Gwendoline he onward led,
Until they parted in the Leigh Woods' Lane,
With a love promise soon to meet again.
There was to be no hindrance to his will—
He always would be welcome on the hill;
And soon he came again, and every time

Brought with it for them both a joy sublime :
For they would stroll in summertide's bright hours,
And gather in Leigh Woods the sweet wild flowers.
While on returning they would gaze with pride
Upon the winding Avon's flowing tide ;
And see the shipping passing Pill with glee,
With heavy cargoes from across the sea.
Thus they would linger, as true lovers do
Who have acquired the aptitude to woo ;
And sometimes they would whisper 'neath the sky
Of coming pleasures in sweet by-and-by,
When they would have a home, and what was right
To make their home a mansion of delight,
And life worth living for, without the dread
Of lacking comfort or the daily bread :
For Providence had blest them in the land—
Bestowed them favours with abundant hand.
And for this they felt thankful side by side—
It did not fill them with unseemly pride.
Heaven's gifts they knew, in order to excel,
To e'er act wisely they must use them well—
For they well knew these gifts were all bestowed
By the Good Giver to be spread abroad :
Not hoarded up with a strong, clutching hand,
While there was so much hunger in the land,
But used for purposes they understood—
The true heart's luxury of doing good.
Thus days and weeks and many months were spent
In true love's quiet and in heart content,
And merry Christmastide was coming on
When two young hearts were longing to be one :
And one of these proposed without a fear
A question to the other all sincere,
Yet in a way that gave her no distress :
For to it soon she sweetly whisper'd " Yes."

And joy had her loved parents on that night ;
For they had faith the answer would be right,
And this they told the happy lovers there,
Which freed them from another anxious care.
They told young Brentoline it gladden'd them
To promise him their precious, treasur'd gem,
Lov'd Gwendoline, who lived for doing good—
To all who knew her this was understood ;
And they would offer her to him with pride,
If all was well, in merry Christmastide :
They felt assured that he would guard her fame,
And she would add a lustre to his name.
Their meeting at the first had been so strange,
As though kind Providence did it arrange ;
How it was done no mortal tongue could tell,
But it was done, and they believ'd done well.
They sought for guidance on the path of right,
And seeking it had brought them inward light
That only comes to those who are sincere,
To useful be in their life's duty sphere.
They pray'd that Gwendoline and he might live
For others' weal, to sad hearts comforts give,
And this to them would a true solace be,
Both at their home and in the woods of Leigh.
They should have wealth when they were domicil'd
With Gwendoline the good, their only child :
Her marriage portion they could safely trust
With him she loved, young Brentoline the just ;
And her loved father would, on Christmas day,
With joy to him, give Gwendoline away.
Thus all was well arranged with true delight,
And loved ones whispered sweet " Good-night."

CONCLUSION.

'Twas merry Christmas morning, and the bells
From old Leigh Church sent music through the dells :
Reminding all around it was the morn
When He, the Babe of Bethlehem, was born ;
While near Leigh Woods a wedding party had
A look'd for Christmas meeting, and were glad—
It was young Brentoline, 'twas understood,
And his heart's treasure—Gwendoline the good.
Their parents joined them on that joyful day,
And then to the old Church soon drove away
With their two loved ones they now look'd upon,
Who, all delighted, would be soon made one.
Good Vicar Fry was there, array'd n white,
All eager to perform the marriage rite ;
While friends from Ashton, Abbot's Leigh, and Pill,
With smiling faces did the old church fill.
Two hands were joined, a prayer was said, and then
The people with loud voices cried, " Amen ;"
And then went home with glee to famed Leigh Wood
A husband loved, and—Gwendoline the good.

DOING RIGHT.

THESE are only two short words,
    Yet what meaning they convey ;
Only those these understand
    Who are walking wisdom's way.
They have found, while heeding them,
    An incessant, pure delight :
Worth more than a diadem,
    This employ of doing right.

POOR FRED.

POOR Fred! And who was he?
Well, he was one well known to me,
And I must write his elegy—
                    Poor Fred.

I loved on him to gaze,
Yes, even in his childhood days,
With all his little winning ways—
                    Poor Fred.

But now, with tear-dim'd sight,
A farewell dirge I have to write:
An In Memoriam indite—
                    Poor Fred.

He had a mother mild,
Who on his infant features smiled,
But died and left her youngest child—
                    Poor Fred.

Then he had a tossing life,
With much of this world's sorrow rife,
And many a pang of inward strife—
                    Poor Fred.

He once gainèd some renown,
In hamlet, city, village, town,
And yet he always tumbled down—
Poor Fred.

Strange things would him retard,
While he felt like many a bard,
That this cold world had used him hard—
Poor Fred.

'Tis said 'twas his complaint :
Keen, fell consumption, that did paint
Him sombre scenes without restraint—
Poor Fred.

Yet somehow failings sore
He had, like very many more ;
Yet these I know he did deplore—
Poor Fred.

And he had, what I deem
Some traits that won him much esteem :
Though transient as a passing dream—
Poor Fred.

But now he 's done with all
The changes of this earthly ball :
He has gone hence at death's stern call—
Poor Fred.

Before he pass'd away,
One lovely autumn Sabbath day,
He had bright hopes of heaven, they say—
Poor Fred.

And now he lies at rest,
With some love roses on his breast ;
It was God's will, and it is best—

Poor Fred.

Near St. Mark's ivied dome,
In Lower Easton's turfy loam,
He sleeps, and has his peaceful home—

Poor Fred.

An elm and chestnut wave
Their outspread branches o'er his grave,
And now from all molest will save—

Poor Fred.

His friends will visit there,
Then o'er him shed the sorrow tear,
And often sigh when passing near—

Poor Fred.

Poor Fred—in peace depart ;
Though thou did'st die from death's cold dart,
Thou liv'st yet in thy father's heart—

Poor Fred.

IS IT RIGHT TO GO TO WAR?

IS it right for men to meet
    On the gory battle plain :
Killing there some brother man,
    'Mid excruciating pain ?
If the Bethlehem angels' song,
    And the welcome Bethlehem Star,
Both were true, it is not right
    Now for men to go to war.

DRUSILLA DORE:

THE HEROINE OF CLIFTON VALE.

N Clifton's charming vale, with trees arow,
There stood erect—some centuries ago—
An antiquated manse in Doric style,
With roof-tree groaning 'neath its dark red tile :
For slating, that now comes by Swansea Bay,
Had not found favour as it has to-day,
To cover mansions in each snug retreat,
And giving unto all appearance neat.
Yet this old manse had an attractive view,
And it was large, as its possessor knew,
Who had it built to gratify his taste :
Not for investment, nor in too much haste,
Like far too many in each crowded town—
Just built for profit and to tumble down !
But this renown'd, lov'd homestead, now is gone,
Though it was built with 'during pennant stone ;
For modern taste, with its unsparing hand,
Has on its site now reared a structure grand
More pleasing to the eye and modern pride,
Though far less comfort may be found inside.
For in this grand old dwelling there was love,
All pure and fervent (we shall shortly prove)—
A love that grew and flourished more and more,
In this sweet homestead of Drusilla Dore.
And who was this Drusilla, with her fame,
That bore a Jewish, yet endearing name?

What was she noted for? We long to hear—
Was she a heroine, with love sincere?
Have patience, kindly reader, you shall know
Drusilla's history, and from "long ago."
Her parents they were both descendants of
A race enduring many a jeer and scoff
From varied peoples underneath the sun—
The seed of Abraham; yet e'en these had won
Immortal honour, that all free descends
From Him whoe'er in pity condescends
To bear with all the creatures in His sight,
And gives them guidance to the path of right;
For they had seen the light dawn from afar—
Had hailed the presence of the Morning Star!
The scales of darkness that once closed their eyes
Had fallen from them with a glad surprise,
And they had found a fair and priceless gem—
Reflected by the Star of Bethlehem:
Had both determined, with a joy serene,
To tread the footprints of the Nazarene.
This firm resolve of theirs soon made a noise
Amid their kinsmen, who with clamorous voice
Denounc'd them as apostate: and with jeers
Pronounced on each "Anathema!" with sneers,
And bade them flee for refuge from their place
Amid the Christian and the Gentile race.
Drusilla's parents bore this taunting for awhile—
Yet welcomed persecution with a smile,
For Him who bore much shame and agony
On Calvary's mountain, on a rugged tree;
Yet their harsh treatment, one remembered day,
Made them resolve at once to flee away,
And seek for peace and shelter in some place
Where they would not be subject to disgrace
For loving Him, whose love to them was such—

They knew, indeed, they could not love too much.
Yet, where to go, to them was somewhat strange,
And long they tried to finally arrange ;
Yet could not settle what could both approve,
Until they sought true guidance from above :
And then their path was clear—they both did see—
Mark'd out for them as plain as plain could be.
And it was this—to sell their varied store,
And sail for Albion's ever welcome shore,
Where all are sheltered from the tyrant's hand
For faith in Christ, and following His command ;
Where consciences are free who take delight
In following what is good, and true, and right.
And one remembered night they quickly left
Their Jewish people as a pair bereft
Of what, to them, was now more worth than gold —
The love of kindred—with a grief untold.
The silvery moon, on this eventful night,
Shed on them beams of her all-welcome light
As they sped on alone with silent lip,
To reach the harbour for a waiting ship,
Which bore them safe from Alexandria's fort,
To seek a homestead in old Bristol's port.
The autumn leaves from Clifton poplars tall,
Near famed Leigh Woods, had just begun to fall,
When her loved parents, in the good ship " Clyde,"
Came sailing onward with the Avon's tide :
And landed, 'mid the chime of evening bells,
Close by the basin at renown'd Hotwells.
Then life with them had to begin anew,
And for a time they scarce knew what to do :
Though Clifton scenery was rich and grand,
They both were strangers then in a strange land !
They felt that life was real, and the sage
Must make provision for a ripe old age.

Two hundred pounds in sterling British gold
They had in store, Drusilla's father told
A friend, who saw them leave their native land.
And this to them was like a bird-in-hand :
For they it wanted, though a small amount,
To use in trade and to the best account.
Drusilla's father look'd around at once to see,
If in Old Bristowe and its company
He could employ what he had saved of yore,
And so invest it as to make it more.
He visited, and oft, the busy quays,
And met with merchants from across the seas ;
Then had some converse with them as to trade,
And where good bargains could at once be made.
For though a Christian, he had Cromwell's eye—
" To trust in God, and keep his powder dry ! "
And so he meant—but only for the right,
And in all trading keep his honour bright.
One day he fell in with some polish'd knaves,
Who did a bus'ness in kidnapping slaves ;
And who long tried to show him it would be
To his advantage, if he could agree,
And join with them to any known extent—
For they could realise in full, and cent. per cent.
The trade in slaves was generally good—
By all who knew it, this was understood ;
And though at times there was a little risk,
This soon was remedied when trade was brisk !
Drusilla's father heard them to the end,
But would no longer time with these men spend :
He told them frankly that he never would
Invest his savings in men's flesh and blood ;
He was a Christian, with a soul to save,
And being this, would never own a slave :
For his Creator made man to be free—

This was man's birthright, he could plainly see ;
Then why should he (by trading) be a knave,
And barter with the poor downtrodden slave?
Oh, no ! If he invested gold, it e'er should be,
Not to make captives, but to set them free.
The smooth-faced villains laughed aloud at this—
It seem'd a moment to create them bliss.
He well knew then their consciences were dead,
And so he left them with a hasty tread.
But he soon found an old sea captain nigh,
Who had the look of candour in his eye ;
And then a converse they began with glee,
On trade and commerce far across the sea.
He heard from this old captain (while they stood)
Some news, he thought, might be for his own good—
That on some islands, by the famed South Sea,
The natives eager long'd for what could be
Produced in Bristol at a little cost,
And this good news was not upon him lost :
For he determined then to do his best,
And in those articles at once invest ;
Then cross the sea in this old captain's boat,
And see those islands while they were afloat.
He hastened home, as though 'twere for his life,
And told the secret to his valued wife,
Who, though all loth to part with him she lov'd—
She e'er to him a faithful wife had proved—
Yet she consented, though reluctantly,
For she was then a mother soon to be ;
But sense of duty overcame her then,
With brightened hopes of meeting him again.
A week from thence his purchases were made
In what he thought would pay him well to trade ;
And kissing his lov'd wife, he soon set sail
With the old captain and a favoured gale :

Where in due time they both, with heartfelt glee,
Safe reached the southern islands of the sea.
The natives throng'd to view this trader come
From o'er the waters and the white man's home;
And when his wares were all exposed to view,
They gazed with rapture on inventions new,
And gladly barter'd ivory and gold
For what the white man offered to be sold.
His profit on their first exchange was great —
He sold all out, and had not long to wait.
Then he resolv'd, as speedy as he could,
To make another venture just as good;
And so he shipp'd at once for Albion's shore,
With well fill'd purse, to fetch another store.
His heart beat high with rapture that was new
When Bristol's well-known channel came in view :
For he saw in it, with a glowing pride,
A many vessels waiting for the tide;
And found, when nearing it, with joy sublime,
Their vessel too, for it was just in time—
Then on the flowing Avon they sped well,
Until they landed at the famed Hotwell.
With bounding heart he soon was on the shore,
And hurried onward to a well-known door,
Where one he lov'd was waiting his return,
And where he hoped all speedily to learn
Some more good news that peaceful summer's night,
To give his mind a rapturous delight.
His well-known foot was heard, and long before
He reach'd the threshold of their homestead door,
By her who loved him with a love sincere—
Yes; his quick footstep caught her waiting ear,
And springing to her feet without alarms,
She found herself soon folded in his arms!
Then fond heart kisses fell on each one's cheek,

And so two hearts were full—too full to speak,
Until the first surprise of love was o'er,
That came o'erwhelming from the heart's deep core.
At length his own true wife breath'd thick and fast—
" At home, my love, at home—safe home at last ! "
" Safe home," he whisper'd ; " and I have done well,
Far better than I dare to some folk tell :
For I must go again to where I've been,
And you will soon be happy as a queen.
But tell me, love, how you have fared, I say,
From first to last, since I have been away ? "
" Oh, I have done as well as you," she said ;
While gently taking from his breast her head.
Then leading him all gladsome by the hand,
But a distance from where they did stand,
They reach'd a little wicker cradle near,
And soon she pointed to a treasure there—
A little jewel, and but six months old,
Yet worth far more than thrice its weight in gold.
It lay all smiling with its bright black eyes,
The darling had a pleasant, new surprise ;
And so had he—for with a rapture wild
He there beheld his lovely first-born child :
And taking it from out its baby nest,
He held the sweet one fondly to his breast ;
Then kiss'd their treasure, for he could not speak,
While tears of gladness trickled down his cheek.
The more he kiss'd, he hugg'd the darling more—
And this lov'd treasure was Drusilla Dore !

PART II.

THREE weeks at home Drusilla's father spent
With two he treasur'd, and in heart content ;
Meanwhile he made new purchases with ease
In Bristol city, and upon the quays,
Of what he knew would an advantage be
To him and other folk beyond the sea.
The profits of the voyage made before
Had largely added to his former store ;
And he invested all he had again,
Assured 'twould treble when he cross'd the main.
With hopes all bright he left his treasur'd wife,
And his lov'd babe, the new hope of his life ;
Then setting sail with a propitious breeze,
He landed safe once more across the seas.
His voyage this time was a glad surprise,
For he soon sold his stock of merchandise ;
And far more profit came to swell his store
Than he acquired the voyage made before :
For what he sold the natives saw, with bliss,
It was for their advantage as for his—
For he had shown, in copper pans and tin,
His object then was not to take them in :
But let them have what would of service be,
And, trading with them, traded honestly.
Then he shipp'd once more home, and on the way
Resolv'd next voyage he would longer stay,
And make arrangements with the firm of NASH,
To have his goods sent on by sending cash :
Then it would give him time, he had no doubt,
To new and better customers find out.
He reach'd old Bristol port all safe once more,
And hasten'd gladly to his well-known door ;

But ere he reach'd it by the garden gate
He hath, forsooth, a little time to wait :
For there was, peering through in perfect bliss,
A pair of little eyes that look'd like his—
A pair of tiny feet had come along
The garden path, although not very strong—
For there stood up his own Drusilla Dore,
Whom he had left a babe ten months before !
He clasp'd the little treasure in his arms,
And she seem'd free from any soul alarms ;
Then kiss'd the prattler with a joy unknown
(Except to parents, when they kiss their own).
This loud commotion at the garden gate
Brought out Drusilla's mother, all elate ;
And then was joyful greeting in this life
Between a faithful husband and his wife.
Their happy home was enter'd soon with glee,
And long recitals made with harmony
By both in raptures, of what they had seen
Since last they parted by the Leigh Woods' green
He then told his true wife of his intent,
And hoped that she would try and feel content,
When he went on his voyage the next time,
To trade and barter in a distant clime ;
For he had thought when he was far away,
It would be best a longer time to stay ;
Then he could give more time to look around
And see where some new openings might be found :
Where he could profits make of useful kind,
To satisfy the body and the mind.
Drusilla's mother heard this with surprise,
And to him turn'd her bright, imploring eyes—
As though she would, with her fond heart inclin'd,
Dissuade him from a purpose thus designed.
He saw her look, and well knew what it meant,

Then tried to show her—with a good intent—
That such a plan would be for both their good,
And she would say it if she understood
As well as him what he had in his mind,
She would not grieve to be thus left behind ;
They sooner would obtain for wealth renown,
And from life's worry sooner settle down :
Their fortune would be made, and he would cease
From business then, and settle down in peace.
She heard him to the end, and without strife
She acquiesc'd, as should a loving wife ;
She saw that though a time true love must bend,
Yet 'twould for both be better in the end.
A few weeks' rest, and many bargains made,
For doing o'er the seas a thriving trade,—
And lov'd Drusilla's father left their home,
Beyond the wide Atlantic sea to roam :
With ship well freighted, and with cargo rare,
For varied uses, and beyond compare.
He went to many islands with his store,
And some that he had never seen before.
Bright fortune smil'd upon him where he went :
(Or rather Providence, with good intent ;)
And he soon sent for more, that quickly came,
Of useful things we have not time to name ;
And thus he traded well, and day by day,
Until three years had quickly pass'd away.
But in the meantime there had often come
Some loving letters from his own sweet home,
And others had been sent with hearty glee
By him, to lov'd ones far across the sea.
Then he resolv'd at last to give up trade,
For he had now a handsome fortune made ;
And on one glowing rich autumnal day
He from the South Sea Islands sail'd away,

And reach'd old Bristol in the opening spring,
When Leigh Wood songsters had begun to sing.
His dear old homestead yielded him delight—
His heart beat quickly as it came in sight;
And hastening to his doorway, there he met
His darling wife and his own little pet—
His sweet Drusilla, looking blithe and hale,
To be the heroine of Clifton Vale.
Then there was greeting never had before,
By father, mother, and Drusilla Dore:
They hugg'd and kiss'd, and free from all annoy,
Till all in concert wept aloud for joy;
Then home, sweet home was felt, what it should be—
The blest abode of love and unity;
And near their welcome fire, with sparkling blaze,
They sang that night a joyful hymn of praise:
And rendered thanks to God with cheerful strain,
For bringing them to meet at home again.
Drusilla's father then his story told,
Of his success in trade, and getting gold:
A fortune he'd secured by labour done—
For trading right, him true success had won;
And now in quiet they would pass their days
In some secluded spot from business ways;
He'd purchase land well sheltered from the gale,
And build a mansion in fair Clifton Vale.
This pleased Drusilla's mother, for she had
Before some thoughts that oft had made her sad,
Lest her loved husband should be lost at sea,
And they no more have his lov'd company:
But now to know that he would with them stay,
Was quite enough to drive her fears away.
Their plans thus settled, all were carried through—
A mansion built, and all within it new:
For ease and comfort it had rich command,

And for the age, it was considered grand.
Then here for years, like love in fairy bowers,
Did lov'd Drusilla spend her girlhood hours—
And days and months, and sundry years, I ween,
Until she had arrived at sweet sixteen.
And when Drusilla had won much esteem,
A change came o'er the spirit of her dream ;
Her education had been minded well :
She was proficient, for she did excel
In music, languages, and needlework, all rare—
And for true culture she was past compare ;
And with it all she foster'd common-sense,
The only standard of true excellence.
No wonder, then, this jewel should excel—
For she, though rich, was beautiful as well ;
And many a youth, aspiring, lent his ear
To her pianoforte's music clear :
And long'd to gaze, while halting near the place,
Upon her sweet, bewitching, smiling face ;
And when her features met his wond'ring eyes
He sigh'd and wonder'd who would win the prize.
Her parents long had seen these gazers stand,
And they had watch'd one, with his hat in hand,
Salute. Drusilla on one summer's night,
As though it gave him an intense delight.
But she regarded this with inward dread,
And lady-like, she quickly turned her head.
She'd told her parents why this gave her pain,
When they had wish'd her briefly to explain :
She'd met this gentleman but twice before,
And now he scarce could keep from off their door.
She never could encourage him to come
To visit her at their own treasur'd home,
Unless her parents first had seen him there,
And heard from him what his intentions were.

She was but young as yet, and should not think
Of marriage with a man who lov'd strong drink,—
For she had seen enough of it to know
That it was the cause of many a blighting woe.
She'd watch'd its workings, though she was but young,
And often heard its praises loudly sung ;
But she could see no beauty in a thing
That had within its cup an adder's sting,
And serpent's bite from its all poisonous breath,
That lured its victims to a drunkard's death.
Drusilla's parents heard their daughter with delight,
For they well knew her reasoning was right ;
And so they told her ere the day was spent,
To give her in the right encouragement,
That she should have attention was to them
Not a surprise, for she was such a gem.
She ne'er had been inclin'd to grow up wild
And it was known she was their only child,
And fortune one day would descend to her,
That she would doubtless cheerfully confer
On him she gave her trusting hand and heart
That only death's cold hand would ever part.
Thus time pass'd on in that sweet home serene,
Until Drusilla had just turn'd nineteen,
When a loud postman's knock fell on their door,
And he four letters brought Drusilla Dore.

PART III.

ER parents, on this long-remember'd night,
    Were not at home—this gave her some delight :
    For she could leisurely, without ado,
Arrange the letters, and then look them through
Ere they return'd from the old seaport town,

Or their long ramble on the Clifton Down.
She hasten'd then unto her neat *boudoir*,
And quick, though silently, she closed the door :
Then on a table where her work was done
She placed the letters, opening number one.
This came from a young gentleman with pride,
And one well-known, she often had espied
When she was walking, or with rapture stood,
To view rich tintings in the grand Leigh Wood :
When autumn leaves were dancing through the day,
And showing beauty even in decay.
He told her, in this scented billet-doux,
How he'd esteemed her—might he be her beau ?
And he now lov'd her with a love sincere,
And had done long ; but yet he had a fear
Sometime to tell it, lest it should be told
That he in his advances had been bold :
But he had money left him, he would wage
'Twas coming to him when he came of age.
Oh ! if she would but see him, he would call,
And of his future prospects explain all :
This letter finished in the usual way,
And had the signature of Edward Gay.
She open'd number two with some surprise—
For opening it had open'd both her eyes
Much wider than they ever were before,
And brought some blushes to Drusilla Dore—
For it had come from a fast-going spark,
That for a time sojourned in Clifton Park
With friends of his, who had from London come,
And who was finding him both food and home.
He was a spark, the wise could truly see,
Without one spark of true gentility ;
He lack'd the useful gift of common-sense,
But had more than his share of impudence :

For every prudent girl, when passing by,
He ogled with his all-lustful eye ;
And if a group of ladies should him pass,
He'd do it grand to them through his eye-glass.
His letter open'd—" Miss Drusilla Dore,
You are an angel that I much adore !
I long have loved you, I can truly prove—
Oh ! will you give me, in return, your love,
And let me have the honour and delight
To take you to the theatre some night ?
Excuse this scribble—it is short and sweet,
And I will tell you more when we shall meet.
Believe me to remain, while life shall last,
Your very great admirer, Randolph Fast."
Then number three was presently displayed—
It open'd out with such a grand parade
Of words, that made Drusilla almost doubt
If with her learning she could make them out—
Especially when he avowed (by Jove !)
That he had fallen awfully in love,
And that his object was Drusilla Dore :
He loved her very shadow more and more.
Drusilla smiled at this one's bold advance,
And vow'd he'd not a shadow of a chance :
And as to love being awful, that was new —
She'd always thought 'twas joyful, if 'twas true.
She placed this letter very near her feet—
For it had come from Harry Great Conceit.
She open'd number four, and in a trice,
Because the plain handwriting was so nice,
And read it o'er with mingled feelings then,
For it had issued from a well-known pen :
The writing she had seen some time before,
And it commenced, " Will Miss Drusilla Dore
Regard this letter from a sincere friend,

For on Drusilla his life's hopes depend ;
He loves her, and she knows it, he believes—
And for her love impatiently he grieves :
Then why withhold it, loved Drusilla Dore ?—
Is it because the lover is born poor ?
If so, he would that he had piles of gold,
To prove a love that never could be told—
A love that only death's cold hand could part
From its indwelling in his faithful heart."
Drusilla read this till she could not speak,
And tears of pity trickl'd down her cheek ;
And there was throbbing in her heart, she knew,
For this known letter came from Albert True.
Awhile she stayed, then, in her neat *boudoir*,
Long musing on what she'd been reading o'er :
These letters seem'd to represent the mind
Of all the senders, she did quickly find :
But were they all sincere in what they wrote—
Was the one thing of which she made a note,
And which she'd fathom on some future day,
As some young ladies can—in their own way !
Meantime she had determin'd on that night
With her lov'd parents to set matters right,
And when they came, who for her weal did live,
To seek advice which they alone could give.
She knew but little of three who had sent
Their letters to her, and for some intent ;
She had seen Edwin Gay just a few times,
While she was hearing Clifton's old church chimes :
She'd seen him passing at a hurried pace
From his own home, which she thought a disgrace ;
And she had further thought, while on he fled,
'Twas time young gentlemen should be in bed ;
And though she had true heaven-born charity,
Yet, when she saw him, oft would sigh, "Ah ! me."

Then Randolph Fast she'd met in Regent Street,
And he'd not always nice shoes on his feet :
His thread-bare coat and his downfallen crest
Betoken'd that of times he'd not the best—
Or he was making worst of them, she thought,
In varied ways of sin that he had sought :
For on his face appear'd, she oft did find,
Some drink-made blossoms of peculiar kind.
And every time that she this young gent pass'd,
She had heart-sorrowing for Randolph Fast ;
No ! she would never blight her future life,
By promising to be young Randolph's wife.
Then Harry Great Conceit was strange to her,
Although her parents she had heard aver :
Had many times observant seen him prance
Through Clifton vale, and with his eyes askance
At one known window of their own domain—
And one day did it in the falling rain.
As though he wished to find a something there
That would, if found, be rich and also rare ;
But he could never find, while he was out,
The one he look'd for, which oft made him pout ;
Then they had noticed him in Portland Street,
Stalking along with very much conceit :
And when young ladies with him tried to walk,
He always was so full of empty talk :
His own opinion (for he could not err)
He wish'd them always, like himself, prefer ;
And all young ladies, when the walk was o'er,
By one consent had voted him a bore.
Drusilla knew, from what she'd heard them say,
For him she must not throw herself away.
But Albert True she had some knowledge of :
At things all sacred he would never scoff ;
Then to his widow'd mother he was kind,

And tried to comfort her in heart and mind :
For he was so industrious, like the ant,
And long had kept her from all pinching want.
" If he was poor," she said, in words sublime—
" Well, poverty itself was not a crime :
Her parents had been poor in early life,
Though now all free from any business strife ;
And she was now their only child, to give
Them consolation while they both did live.
She thought they would not thwart her, if she told
That Albert's love to her was more than gold :
And she would tell them this when they had come
Within the precincts of their own sweet home."
Her plans were finish'd, with a joy complete,
Just as the hall door-bell rang from the street.

PART IV.

THE ringing bell announced, as oft before,
Drusilla's parents waited at the door ;
And, sooner than the maid who was within,
Drusilla hurried forth to let them in.
They saw something unusual in her looks,
And thought she had been busy with her books ;
Yet, while they look'd upon her they did find
That something else had occupied her mind :
For near the entrance door, where they did stand,
They saw she had some letters in her hand ;
And when within the room the three were gone,
She opened out the letters one by one.
Her father read them to her mother dear,
And read them as a father should—with care ;
At times he smil'd, and sometimes look'd down,
As though there gather'd on his face a frown—

For many thoughts were passing through his mind,
Because he'd read, and often, love was blind!
So he was wishful, and at any price,
To give his only child the best advice.
Riches, by him, was not consider'd first—
He had known marriages by these accurs'd.
Gold in its place he knew was useful here,
If character was right, and heart sincere ;
But without this—why, wealth was but a bane
To make its owners wretchedly insane,
By leading them to paths where sin abounds,
As they walk on them in their daily rounds,—
While all whom they have lured to married life
Are subjected to misery and strife.
A few more days then pass'd without a quail
In that lov'd home in queenly Clifton Vale ;
For lov'd Drusilla, acting on advice,
Had answered the four letters in a trice.
Her parents thought it best that she should write,
And tell them all that she considered right :
For she could do it with her ready pen,
What her heart-feeling was to each one then.
To Edwin Gay she wrote : " Dear Sir, I send
A brief reply to what of late you penn'd
To Miss Drusilla Dore, on what you knew
Would make you happy, if she'd look on you :
And further hinted it would cheer your life
If she would love you and become your wife.
With one request of yours she will comply :
To look upon you—and you may rely
She has done this for your own mother's sake :
Long looked upon you, till her heart did ache—
To see you hurry, both at night and noon,
To seek for pleasure in the gay saloon.
With pitying eye she has beheld you long,

When she has known you loved the siren's song :
And with the giddy dancers joy'd to dwell,
That yet keep dancing on their way to hell.
With pity she looks on you, Edwin Gay,
And here would warn you now to turn away
From all such scenes, that bring ignoble strife,
And enter on a purer, better life.
Become your wife ? No ! never, Edwin Gay ;
Drusilla Dore wont throw herself away.
The man who claims her for his love and bride
Must be a gentleman with decent pride—
A gentleman with love, true love, at home—
Not one who in forbidden haunts doth roam ;
And one who will from all known evil shrink—
A true abstainer from the drunkard's drink,
And a true Christian in this world of strife :
To such an one she would become a wife.
But not to you—for you would not be true,
And now to Edwin Gay she writes ' Adieu ! ' "
To Randolph Fast she wrote with trembling hand,
" Sir, this is sent that you may understand
(Though it perchance may make you stand aghast),
Miss Dore can never welcome Randolph Fast ;
The reason why, she calmly doth aver
Is this—that he is much too fast for her :
A fast young gentleman that's always dry
Would never be the one to please her eye ;
And further she would state, as she's not blind,
Would never be the one to please her mind.
Her reasons here to Randolph she will give,
To urge him soon a nobler live to live.
Young ladies who have wealth do not wish strife
When they have enter'd into married life ;
And they would always have it with a man
Who was fast living, for he is a ban

To all that should make life what it should be—
A festal homestead of soul-harmony:
For he would want to spend with lavish hand
What he had never earn'd, to do the grand.
Drusilla Dore would have, when she was wed,
Much golden store, her honour'd parents said;
But this was wealth acquir'd by honest toil—
Not the long savings of a robber's spoil;
And she'd resolved, throughout her life's own day,
That it should not be squander'd far away:
But usefully employ'd, as wealth e'er should,
In heaven's true service—that of doing good."
And then she bade him think on life he'd pass'd,
And bade a long farewell to Randolph Fast.
Then soon to Harry Great Conceit she wrote,
In answer to his very fulsome note,
That she, through life, could never condescend
To recognise him, even as a friend:
For he and her would never well agree—
This anyone, with common sense, could see.
Drusilla Dore had all her dresses neat,
And this might umbrage give Sir Great Conceit:
For in the choice of pictures he was don—
Great Harry always would be number one.
He knew the best, and would have full command,
Because he always liked to do the grand
In company—when moving in high life,
He'd always keep the thumbscrew on his wife;
And if then needed anything to say,
He knew best how to do it in his way;
And when returning home she'd have a treat,
Accompanied by Harry Great Conceit.
She then told this Sir Harry, who loved wine,
That she his kind advances must decline;
And further wish'd him, for wise people's treat,

To be in his behaviour more discreet.
Then last of all she answered Albert True,
For she had watch'd him from a boy, she knew ;
And on some few occasions for awhile
Would greet him, when she met him, with a smile :
For she saw in him once what won esteem
From her, while walking near the Hotwell stream,—
Some rude boys had surrounded, on the way,
A poor old traveller, whose locks were grey,
And to their insults would have added blows—
For they were rude young rascals, goodness knows—
When Albert True to him all swiftly ran,
And shelter'd from these brutes the poor old man.
This simple act of kindness did its part
To find a place for Albert in her heart ;
And so she wrote him in a different key
To what she'd written to the other three.
Her letter thus began—" Dear sir, I write
You a reply, and with true-heart delight.
Your letter was receiv'd, I liked its tone,
And I read it with joy. I'm free to own
I've had three more from some unwelcome bores,
The very night that I received yours.
I read them to my parents in a trice,
As well as yours, then sought their wise advice :
Soon they permitted me to write again,
And answer all the four in my own strain.
I've written to the other three, and told
Them not to think, though I have stores of gold,
That I have not discretion in my mind—
And their mistake in this they soon will find.
I did not wish to give them needless pain,
So wrote them not to trouble me again ;
And now to you I'll tell, without reserve,
What I have thought you honestly deserve :

Your letter, it was welcome as the May,
And future letters will be any day.
Drusilla Dore will, with a true heart fond,
Delight with Albert True to correspond.
Her parents lik'd your letter, though you're poor.
And so did their lov'd child, Drusilla Dore :
She likes your frankness, you may well depend,
And thinks more of you than a treasur'd friend.
Your poverty will never be a ban ;
For 'neath its garb Drusilla sees a man
With honest heart and an expansive mind,
And with these, Christian principles combined.
And further—it doth give her joy to think
You never touch the blighting drunkard's drink :
For she had long determin'd it should be,
The one she lov'd should love sobriety.
And if this letter he can understand,
She offers Albert True her heart and hand,
And would be glad to see him on some night—
'Twould give her parents and herself delight.
If he has no engagement, she would say
His visit may be made on next Tuesday—
If at their mansion he will make a call,
He then to her can fully explain all."
She closed the letter with "I wish you well ; "
And then she had more joy than tongue can tell.

PART V.

NEXT Tuesday night to Clifton Vale there came
A wise young man with an enduring fame,
And at a mansion door he stay'd with pride :
The bell he rang, the door was open'd wide—
When a young damsel waited at the door,

And introduced him to Drusilla Dore.
Their meeting, it was cordial now he'd come,
And Miss Drusilla made him feel at home.
Though she in station was above him far,
She never tried his happiness to mar :
He felt at home, he readily confess'd—
Drusilla did the same, she soon expressed ;
And he was introduced to her lov'd friends,
On whom so much of happiness depends ;
And these received him—as was meet and right—
With feelings of heart-thrilling, pure delight.
Drusilla's father had observed his ways
From his youth upwards, to his manhood days ;
And he had heard from others he was just,
And one they might all confidently trust :
For queenly Clifton own'd him from his youth,
And never was ashamed of him, forsooth.
His father had died young, and he was left,
As was his widow'd mother—all bereft ;
But she had struggl'd hard to rear her boy,
Who had to be her future hope and joy.
And he had well repaid for care she had :
For he grew up, and not to make her sad,
But was a consolation in her fears—
A glory for her in declining years.
When he could toil he worked hard for her bliss,
And when he left her with a morning kiss,
And sweet " Good-bye, till I return at night,"
It fill'd his widow'd mother with delight.
Drusilla's mother then beheld with joy
Drusilla lov'd this mother's only boy ;
And now their daughter he had come to woo,
That she, ere long, might be his mother too.
Thus all went sweetly as the marriage bells,
In that known manse o'erlooking the Hotwells :

For Albert and his lov'd Drusilla spent
The night with her dear parents in content ;
And when the hour for parting them had come,
Young Albert hastened to his own lov'd home,
And told his mother of his great success,
When he had given her a love caress.
This caused the good old widow to rejoice,
And praise him for his pure affection's choice.
She told him this had all been brought about
By trying to live right, she had no doubt :
For they who honour'd God in all their ways,
He would safe guide them through life's passing days :
Those honouring Him would honour parents here,
Fulfilling heaven's own law in duty's sphere,—
Receive the promise made to all the young
By Heaven itself—that their days should be long.
He heard his mother with intense delight,
And vow'd again his future should be right.
A few more days pass'd on, and Albert thought
He'd pen his lov'd Drusilla a sweet note,
And tell her how he had delighted been
Since he at her lov'd mansion had been seen,
And how her parents had delighted him :
His cup of joy was full —yes, to the brim—
For he had got from her, with true intent,
What was his joy for life—encouragement !
He dared not hope it once, for inward strife :
But that was past, and with it a new life
That gave him an untold, inherent bliss,
Since she had breath'd the promise to be his.
He lov'd her father much, and mother too—
They were not cold at his first interview :
They did not look upon him in disdain,
Nor give to him unnecessary pain ;
But gave him proof their child should have her choice,

And this would ever make his heart rejoice.
His future life should never be disgraced,
He'd show their confidence was not misplaced :
Then lov'd Drusilla should be free from strife,
When she had claim'd the honour'd name of wife.
He sent the letter with a new delight—
And faithful promise he would come at night.
At the appointed time, with heart content,
Blest Albert True to his Drusilla went,
And found her waiting in her graceful bloom
To give him welcome in a cosy room.
'Twas wintertide ; and she, with heart elate,
Had a nice blazing fire within the grate ;
And bright wax tapers, that remember'd night,
Shed in the peaceful room a lustrous light,
While on a tinted couch Drusilla sat,
And welcom'd Albert for a pleasant chat :
Then for some hours, as lovers do at ease,
Told pleasant stories to each other please ;
And they had kisses, pure as lovers give
Who have resolv'd in purity to live ;
And then Drusilla did, in her own way,
Her grand pianoforte sweetly play,
And sang to Albert, with her warbling tongue,
Some pleasant stanzas of a favourite song.
And he would give his lover meed of praise,
Just as young lovers do, with winning ways.
Thus days and weeks and months pass'd on in glee,
And love was tested, as true love should be ;
Yet it grew stronger, as 'twas tried the more,
In Albert True and sweet Drusilla Dore,
Until two years had gone since first they met,
And on each other their affections set ;
And but one blight meanwhile to them had come,
To throw a shadow on each treasur'd home—

It was that Albert's widow'd mother died,
And left her boy, who was her joy and pride.
She had to quit for aye the earthly scene ;
Yet she had left her son with hope serene,
That by-and-by she'd meet him on the shore
Where death and grief and parting are no more.
Drusilla sooth'd him in his sad bereave,
And told him that it would be wrong to grieve :
His mother had escaped from all her pain,
And in God's time they all would meet again.
Drusilla's parents, too, assuaged his grief,
And in due time they gave him heart relief,
By telling him they thought the time had come
That he and their Drusilla had one home.
They had been planning for their future bliss,
And the conclusion they came to was this :
That as Drusilla was their only child,
With them they both might well be domicil'd :
Their mansion, it was large enough, indeed,
For ease and comfort and for every need ;
And they well hop'd that it would be through life
For all of them a home, all free from strife ;
That each, through time, would try and do their best
To make that home more beautiful and blest :
By ever striving, with a soul-delight,
To practise only what was true and right—
Then all of them most certainly would prove
That theirs was only the " Abode of Love."
They then concluded what they had to say,
By fixing soon the welcome wedding day.

CONCLUSION.

THE Leigh Woods' songsters had begun to sing
Their matin notes to welcome virgin spring,
While down the valley, by the known Hotwells,
There came the merry sound of wedding bells.
Fair Clifton was astir some hours before,
To see the marriage of Drusilla Dore.
Old Clifton Church was full as full could be—
For old and young found there were glad to see
The happy couple standing side by side—
The mother's hope, the father's joy and pride ;
And soon the good old Vicar's work was done,
By joining two in bonds that made them one :
The people said, " Amen," and all was o'er :
Then as with one consent they sought the door
To see them start, that sunny sweet forenoon,
For Ilfracombe to spend their honeymoon.
Many had gather'd round the old Church gate,
Where they a time all patiently did wait
To see this new-wed couple the first time,
And give them greeting with a joy sublime.
A short way from the multitude that day
Stood gazing pensively young Edwin Gay ;
And when he saw them with his redden'd eyes,
He mutter'd slowly that he'd lost a prize.
And then another there was seen downcast—
It was that noted scapegrace, Randolph Fast :
He trembl'd like the poet's aspen leaf,
And felt at last that he had come to grief.
Near him, again, stood gaping in the street
That boring know all—Harry Great Conceit,
Who vow'd, by Jove, this wedding was a sell,
And Albert True had managed matters well.
Then from the Church and friends, and their lov'd home,
The happy couple sped for Ilfracombe.

LITTLE JEWELS.

HAVE two little jewels to brighten my home,
From one who is precious to me ;
They seem like a welcome surprise to have come,
Where I have to retain them in fee.
They are costly, I know, but they pay it in love :
For I love much to have them in sight ;
These are treasures to me, I can readily prove,
And give me exquisite delight.

Now one is a sweet little prattling boy,
With hair that is flaxen and bright,
And cheeks where the Queen might plant kisses of joy—
So thinketh my queen, who is right.
Then he has two feet that can toddle about,
And a pop horse to which he says " Gee " :
I would rather have him than a bottle of stout,
For he 's a choice jewel to me.

The other 's a darling like waxwork, I know :
'Tis baby, of course, all serene,
With eyes that would gladden a princess below ;
We have named her our Evangeline.
She 's a smile in the cradle for every one,
And a good little cherub is she :
Yet never so right, as when she can look on
Her own beloved mamma and me.

Do you ask me the price of my jewels all rare ?
Then I answer, it cannot be told ;
They are stored in my heart are the prized precious pair,
And they cannot be purchased with gold.
May I but retain them in homestead of health,
To cheer me on life's passing way,
Rich Clifton, with all its abundance of wealth,
Cannot purchase my jewels to-day.

MATTIE'S GRAVE.

THE holy Sabbath's dawn had come,
   With hallow'd unction blest,
And I had left my own sweet home,
   Near city of the west,
To toil for One who died for me,
   And all the world to save,
When, lo ! I turned aside to see
   My own loved Mattie's grave.

'Twas springtide ! I remember well,
   And in its golden hours
I bore with joy no tongue can tell
   For her some treasured flowers.—
A loving wife had wreathed with care,
   And pure affection gave,
For me with love to place upon
   My own loved Mattie's grave.

I laid them on the turfy sod
   Above her quiet breast,
Then thanked my loving Father God
   My loved one was at rest.
She'd reached the home of no more sin,
   A little jewel brave ;
Only the casket was within
   My own loved Mattie's grave.

That night, in an all peaceful nook
   And sweet forget-me-not,
I went to take a farewell look
   Of this thrice hallowed spot.
When, lo ! some strange yet kindly hands
   To me new comfort gave :
For they had strewn with more love flowers
   My own loved Mattie's grave.

THIS OCTOBER DAY.

ERE I am upon the Downs,
   In my little box ;
Far away from noisy towns,
   On St. Vincent's Rocks.
Rain is coming down apace,
   And the morn is grey,
Giving nature sombre face,
   This October day.

Lonely here I sit and write,
   Yet I am not alone :
For the poet hath delight
   In a path his own ;
And he doth his sorrows find,
   In a poet's way :
For the two are on my mind
   This October day.

I have joy that I possess
   Wife and children dear—
Little darlings to caress
   With a love sincere.
And my sorrow it is this,
   That that the world don't pay
More regard for what is good
   This October day.

Had I written foolish themes—
   Ballads to inflame
Passions that are worse than dreams,
   I might win a name;
But because my lines are pure,
   I am kept away
From what is a poet's right
   This October day.

I S A B E L.

POOR Isabel! And who was she?
Well, she was one well known to me
    I'll freely tell;
And I must write her elegy—
    Poor Isabel.

I knew her many years ago,
When she was tripping to-and-fro,
    And looking well,
On Clifton Down, with heart aglow—
    Poor Isabel.

She had in charge a darling child,
With flaxen hair and manners mild,
    From Clifton dell:
One on whom its loved parents smiled,
    And Isabel.

For she was training it for good
Soon as its powers began to bud,
    With a love spell;
And this was rightly understood
    By Isabel.

But time brings changes unto all,
And Isabel with some appal
    Left Clifton dell;
Gave up her charge at duty's call—
    Poor Isabel.

She dreamt of happiness for life,
And living from a world of strife,
    Her heart did swell
With joy that she would be a wife—
    Poor Isabel.

And she became one in due time,
But, ah ! her joy was not sublime,
    A many tell ;
She found sore trials in life's prime,
    Did Isabel.

For reason fled one evil day,
It could no longer hold its sway,
    I grieve to tell ;
And she, alas ! was put away—
    Poor Isabel.

Awhile she lingered there, and sigh'd,
She who was once her village pride—
    This is known well—
And then she quickly droop'd and died—
    Poor Isabel.

One little precious lamb she bore,
But she will see it here no more—
    She's gone to dwell
With angels on the peaceful shore—
    Has Isabel.

For she was Christian in her life,
Too good for this world's noise ; and strife
    She would repel,
And she was doting as a wife—
    Was Isabel.

But she has done with earthly things,
And now she with the ransom'd sings
    That all is well;
Safe landed with the King of kings
    Is Isabel.

She now has reach'd the heavenly home
Where sore distresses cannot come,
    Nor lonely cell,
But a loved mansion with a dome
    For Isabel.

Yes ; she is dwelling with the blest,
Where no dire troubles can molest,
    Or sorrows swell :
For she hath found eternal rest—
    Loved Isabel.

EARL SHAFTESBURY.

NOBLE man with noble name,
    One with an enduring fame ;
    One that will through time endure,
    For thy kindness to the poor,—
Thy long life, now understood,
Was a life of doing good ;
And thy death has brought thee rest
In the mansions of the blest.

THE ANGELS MIND HIM NOW!

E used to watch the sunshine
   Beam on the baby face,
His bright blue eyes would sparkle
   With such a winning grace ;
But when the flowers of autumn
   Did in their beauty grow,
Our flower was borne to Eden,—
   And angels mind him now !

Our hearts were well-nigh breaking
   The morn we saw him die ;
But when in snowy whiteness
   The fragile form did lie,
We thought our tears of sorrow
   Could never cease to flow,
Until a voice came whispering,—
   The angels mind him now !

The cradle-bed is empty
   Where he was wont to rest,
And socks are neatly folded
   His tiny feet once press'd ;
But to the will of Heaven
   Submissively we bow,
And hope to meet our darling—
   Where angels mind him now !

MATTIE GABBITASS.

NOVEMBER.

'T is dull November,
  Skies are overcast ;
On the street and rooftree
Rain is falling fast.
Autumn leaves are drifted
  From the woodland trees,
Sported with like bubbles
  By the fitful breeze.

Many hearts are quailing
  With portentous fear—
Gloomily bewail it,
  Sad month of the year.
Men have deem'd it cruel
  In their woe-betides—
Nam'd it, and for ages,
  Month of Suicides.

We will not reproach it
  With that loathsome name—
We have no just reason ;
  It is not to blame.
It is but obeying
  A Divine behest—
In it's Maker's service,
  Doing what is best.

Did we view it rightly,
  Man would not complain ;
But 'mid fog and rainstorm,
  Chant a grateful strain.
All may sing of mercies—
  Mercies of the past,
And that dull November
  Will not always last.

We may make it joyful,
   Chasing mourners' fears—
Bereft widows soothing,
   Drying orphans' tears ;
Bringing city arabs
   From their wretched delves,
Showing we are living,
   And not for ourselves.

We have all life duties
   Varied in their ways ;
Yet we each may brighten
   Dark November days.
In the cot or palace
   All may faithful prove—
Keep the path of duty,
   And the law of love.

Have we wealth abundant
   Flowing like a flood,
We may find true pleasure—
   That of doing good ;
And if we are feeble,
   We may write a lay,
That some heart will gladden
   When we're pass'd away.

Let us then be filling
   Well our duty sphere ;
Chilly, dull November,
   Soon will disappear :
And while it is passing
   It will yield delight,
While our life is useful,
   And our heart is right.

WE SHALL MEET HER ONCE AGAIN.

MILY has gone to rest,
  Like the lily, in her prime ;
She is blooming with the blest
In a pure unchanging clime.
We shall meet her once again,
  Love her as in days of old,
In a city o'er the main,
  Where the streets are burnish'd gold.

How we miss the gentle voice,
  Singing with a cadence sweet ;
Yet we cannot but rejoice
  That her bliss is now complete.
We shall meet her once again,
  Love her as in days of old,
In a city o'er the main,
  Where the streets are burnish'd gold.

Angels came one summer night,
  While the stars shone 'mid the flowers,
And they bore her with delight
  To a better world than ours.
We shall meet her once again,
  Love her as in days of old,
In a city o'er the main,
  Where the streets are burnish'd gold.

MATTIE GABBITASS.

WITH MY LITTLE TREASURES.

MANY joys I have on earth,
　　And my share of sorrow ;
　Sometimes I am full of mirth,
　Then it goes to-morrow.
Yet there is one welcome time
　Always brings me pleasures—
It is spending twilight hours
　With my little treasures !

From a cot, at early morn,
　One will come beguiling ;
And if he's his night-dress torn,
　This will set him smiling.
Walter Charlie he is named—
　Two feet six he measures ;
And one day he will be famed
　With my little treasures !

Then the other I know well,
　'Tis my darling Eva,
Peering from her cradle bed—
　Hoping I won't leave her.
She is cooing like a dove,
　Giving me heart-pleasures :
For I feel a father's love
　With my little treasures !

Little treasures, bless them both !
　Though I have another ;
And to tell it I'm not loth—
　'Tis the darlings' mother.
Heaven guard them with its might,
　Give them true heart-pleasures ;
'Till I come again at night
　To my little treasures !

2 D

WATCHING BABY SLEEP.

HAD joy this morning,
  Passing all compare,
  Near my little treasure,
  With his flaxen hair.
Baby boy was sleeping—
  I did vigil keep
By a tiny cradle,
  Watching baby sleep.

Long I gazed upon him
  With a father's joy,
He was such a darling,
  Was my baby boy ;
And he seem'd so happy
  While in slumber deep :
It gave me new rapture
  Watching baby sleep.

Soon he moved the fingers
  On one little hand,
As though he were sketching
  Scenes in fairy land.
Smiles came on his features,
  Made his young heart leap ;
Smiles that pleased the watcher,
  Watching baby sleep.

Then two blue eyes open'd
  On a cradle bed,
Sleep was changed to laughing—
  Baby had no dread :
For it threw me kisses,
  And we play'd Bo-Peep,
Where I was that morning
  Watching baby sleep.

CAN'T YOU MAKE SOMEBODY HAPPY TO-DAY ?

WHAT are you grumbling and fretting about ?
    Oh ! what commotion you 're making at home—
Just as though you had a fit of the gout,
    Or were inviting some trouble to come.
Pray look around you for something to do,
    And give attention to what I shall say :
Here is a question to study for you—
    Can't you make somebody happy to-day ?

Do you think life was bestowed upon men
    E'er to be spent in a don't-caring mood ?
If you think this you shall know from my pen,
    Living for lounging will do you no good.
I would advise you to just look around,
    That you may find a more excellent way :
One that will long to your credit redound—
    Can't you make somebody happy to-day ?

Are there no hearts that are bleeding with pain,
    In the cold attic or down in the slums ?—
Hearts that are rended and rended again,
    Just because somebody keeps from their homes.
Here is a sphere you may labour in well ;
    Speak to them kindly, then with them pray ;
On these sad hearts let your influence tell—
    Can't you make somebody happy to-day ?

Up, then, no longer your talents abuse,
    You can do something, I know, if you try—'
Something to cheer you, and be of good use
    While you are living and when you shall die
Try to make better the desolate homes—
    Rise, for the time is fast flying away ;
Don't say to-morrow, for that never comes,
    Can't you make somebody happy to-day ?

WELCOME TO GARIBALDI.

WELCOME, Garibaldi ! name to England dear;
English tongues and English hearts bid thee welcome here :
Spring-time with its perfumed flowers,
Feathered songsters in their bowers,
Flowing rills and humming bee,
All unite to welcome thee !

Welcome, Garibaldi ! despots' mighty foe ;
Forward urge thy work, begun ; tyrants overthrow ;
England's daughters garlands bring :
England's sons with joy shall sing—
Thy loved name their theme shall be ;
England's homes all welcome thee !

Welcome, Garibaldi ! England's soil is free ;
Stands thy foot on hallowed ground—land of liberty.
Here 'twill find some mystic font
To heal the wound of Aspromonte.
England's heart that cure shall be ;
England's people welcome thee !

MY EVANGELINE.

WHAT ! begun to trot about
On the kitchen floor ?
Mind, or you'll be put to rout :
Steady ! You'll be o'er.
Try again, that 's not amiss—
Well done, little queen ;
You shall have a poet's kiss—
My Evangeline !

DON'T MAKE TROUBLE OF TRIFLES TO-DAY.

H! don't you make trouble of trifles to-day—
 Yes ; this is the title to-day of my song :
 For I have to sing to send trouble away,
And that all the weak-minded folk may be strong.
E'er helping each other our motto should be,
 For in this cold world we have not long to stay ;
And far the best thing for mankind I can see
 Is not to make trouble of trifles to-day.

No, pray don't make trouble of trifles to-day,
 But try to get comfort when threatened with woe :
For you may find thousands far worse off, I say,
 Whate'er be your station, or where you may go.
Oh ! think this well over when trials assail,
 'Twill give you much soothing in time's chequer'd way :
Like the healing medicine it never will fail,
 Then never make trouble of trifles to-day.

Oh ! don't you make trouble of trifles to-day,
 For you are not under the guidance of fate ;
If you are but treading the safe narrow way,
 Well, you can tell trouble to stay at the gate.
'Tis true it may try then to harass your mind,
 Yet you shall escape, if you heed what I say :
By looking above for the help you can find,
 You need not make trouble of trifles to-day.

Then do not make trouble of trifles to-day,
 But always look trifles right full in the face,
And you shall be pleasant and cheerful as May—
 All free from mistrust, with its lasting disgrace.
Put off till to-morrow the trouble that comes,
 Then labour all earnest to keep it away :
'Twill bring you much comfort and joy in your homes,
 If you will not make trouble of trifles to-day.

LITTLE MISCHIEF FINGERS.

ITTLE Mischief Fingers,
   I have watch'd you long :
   And upon your doings
I must write a song.
Mamma bade me watch you,
   And to give alarm,
If the Mischief Fingers
   Should be doing harm.

On the breakfast table
   You were seen at play,
Turning cups and saucers—
   In a baby's way ;
While the salt and pepper
   Seem to baby please—
Only one is making
   Little baby sneeze !

Soon the Mischief Fingers
   Seek for something more,
And are swiftly tossing
   Egg cups on the floor.
Then the bread and butter
   They stretch out to take—
And I'm thinking baby
   Wishes it were cake !

Now they clutch the cream jug,
   With a baby's pride ;
Turning it right over,
   Then—oh, woe betide !—
Mamma came and saw it,
   For I heard her shout—
" Little Mischief Fingers,
   What are you about ? "

WE HAVE LABOURED IN OUR DAY.

E must toil while we are here,
  Idle hands will mischief find ;
And to find a useful sphere,
  We must well employ our mind.
Active—yes, in doing good ;
  Let those left behind us say,
That to make a better world,
  We have laboured in our day !

Labour brings its own reward,
  If it be for others' good :
Soon a better world we'd have,
  If this were but understood.
Many a toiler sleeps in peace,
  In God's acre far away,
With this blest memoriam—
  We have laboured in our day !

Honest labour wins a place,
  In whatever state we 're in :
For no labour will disgrace,
  But the drudgery of sin.
From the base, the vile, the low,
  Let us ever keep away,
That for good mankind may know—
  We have laboured in our day !

Working time will soon be o'er
  In this world some dote upon ;
And to yonder silent shore
  We shall gather one by one.
Let us well employ our time,
  Walking in true wisdom's way—
Then we shall have joy sublime,
  That we laboured in our day !

THE SILVER CLOUD.

ATHER, how can it be
That I, Thy child, now passing o'er life's troubled sea,
Should see above a dark and cloudy sky,
Whose sombre shades I mournfully descry?
And eager ask from Thee the reason why:
My Father, answer me.

I know that Thou art kind,
And would not willingly afflict Thy helpless child;
Thy character I see, and mercy prove
In all Thy works—and yet how soon would rove
My mind from Thee, Thou source of purest love:
Let me Thy pity find

I will not lingering stay
To tell Thee all the darkness that surrounds my soul;
Thy searching eye, omniscient, it hath seen
How deep-wrought anguish, with unerring spleen,
And sorrow's waves hath dashed, with fury keen,
On me their falling spray.

My Father, undertake
Around that cloud of darkness: for Thy mercy's sake
Throw silvery rays in each distressing hour,
To light me onward to that peaceful bower
Where sorrow dwelleth not, nor cares devour,
Or fainting spirits quake.

I will, with faithful hand,
Indite the promise graven in Thy precious Word—
That Thou alone dost give the clouds their course,
And blend the light with shade from heavenly source,
That reasoning man may feel their potent force,
And seek the better land.

If that be Thy design,
Be hushed, my spirit—what my Father wills is best;
Cheerful from Thee I take the trial cup—
Thy sorrowing child its bitter draught will sup;
If Thou Thy face won't hide, I'll drink it up,
    And to Thy will resign.

My Father, now I see
Thy wisdom hath ordained the rugged path I tread;
But Thou my feeble flesh will sure sustain,
And guide me through this trackless land of pain,
Till Beulah's heights of rapture I shall gain
    In blest eternity.

This suppliant cry aloud
I now will send; my Father, pray forgive Thy wayward child—
From henceforth shall my feet to Theeward tend,
And to Thy yoke my tractive spirit bend,
That light and shade may yet all richly blend
    To fringe the silver cloud.

MODERN THOUGHT.
A SONNET.

YES! What is modern thought? 's the question of the day—
    It takes such shapes and forms, the people say,
    For in our age we 're thinking such strange things:
They come to meet us as on lightning wings.
Some modern thought there is that sages pall,
For it would spurn the Maker of us all,
And give to fate's fell goddess, who is blind,
The full surrender of the heart and mind.
Where'er such modern thought vain man inspires,
And leads him on through sceptical quagmires,
Away from paths of life the good have trod,
To doubt the Being of creation's God,—
It proves itself, despite the modern schools,
That modern thought can fashion modern fools!

THE JOY OF HARVEST.

HE fields are now vocal with gladness,
  And ring with melodious strain ;
They have put off their mantle of sadness,
  For Harvest is coming again.

How rich and abundant their treasure,
  So plenteous the bright golden grain,
Presented to man without measure,
  For Harvest is coming again.

See, reapers the joy too are sharing,
  Nor shall their rejoicing be vain,
While sickle and scythe are preparing,
  For Harvest is coming again.

With joy shall the husbandman gather
  His seed in the garner from rain ;
The gifts of a bountiful Father,
  For Harvest is coming again.

Soon gleaners shall gladsome be singing,
  Not caring for labour or pain :
Their songs through the woodlands be ringing,
  For Harvest is coming again.

Then let all our songs, while ascending,
  Be pure as the light is from stain :
For we read, when this life is ending,
  That Harvest is coming again.

I AM SHELTER'D BY A ROCK.

HERE am I in boisterous weather
  With my little poet's stand,
  Yet I keep it well together
On a mountain that is grand.
Old Boreas loud is roaring
  Like a pealing thundershock,
Yet I heed not his outpouring—
  I am shelter'd by a rock.

Storms are making deathly havoc
  With the silver birchen trees,
Driving them like madden'd horses
  Plunging from each fitful breeze ;
Yet 'tis well these storms should know it,
  I can at their doings mock—
They to-day can't harm the poet—
  I am shelter'd by a rock.

Early this October morning
  How they shriek'd and raved and tore,
As though they the world were scorning
  With their loud, terrific roar ;
These in years gone by have plagued me,
  Dash'd my stand with fearful knock ;
But this morning I defy them—
  I am shelter'd by a rock.

Yet there 're other storms assail me
  On this rough October day,
Pelting ones that would appal me,
  If I'd let them, on time's way ;
Yet I have no need to fear them,
  Though like birds of prey they flock,
And I sing whene'er I hear them—
  I am shelter'd by a rock.

ON THIS COLD NOVEMBER DAY.

T is drizzling, foggy weather,
  With the sere leaves on the ground—
What a pack of ills together,
  Bringing sadness all around.
And I have to write a poem,
  Come what inspiration may —
It must come from Clifton's poet
  On this cold November day.

Who would envy my position,
  Writing in the fog and damp—
Mine is but a sore condition,
  Being subject to the cramp.
But I'll try to now forget it,
  Or to ease it, any way :
For 'twould plague me, if I'd let it,
  On this cold November day.

Farewell, then, ye pains and crosses
  I am call'd to bear in life—
Ye are not my greatest losses
  On the battle-field of life.
I have one that will cling to me,
  One I cannot put away,
And it is a heavy burden
  On this cold November day.

Having this, then, I must bear it,
  While I lonely sit and write —
For no other heart can share it,
  Or its agony indite.
It is that so great a number
  Hate the good and love the gay—
Keeping from the path of wisdom
  On this cold November day.

ROUNDELAY TO A SKYLARK.

One Sabbath Morn at Frampton Cotterell.

ARBLE on, sweet singing bird,
  Thy glad notes my soul have stirr'd ;
  And I'll halt in this retreat
  With the daisies at my feet.

Warble on, I love to hear
The new anthem pure and clear ;
It hath charms in every part,
And an echo in my heart.

Warble on, this day of rest,
High above thy lowly nest ;
Send some strains, while thou 'rt above,
To my Father's home of love.

Warble on, thy trilling tells,
While I hear yon Sabbath bells,
That thou sing'st in temple grand,
One not made by mortal hand.

Warble on, thy song begun—
It came with the rising sun ;
And it brings without control
Such sweet music to my soul.

Warble on, and sweetly sing
Soaring on thy fluttering wing :
While I heavenward try to rise
Like a singer for the skies.

Warble on, for I must go—
Work is waiting me to do ;
He who hears the angel throng
Won't despise thy morning song.

MUSINGS FOR THE OPENING YEAR.

THE budding year has open'd o'er time's declining hill,
And myriad happy voices sang its advent with good will ;
The waves of mighty ocean have borne the joyful strain,
While gushing rivers, flowing rills, the echo bring again.

The budding year has open'd ; and birds in choral song
Throughout their woodland homes the pleasing theme prolong ;
They wait for sylvan shading, and gladsome anthems bring—
Hailing this welcome new-born year, the harbinger of spring.

The budding year has open'd ; the patriot now inquires
For honour'd path of duty—the wish his breast inspires :
To live to noble purpose, and strive for virtue's crest,
His country's weal pursuing, to make her truly blest.

The budding year has open'd ; wide fields of labour wait
Where willing hands may find employ to make sad hearts elate ;
What homes of desolation still crowd our fatherland,
What widows' woes and orphans' tears yet need the soothing hand.

The budding year has open'd ; and there is work for all—
For mis-named Christian governments, would they obey the call—
Fulfil their mission as they ought, from warlike passion cease,
And help to fill this sin-cursed world with righteousness and peace

The budding year has open'd ; will you, ye ruling men,
From henceforth let your weapons be the potent press and pen ?
labour that those glittering swords may in their scabbards rust,
Which far too long have help'd to lay God's image in the dust ?

The budding year has open'd ; then turn the current tide
Of flowing wealth you've wasted long on Mammon's grasping pride,
And !et it flow in mercy's streams throughout the passing year,
And ere its close one gladsome song shall fill our hemisphere.

The budding year has open'd ; oh, will you try to stem
This torrent rush of wrong's black stream, and lift the diadem
Of lovely truth and righteousness from out the trampled dust,
And write each Christian country's name—" The beautiful, the just ! "

The budding year has open'd—the moments quickly fly :
To work at once, ye Templars true—life's seed-time well apply ;
Your coming harvest will be rich, and crown'd with angel song ;
For all who labour now shall reap with Him who labour'd long.

The budding year has open'd ; then sing the joyful strain ;
Let Queen, Prince, peer, and peasant, swell the jubilant refrain—
In palace home or humble cot, through life's uncertain lease—
And labour that the world may come and kiss the Prince of Peace.

GENERAL GORDON.

ERO for the true and right,
       Foremost in the hottest fight ;
England's long-remembered son,
Thou hast her heart's guerdon won.
Though in Khartoum thou did'st fall,
Serving at thy country's call,
English hearts will fin l thee room,
For thy service at Khartoum.

HOW IS IT?

THIS world is adapted for pleasures of mind,
    If people would use it aright ;
  I long have been thinking, a many might find
  Even here an abundant delight.
And yet there is much that 's depressing, I see—
  All cannot partake of its bliss ;
It seemeth to me a shame it should be
  In a beautiful world like this.

There is plenty around for the rich and the poor—
  Yes, plenty of clothing and food ;
Kind Providence gives an abundance of store,
  That all may have share of the good.
And yet there is hunger and sorrow, we see,
  What is it that 's going amiss ?
It seemeth to me a shame it should be
  In a plentiful world like this.

The valleys in season are clothèd with corn,
  The mines richly laden with coal ;
How is it that myriads are sighing forlorn,
  And haggard in body and soul ?
What hinders them having sufficient, I ask,
  From out the abundance there is ?
It seemeth to me a shame it should be
  In a bountiful world like this.

Are there deep schemers abroad in the land ?
  Is jobbery bolting the door ?
Keen selfishness grasping, with its iron hand,
  What ought to be feeding the poor ?
There is something gone wrong in the Church or the State—
  I'm anxious to know what it is ;
For it seemeth to me a shame it should be
  In a beautiful world like this.

NOW MY LOCKS ARE GREY.

HAVE just been looking
   In my mirror'd glass,
And I see I'm changing,
   Fading like the grass.
How my cheeks have furrow'd
   On my life's rough way,
And I 've silver threadings—
   For my locks are grey.

Where's the hand that smoothed them
   In my childhood years—
Father's hand, that stroked them
   When I 'd boyhood fears?
Ah! 'tis cold and frigid,
   Many miles away,
Death's cold hand doth hold it
   Now my locks are grey.

Yet I dare not murmur,
   Nor will I complain:
For my good old mother
   Kissed me once again.
Eighty-four bright summers
   She has seen decay,
And I love her better
   Now my locks are grey.

Then I've children near me
   In this world of strife,
And in my loved homestead
   A true-hearted wife.
I have many mercies
   Though a chequer'd way,
And sweet hope of heaven,
   Now my locks are grey.

2 E

MARRIED LIFE.

WHAT a fuss there is made in the world now-a-days,
About married life, I am hearing ;
It is chattered about in some wonderful ways,
And making much mischief, I'm fearing.
Now I've had experience in this kind of thing—
Far more than some men who forsake it ;
And while they are grumbling, I'll pleasantly sing,
It is just what we married folk make it.

It is all very fine to be blaming the wife,
And saying you don't care about her ;
That you have with her such a troublesome life,
And you could do better without her.
Now, don't you think, Thomas, there's some fault in you?
Here's a suitable pill, if you'll take it :
For I've an opinion on marriage—and true—
It is just what we married folk make it.

I know it's not right for Eliza to pout,
When everything don't meet her wishes ;
There will always be something to put her about
In cooking, or washing the dishes.
Yet she must remember that Thomas as well
Has trials, howe'er she may take it ;
And all married life may be heaven or hell —
It is just what we married folk make it.

But true married life is always the best,
It will make true hearts light as a feather ;
Where there is pure love, it will ne'er be a pest,
When husband and wife pull together.
Then never blame wedlock for troubles that come,
And though there are some who forsake it,
I shall always be singing, wherever I roam—
It is just what we married folk make it.

LITTLE LILLIE DALE.

N a new-made turfy grave,
   Down in Arno's Vale,
Sat a little orphan girl—
   Little Lillie Dale.
She was grieving there alone,
   With a bitter wail,
For two loved ones who had left
   Little Lillie Dale.

Once she had a home all bright,
   One true love had made :
Found in it true heart delight,
   Where she sang and play'd.
But a vessel had been lost
   In a stormy gale,
While the Bristol Channel cross'd—
   Little Lillie Dale.

On this fatal ship was found
   Lillie's parents dear :
These to distant port were bound—
   But that storm severe
Sent them to the silent dead
   With a loud bewail :
Only one was saved 'tis said—
   Little Lillie Dale.

Now she wanders up and down
   Bristol city's street—
Do not pass her with a frown
   With her shoeless feet.
She is friendless and forlorn,
   Haggard, wan, and pale :
Will you search and find her out—
   Little Lillie Dale.

TO EMILY.

BY MATTIE GABBITASS.

A T your request this theme I write ;
    And if some plain truths here appear,
    Pray do not deem me rude, or fear
'Tis meant to please the public sight—
For it shall in oblivion die,
If such your wish, you may rely.

" A faithful friend," a king once said,
    " Is better than a secret foe ;
    And he who flatters well may know
He will, by honest minds, be read,
    And treated by them with disdain,
    'Till he a better name obtain."

So to my task I now proceed,
    The good and bad alike note down ;
    But if, when reading it, you frown,
And say, " It is not me, indeed,"
    My pen henceforth shall idle stay—
    No other character portray.

    o   o   o   o   o

A gentle girl, of modest mien,
With carriage suited to a queen,
Would you her virtues here descry :
Then take a glance at Emily.
'Round those she loves affections twine
Like tendrils to the leafy vine ;
Nor will that love with time decay,
But grow and strengthen day by day.
Her penetrating power is keen,

And also good, as I have seen ;
While if on converse you are bent,
You'll find her quite intelligent ;
But lest from faults you think her free,
I now will mention two or three.
First, then, suppose in pleasantry,
You cannot both see eye to eye :
A cool, sarcastic speech will flow
From out her lips, you soon will know,
Which gives to you a smarting pain,
That will not quickly heal again.
Or when some favour you would show,
To mitigate her cup of woe—
For she has long an orphan been,
And suffering has been hers, I ween—
Without a moment's thought or care,
She'd answer, passing all compare,
" If I have favours I must buy !"
Then toss her pretty head, and cry,
" On paying you I must insist,
Or I your favours will resist :"
Thus oft her dearest friends she'd pain,
By what they term'd " her pride again."
Then sometimes they would her reprove,
As all true friends will one they love.
Then they would have to coax awhile,
To bring from her a pleasant smile ;
But when it came, there was no fear
But it was welcome and sincere :
For she would say, to quell their pain,
" You think you've conquer'd me again."
'Twas thus she lived from day to day,
My life-long treasur'd Emily ;
And though her faults were great and small,
Her virtues far outweigh'd them all.

OUT IN THE COLD.

UT in the cold, young and the old,
　　Thronging each city and town ;
Oh, how they come, some have no home—
　　Visit them not with a frown.
Scores are bereft, not a friend left,
　　Now let it cease to be told :
In this our day, on the highway—
　　Poor are left out in the cold.

Winter is here, oh, how severe ;
　　Thousands are pleading for aid :
Let them not die, hark, how they cry
　　For a revival of trade.
Who will give heed to their great need ?
　　Who will distribute their gold ?
While it is said many want bread—
　　Poor are left out in the cold.

Out in the cold, no shelter-fold ;
　　Shivering in alley and street
Arabs are seen, in the frost keen—
　　Pity them with their bare feet.
Each Arab wild, is somebody's child,
　　Worth more than jewels and gold ;
Oh ! go about, search them all out,
　　These are left out in the cold.

Christmastide's near, season all dear—
　　Dear to the owners of health ;
Let it be such as soon will touch
　　Hearts of the owners of wealth.
Christ of the poor, open the door
　　'Till it shall no more be told,
As it is here, in the old year,
　　Poor are left out in the cold.

SPECIAL NOTICE.

—◆◆—

Thirteen Copies of the undermentioned Penny Sheet Poems, assorted, will be sent to any address post free for six stamps, until sold out.

Address : P. GABBITASS Clifton Poet, Bristol.

1—" Teignmouth Catastrophe " (20th Thousand).
2—" Tower Street Tragedy."
3—" The Burning Ship *Cospatrick.*"
4—" Oxford Railway Catastrophe."
5—" Terrible Colliery Catastrophe at Abercarne."
6—" Tay Bridge Catastrophe."
7—" Loss of the *Princess Alice :* Thames Disaster."
8—" Southey's Memoriam Centenary Wreath."
9—" Merry Christmastide."
10—" Won't you go to the Races, my Brother ? "
11—" Bath Bridge Catastrophe."
12—" Dockise the River, old Bristol."
13—" Vaticanism : a Parody."
14—" The War Fiend and the Angel of Peace."
15—" The Risca Colliery Explosion."
16—" Death of the Children at Sunderland."
17—" Marriage Ode for England's Prince and Prussia's Pearl."
18—" The *Daphne* Disaster on the Clyde."
19—" The Terrible Earthquake in Italy."
20—" Death of the Duke of Albany."
21—" Hurrah for the Coming Election."
22—" Uncle Peter's Welcome to the Juvenile Cold Stream Guards."
23—" Death Song for Gordon the Brave."
24—" Birthday Song for the Queen."
25—" Death of Lord Shaftesbury."
26—" Charles Peace, the Banner Cross Assassin : his Life Lessons."
27—" Come and take the Ribbon."

———————————

Also the following Acrostics until sold out, as Memoriam Cards, same price, assorted.

1—" Our Princess Alice."
2—" Prince Louis Napoleon."
3—" Earl Beaconsfield."
4—" President Garfield."
5—" The Rev. W. Morley Punshon, M.A."
6—" Captain Webb, Champion Swimmer."
7—" Miss Mary Carpenter, Bristol."
8—" Rev. David Thomas, M.A., Bristol."
9—" Lady Haberfield, Clifton."
10—" Dr. Moffatt, the Friend of Southern Africa."
11—" Samuel Bowly, the Gloucester Friend."
12—" Longfellow, the World's Poet."
13—" Dr. Livingstone, In Memoriam."